DECORATIVE ART
1880 – 1980

DECORATIVE ART
1880 – 1980

Dan Klein and Margaret Bishop

Phaidon · Christie's

OXFORD

Phaidon · Christie's Limited
Littlegate House
St Ebbe's Street
Oxford OX1 1SQ

First published 1986
© Phaidon · Christie's Limited 1986

British Library Cataloguing in Publication Data:

Klein, Dan
Decorative art 1880–1980 – (Christie's pictorial histories)
1.   Decorative arts – History – 19th century   2.   Decorative
arts – History – 20th Century
I.   Title   II. Bishop, Margaret
III. Christie's International Group
IV. Series
745'.09'04   NK775

ISBN 0–7148–8025–6

Design by Gecko Ltd., Bicester, Oxon.

Printed in Great Britain by Blantyre Printing and·Binding
Company Limited, Glasgow.

Frontispiece: an Ernest Gimson walnut inlay fishing tackle
cabinet with barber's pole inlay, 1913; 197 cm. high, 144.6 cm.
wide, 52.1 cm. deep.

Contents

(*Above*)   A painted chest on stand by William Burges, 1875, with the inscription 'Willielmus Burges Me Fieri Fecit Anno Salutis MDCCCLXXV'; 190 cm. high, 120 cm. wide, 71.5 cm. deep.

(*Opposite*)   A Liberty pewter and enamel clock designed by Archibald Knox, the turquoise face with red enamelled design, the case embossed with a border of stylized honesty; 14 cm. high, stamped 0608 Rd. 426015.

Introduction

The last hundred years of design history have probably included more radical change than any other similar time-span in the history of the decorative arts. It is usually social change that brings about new directions in the design world, and of that there has been no shortage, with two world wars as well as a strong reaction against the long and settled traditions of the Victorian era. The consensus of opinion seems to be that the first pointers towards modernism came with the radical thinking of William Morris and his followers during the last two decades of the nineteenth century. His followers were mainly a group of architect-designers who, like Morris, took a fresh look at aesthetic values, and wanted to attack the problems of everyday life at source. Their somewhat devout and often over-idealistic aims were essentially Victorian, and Morris's deep concern with honest craftsmanship is an example of this. But the solutions of these architect-designers, almost despite themselves, were progressive in the extreme. Morris yearned to 'manufacture' honest design that would be available to all; it was a source of great distress to him that this proved impossible and that what he ended up with was a range of products affordable by only a small group of rich and discerning admirers. But his efforts changed the course of design history, creating a new syntax which inspired his followers so that there is a direct link between his thinking and the realization of his aims in modified terms by the Bauhaus designers.

What has distinguished the last hundred years of design is the sheer number of different styles, all of them related even if it is principally because of reaction against one another; Arts and Crafts turned into Art Nouveau, which led to the geometry of Art Deco and Modernism, only to be superseded by the studied asymmetry of the 1950s, which was replaced by the gay abandon of a hippie generation and Pop Art, and has now evolved into the escapist attitudes of anti-design and the Post-moderns. It has not been a simple path but always an interesting one. No previous century has been so preoccupied with design, and the sheer number of people interested in the quality of their surroundings has multiplied many times over. The continuing explosion of the middle classes in this century has been the main factor in our present obsession with design. In the modern world every nut and bolt should ideally be a perfectly designed detail worthy of the designer's comment. In previous centuries good design was almost exclusively for the upper classes. It was enough for things to be functional below stairs, and aesthetic value only began on the ground floor. Designers and craftsmen created within a much narrower field. The expansion of the middle classes coincided with the effects of the Industrial Revolution, and the combination of these two elements has resulted in the vastly wider spectrum covered by modern-day design.

With such diversity it is difficult to write a straightforward chronological account of design. There have been a number of different simultaneous elements in the decorative arts, none of them beginning or ending at the same time. Broadly speaking, there have been three principal categories of designer, the traditional, the fashionable and the avant-garde. As a result some of the chapters in this book might seem to overlap; in the case of traditionalism this is because tradition lasts longer and dies harder than either of the other two categories, and is also slower to develop. Innovation in traditional design is harder to detect; an oak chest designed by Ambrose Heal or Ernest Gimson, for instance, is closely related to much earlier styles, but it is interesting because of a modified attitude not so much to design as to

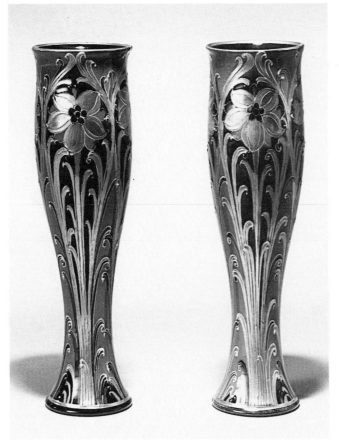

craftsmanship. The tradition of 'honest craftsmanship' in furniture, pottery, glass or metalwork is a matter of making a modified statement within an already existing framework.

In the decorative arts there is always an area where craftsmanship counts most, and this has been particularly noticeable in the last hundred years, when it has been important as never before to distinguish between hand-made and machine-made. Before the age of mass-production there were craftsmen and master craftsmen in the field of decorative arts, but the Industrial Revolution caused major changes in this respect. Design and craftsmanship began to drift apart with alarming speed, and there was a feeling at the Great Exhibition of 1851 that industry would soon swamp design. Many of those working in the decorative arts were afraid of the machine, and during the last century of design the aim of many craftsmen has been that their skills should be evident in the finished product. Many of them would bitterly contest any attempt to class their work as traditional. Are either Lucie Rie or John Makepeace contemporary or traditionalists (one an outstanding contemporary potter, the other as distinguished in the field of contemporary furniture making)? Were Charles Robert Ashbee or Georg Jensen traditionalists? The answer is that they are or were neither fashion-conscious nor part of the avant-garde. Their aim has been to express themselves through their skills as craftsmen. Some take fashion or new thinking more into account than others, but they all belong to a category of

(Left) An Arts and Crafts rectangular brass and enamel mantel clock in the manner of George Walton, made by Goodyer's; 33.5 cm. wide, Stamped Regent St. Goodyer's London W.

(Lower left) A pair of Moorcroft Macintyre pottery vases, painted with gilt and blue flowers on an olive green ground; 24 cm. high, painted artist's monogram WM des. and printed firm's marks Macintyre Burslem England Rd. No. 40417.

(Right) A Tyrian glass vase by Steuben, decorated with iridescent gold foliage; 14 cm. high, inscribed Tyrian

(Lower Right) A double overlay glass vase attributed to Thomas Webb & Sons; 31 cm. high, unsigned.

craftsman-designer which has remained faithful to the craft tradition. Some of them have worked as individuals, and others, like Ambrose Heal, Gustav Stickley or William Moorcroft, have been involved in industry. What distinguishes them all is their common endeavour to get the best out of their chosen material, and more often than not they have worked within a narrow field.

Fashion has played perhaps an even more important role in the history of late nineteenth- and particularly twentieth-century design. Both Art Nouveau and Art Deco demanded total commitment to a particular look. Art Nouveau was highly distinctive and seduced designers from all fields to adopt its imagery of whiplash motifs and stylistic exaggeration. Art Deco was virtually a way of life and went even further in an attempt at transformation. But both styles were about decoration rather than structure. Art Nouveau and Art Deco designers were not philosophers like William Morris or Le Corbusier. They tended to accept middle-class values and sought to embellish life with new surface decoration. They were dictated to by the times rather than the other way round. In a sense they were all innovators, but fashion trends happen fast and without the time for ponderous research. Both Art Nouveau and Art Deco were instinctive responses to the spirit of the times, borrowing freely from a wide field and creating a new look by inventing a new grammar of ornament. Ruhlman did not ask any questions about posture when designing a chair; he just made it as comfortable and as luxurious as possible. Lalique was not concerned with changing the history of glass, he merely found as many uses for it as possible, enjoying the new possibilities offered by electric lighting and finding new contexts (car mascots and fountains for instance) in which its decorative qualities could be seen to advantage.

As the fashion centre of the world moved away from Paris, the French also lost their flair for style. 'Stylishness' is so bound up with fashion, and fashion so much a reflection of the times, that the centre tends to be wherever the mood of the moment is best expressed. During the 1960s Carnaby Street was the epicentre of fashion, and as an offshoot Pop Art became a decorative trend that was adopted in the decorative arts worldwide. During the 1970s the action moved to Rome, and Italian taste was dominant in the world of design.

A peony leaded glass and bronze table lamp by Tiffany Studios;
81 cm. high, shade 56 cm. diam., stamped Tiffany Studios New York
7984.

A 'Wisteria' leaded glass and bronze table lamp with 'tree trunk' base
by Tiffany Studios; 68.5 cm. high, 46 cm. diam. of shade, impressed
marks.

A dark patinated bronze and alabaster lamp, the bronze stylized stag cast after a model by A. Kelety, circa 1925; 55cm. high, signed in the bronze A. Kelety.

Styles connected with fashion have come and gone very quickly during the twentieth century, each lasting barely a decade and pushing its predecessor sharply to one side. A romantic piece of Majorelle furniture looks jarring next to the cool elegance of a Dunand lacquer table, and the clean lines of Art Deco geometry cannot coexist in harmony with the asymmetry of the 1950s look. This rapid progression of style has been responsible for a great change of attitude, particularly over the past twenty-five years. In the 1950s Regency was just old enough to be considered safe taste but Victoriana, particularly late Victoriana, was considered too close for comfort. A hundred years in time seemed to constitute the safe zone where taste was concerned. In the 1960s the gap closed with the revival of Art Nouveau and Art Deco, some of it less than fifty years old. Today collectors are looking seriously at the 1970s, and it is difficult to imagine what the next step will be.

Whilst the race for fashion runs its course, the avant-garde moves at a slower pace, mainly because it is much harder to accept. By definition avant-garde means ahead of its time, and is a state that most of the world tends to avoid until time moves on and it becomes the norm. There are many different opinions as to what should constitute an avant-garde. One of its most recent

exponents, Andrea Branzi, says, 'the need to win back, in traumatic and rapid manner, the reigns of a history in flight has caused the birth of the new cultural category of the avant-garde movements. These have always performed the forward leap of breaking away from the old cultural equilibrium to introduce the terms of the new outside reality, of languages that had come into existence outside the official culture. This rapid decompression-chamber has been so integral a part of cultural life during this century that it has become a truly permanent characteristic of modern intellectual production.' Other members of the twentieth- or late nineteenth-century avant-garde have expressed themselves differently, but a common factor in all their thinking is the need to question the status quo, a dissatisfaction with accepted standards.

In the late nineteenth century William Morris and his avant-garde circle came into being as an indirect result of the Industrial Revolution. Technical discovery had in their eyes interfered with values of honest craftsmanship, and with evangelical fervour they set to redress the balance. The Bauhaus designers felt that the new approach should be one where modern design at last came to terms with the machine age, looking to it for a new set of aesthetic value judgements. Today the avant-garde hits out at the century-old obsession with design in industry; the anti-design theories of Post-modernism might seem for the most part perverse, but the history of twentieth-century avant-garde also makes one aware that they will probably provide the way forward out of the maze of safe Italian design that has held the world in its grip for the last twenty years. Just as with William Morris and Walter Gropius, the theories of Post-modernism will one day soon become accepted as the norm in the design world, though diluted so as not to offend the consumer classes.

Within each of the categories outlined so far, an extra category exists which transcends all barriers, and that is sheer excellence. Wherever it appears, there seem very few questions to ask. The results speak for themselves. There is little doubt about the brilliance of William Morris, Emile Gallé, René Lalique, Walter Gropius, Jacques-Emile Ruhlmann, Paolo Venini or Ettore Sottsass. They are all designers with a clarity of vision that has made them superstars whatever their chosen idiom.

Just as design itself can be categorized, so can its appreciation. For some Bauhaus is too modern even today, for others Art Deco has remained unsurpassed, and for others still the 1950s was the only period with any real originality. Art appreciation is after all no more than a matter of taste, and any judgement is valid providing the facts have been taken into consideration. But too often artistic judgements can be uninformed. No period of design can be altogether bad. As often as not those who say they hate modern art can in fact be proved to like it rather a lot by their choice of something simple like a car which they say they love without realizing that its design sources lie deeply embedded in the areas they profess to hate.

A lacquered and giltwood commode with black marble top, executed
by Süe et Mare, decorated by Paul Véra, circa 1920, the foliate knobs
of carved ivory; 127 cm. wide, 88 cm. high. This model was exhibited
at the Exposition Internationale des Arts Decoratifs et Industriels
Modernes, 1925.

(*Above*)   A Morris & Co. hand-knotted Hammersmith wool carpet designed by John Henry Dearle, circa 1890; 497.5 × 457 cm.

(*Opposite*)   A Maw & Company pottery vase designed by Walter Crane, painted with classical figures in ruby lustre on a cream ground; 32.8 cm. high, painted artist's monogram and crane device, dated 1890.

CHAPTER 1

Arts & Crafts and Late Nineteenth-Century Modernism

The history of nineteenth-century decorative arts is neatly separated into two halves by the Great Exhibition of 1851, which marked both the height of over-decoration and the start of a reaction towards simplification and functionalism. The writings of John Ruskin, one of the chief critics of the Great Exhibition, played a major role during the second half of the nineteenth century in shaping artistic ideals. He was preoccupied with a 'new style worthy of modern civilization in general, and of England in particular'. He was worried by the Industrial Revolution, while at the same time realizing fully the importance of the machine age he so deplored. His dilemma is illustrated by two contrasting ideologies, for on the one hand he wrote, 'Life without industry is guilt'; and on the other, 'Industry without art is brutality'. His vision was of a world where beauty was one of the bare essentials of life – an ideal that could only be achieved 'within a society in which all men would work, take pleasure in their labour and share their delight in its results'. This socialistic attitude was fully endorsed by William Morris, who first came across Ruskin as an Oxford undergraduate when he read The *Stones of Venice*, a book considered 'to form the cornerstone of the Arts and Crafts Movement'. Arts and Crafts is the term used to describe the revival of hand-crafting in the decorative arts during the last two decades of the nineteenth century. The term was coined by a new group of architect-designers who waged war on 'machine power'.

It was William Morris who did more than anyone else for design in the nineteenth century, and he is now generally referred to as 'the father of the Modern Movement'. A great deal was written at this time about artistic reform and Morris was among the many commentators, but he was above all a practitioner. He was

involved in the formation of Morris, Marshall, Faulkner & Co., founded in 1861 and reorganized in 1875 as Morris and Co. with William Morris as sole proprietor. The company was involved in the manufacture of wallpapers, textiles, carpets, stained glass and furniture, carrying out important decorative commissions such as the Armoury and Tapestry Room at St. James's Palace, the Green Dining Room at the Victoria and Albert Museum, and Stanmore Hall, but working principally as a retailer. Morris designs lasted well into the twentieth century with ever-popular classics such as the Sussex chair and the famous wallpapers and chintzes. His aim was to produce good design on as wide a scale as possible, and it was a source of frustration that his high ideals got in the way of his socialist principles. During his lifetime his attitudes and ideas changed: whereas he had begun by treating the machine with the utmost suspicion and favouring honest craftsmanship, he came to realize its importance in the modern world, and in the 1880s talked of 'those miraculous machines, which if orderly forethought had dealt with them, might even now be speedily extinguishing all irksome and unintelligent labour, leaving us free to raise the standard of skill of hand and energy of mind in our workmen'. Although Morris never felt personally fulfilled, his work and his ideas brought about a revolution in design during the later part of the nineteenth century. Throughout his career he adhered to the principle that form should be dictated by function, and this became the central theme of progressive design in the late nineteenth century.

Apart from the philosophical ideals which shaped the work of Morris and his followers, there were various popular decorative trends during the second half of the nineteenth century, the most prevalent of which was a

A pair of William de Morgan tiles with an Isnik style decoration of stylized flowerheads and foliage, enclosed in a brick pattern tile surround; framed, each tile 20.5 cm. square.

jumbled Eastern influence which started when Japan's frontiers were reopend to the West after Commander Perry's expedition of 1854. Influential critics and collectors such as Whistler and Rossetti collected Japanese artefacts, and 'Japonisme' left its mark on European design, particularly in France and England. At first designs merely imitated oriental styles, but gradually these styles were adapted and incorporated to create a new Western style which has come to be known as 'Aestheticism'. In France it is discernible in the work of Symbolist painters such as Ferdinand Khnopff, and the mystique of Symbolism was considered fashionable; in England Aestheticism was to be found in the lifestyle and writings of Oscar Wilde and later Aubrey Beardsley, both of whom typified a kind of decadence that characterizes one important aspect of the end of the nineteenth century. Aestheticism embraced not only Japanese and Chinese, but also Middle-Eastern influences. The work of William de Morgan and Christopher Dresser springs immediately to mind. Such decorative emblems as the sunflower, flying cranes and dragons are characteristic of the style. William de Morgan, along with William Morris, mixed with the Pre-Raphaelite circle and set out to be a painter, but soon abandoned this ambition in favour of a career in decorative design, and began working for Morris and Co. He set up his own kiln in the late 1860s, and for the next forty years produced pottery, including his richly decorated lustre ware, in conjunction with a number of different partners including Fred and Charles Passenger and Halsey Ricardo. Like Dr Dresser, he was an individualist, preferring the freedom of his own studio to membership of one of the many 'Guilds' that characterized the Arts and Crafts movement.

Christopher Dresser was a true pioneer of modern design, searching for clues to simplicity and functionalism in nature. He was trained as a botanist, and applied his learning to the world of ornament and design. He designed metalwork (for Hukin & Heath, James Dixon, Elkington and Benham & Froud), as well as furniture, fabrics and pottery (mainly for the Linthorpe Pottery) and glass (for James Couper & Son of Glasgow, probably pioneering their range of 'Clutha' glass).

There was a strong sense of association among the group of progressive designers inspired by the teachings of Ruskin and Morris, and the spirit of co-operation as seen in the Pre-Raphaelite Brotherhood led to the formation of a number of guilds and alliances during the 1870s and 1880s. Many of the designers involved in the formation of these groups were from a new group of architect-designers, including Charles Voysey, Mackay-Hugh Baillie-Scott and Arthur Mackmurdo. In 1882 Mackmurdo had established his Century Guild; by this time he had been working as an architect for seven years, founding the Guild 'in order to render all branches of art the sphere no longer of the tradesman,

A mahogany display cabinet designed by Carl Davis Richter, mounted with pierced metal panels; 198.2 cm. high, 163.7 cm. wide.

but of the artist' and to 'restore building, decoration, glass painting, pottery, wood-carving and metal to their rightful place beside painting and sculpture'. The Century Guild gave birth to the Art-Workers Guild, 'a Guild of Handicraftsmen and Designers in the Arts' which attracted like-minded artists, architects and designers whose aim was to set new standards; the Art-Workers Guild is still in existence today and recently celebrated its centenary. Later came Charles Robert Ashbee's Guild of Handicraft, founded in 1888, and now remembered principally for its distinctive silver-work. These are just some of the many 'co-operatives' set up by the new Victorian architects and craftsmen, intent on establishing modern standards. A platform

was also provided for these men to show their work publicly by the Arts and Crafts Exhibition Society, which held the first of its annual exhibitions in 1888 under the chairmanship of Walter Crane. In 1893 *The Studio* was launched under the editorship of Charles Holme and has remained in various guises the most important of the decorative arts magazines. At the time of its launching *The Studio* was the first magazine devoted to modern decorative and applied arts, and was widely read in Europe and America as well as in the United Kingdom.

Apart from individuals like William de Morgan and Christopher Dresser and the architect-designers like Philip Webb, William Lethaby and Richard Norman

Shaw, the various industries involved in the decorative arts also showed a marked change of attitude, and this was particularly noticeable in the potteries, many of which set up small 'studio' departments. Among the old-established firms, Minton and Worcester produced 'Art Pottery' along with their commercial ranges, intended to appeal to more refined tastes; Minton opened an art-pottery studio in South Kensington in 1871. Royal Doulton, however, was the most committed to the idea of studio pottery, working in close collaboration with the Lambeth School of Art. Among the many designers working for Doulton in the last decades of the nineteenth century were the Barlow family (Hannah,

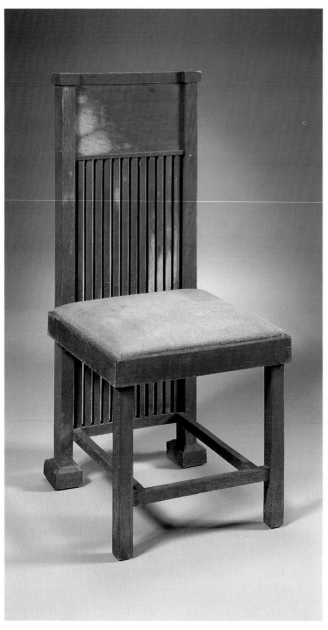

An oak dining chair designed by Frank Lloyd Wright for the Darwin D. Martin House, Buffalo, New York, circa 1904; 100.3 cm. high, 44.5 cm. wide.

Florence and Arthur), Mark Marshall, George Tinworth and Frank Butler. But perhaps the best-known Lambeth students were the four Martin Brothers, Wallace, Edwin, Charles and Walter, who set up their family company in Fulham in 1873 and worked as a team of artists and craftsmen for over forty years. They produced jugs and vases with moulded and incised decoration, but are best remembered for their eccentric 'tobacco-jars' in the form of grotesque birds caricaturing famous political personalities of the day.

Of the smaller 'Arts and Crafts' potteries, one of the most characteristic was the Della Robbia Pottery, established in 1894 by Harold Rathbone, a painter and former pupil of Madox Brown. Another characteristic style of the period was the hand-painted wall charger; some of these were done by professionals, but many good ones were also made by talented amateurs, entering the numerous competitions in this category. Of those made by professional painters, W. S. Coleman's pieces are the most evocative of the Aesthetic taste.

Furniture, glass and metalwork of the Art and Crafts period adhered to the aesthetic and functional criteria already outlined. It was made principally by the guilds or alliances, a closely knit and somewhat incestuous community. The best-known glass was made by James Powell & Son, who executed designs for Morris & Co. including some by the architect Philip Webb, and the best-known metalwork was by William Benson, who set up his own workshop in the 1880s. And perhaps the most important design text-books used by all these designers of the period, apart from *The Studio*, were Dr Dresser's *Principles of Decorative Design* and Charles Eastlake's *Hints on Household Taste in Furniture, Upholstery and other Details*.

The Arts and Crafts Movement also changed the course of American decorative design, although the United States had no figures comparable to the great British artist-philosophers like Ruskin and Morris. When Oscar Wilde visited America in the early 1880s, he commented, 'I find what your people need is not so much high, imaginative art, but that which hallows the vessels of every day.' What has become known as American Arts & Crafts is somewhat later in date than its British counterpart, although as early as the late 1870s there was Arts & Crafts furniture by Isaac Scott and Herter Brothers. There were distinctive styles in various parts of America, and they can be divided into three main areas, the Eastern seaboard (New York, Boston and Philadelphia), Chicago and the Midwest, and the Pacific Coast. The world of decorative artists in New York was dominated by Louis Comfort Tiffany, known chiefly during this period for his leaded glass windows. Tiffany also manufactured metalwork in the Aesthetic taste, but the martelé wares of the Gorham Manufacturing Company are perhaps the best-known work in this category. It is sometimes difficult to draw a line between Arts & Crafts and Art Nouveau in America, for there as elsewhere the two styles overlapped, and much of what is termed American Arts and Crafts belongs to the twentieth century and will be dealt with later on.

There were, however, direct links between the American and the British Arts and Crafts Movements, and these were mainly with the Midwest, giving birth to a style in architecture and decorative arts that is known as the Prairie School. Walter Crane and C. R. Ashbee both visited Chicago and lectured there, and the work of William Morris was well-known in Chicago. The decorative designs of the Prairie School, the best known of whom was Frank Lloyd Wright, grew directly out of the Arts and Crafts Movement, with an 'emphasis on unity of exterior and interior, the respect for natural materials, a desire for simplicity, the interest in Japanese art, and a geometric, rectilinear style'.

It was a rectilinear style as evolved in Europe and particularly in Scotland that on the one hand led the way to modernism and clean lines, and on the other to the worst excesses of 'Spaghetti' Art Nouveau. The more restrained 'Glasgow Style', as seen in the work of Charles Rennie Mackintosh, Margaret McDonald and Herbert and Frances McNair, was the more intellectual of the two developments and had a great effect on design in Germany and Austria. During the 1890s articles in *The Studio* about modern developments in Britain greatly influenced key figures such as Josef Hoffmann and Koloman Moser in Austria and Joseph Maria Olbrich and Peter Behrens in Germany. In Vienna 'The Secession', a breakaway from the establishment, came about when in 1898 Gustav Klimt led a group of architects, including Josef Hoffmann and Otto Wagner as well as the artist-designer Koloman Moser, to exhibit their own work and that of their foreign avant-garde contemporaries away from the venerable Academy of Fine Arts. In Germany and Austria there was talk of a revolution in design, but in Glasgow and further south in Britain the new style was a logical evolution in the field of decorative arts.

The Glasgow School of Art, built between 1896 and 1909, was the crowning glory of the 'Glasgow Style' which had begun to emerge some years earlier. Mackintosh and the other Glasgow artists were inspired by Francis Newberry, the head of Glasgow School of Art, and by his wife Jessie Newberry. Once again the influence of *The Studio* on these artists was considerable, particularly the drawings of Aubrey Beardsley and in sharp contrast the stark simplicity of the architecture and decoration of C. F. A. Voysey. They were impressed too by the mysticism and strange sinuous style of the Dutch painter Jan Toorop, with its elongated figures and stylized gestures. These influences gave rise to what was affectionately known as the 'Spook School'.

While being the central figure of this movement, Mackintosh created a style all his own, with a genius too individual and outspoken ever to be copied closely. But his influence on twentieth-century design cannot be stressed too much, and his geometrical approach had the same sort of influence on the applied arts as Cubism had on painting. The Glasgow School of Art has justifiably been referred to as 'the first really modern building'. The dozen or so years between the design of the School of Art in 1896 and its final phase in 1909 were the

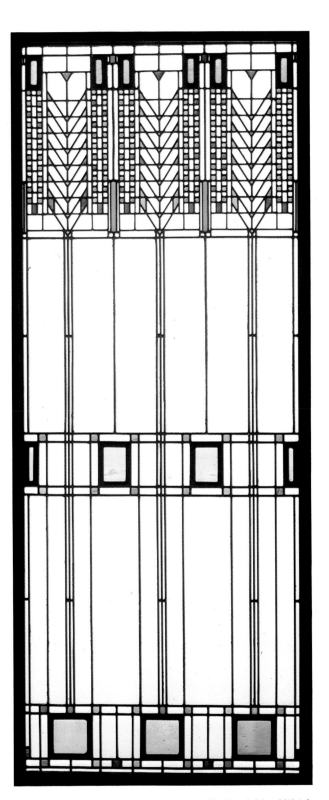

A 'Tree of Life' leaded glass door, designed by Frank Lloyd Wright, executed by Linden Glass Co. for the Darwin D. Martin House, Buffalo, 1903–1905; 165 × 66 cm.

(*Right*)   An oval gilt metal pendant decorated with stylized foliage on a white enamelled ground designed by Josef Hoffman for the Weiner Werkstätte, circa 1910; 3.3 cm. wide; stamped WW monogram.

(*Below*)   A frosted glass vase overlaid in blue, designed by Josef Hoffman for Loetz, circa 1909; 23 cm. high, signed Loetz.

most prolific years of Mackintosh's life, during which he designed several private houses and collaborated on the decoration of Miss Cranston's Buchanan and Argyle Street tearooms.

The Glasgow School made a greater impact on design in Germany and Austria than in Britain. It was in a sense too extreme for the home market, where it was viewed with a degree of scepticism. But the Austrians in particular reacted enthusiastically, and the stylistic change that occurred around 1900 in Vienna was radical enough to merit the first real claim to twentieth-century modernism. Decoration was reduced to the minimum and contained within a geometry that did not interrupt clean lines. The new designs were exhibited at the annual Secession exhibitions, the first of which was held in 1897; by the second exhibition in 1898 Joseph Maria Olbrich's renowned Secession building with its bronze cupola in the shape of a bay tree had been erected. In 1900 the exhibition included an important display of British and Scottish Arts and Crafts, and it was the work of Charles Rennie Mackintosh that attracted special interest. Viennese modernism was in the hands of Otto Wagner, regarded as the 'father of Viennese modernism', and his pupils at the Vienna Academy (where he taught), Josef Hoffmann and Joseph Maria Olbrich. They were later joined by Adolf Loos, the greatest purist among the Viennese architects and designers, who continually stressed the priority of function and bitterly condemned ornament for its own sake. Koloman Moser opposed ornament too, reducing it to pure geometric forms, and it was he who was responsible for introducing the checkerboard motif so typical of 'Constructive Jugendstil' (Constructive Art Nouveau). In 1903 Moser amd Hoffmann founded the craft studio known as Wiener Werkstätte.

It was the clear geometry of the Wiener Werkstätte that earned this new trend in design its nickname 'The

(Chess) Board Style'. The starkness of this geometric effect was offset by the use of luxurious inlays of rare woods, ivory, mother-of-pearl and semi-precious stones, and much of the geometry was figurative. Uniformity was considered all-important, leading to the concept of total design where everything from the door handle to the furniture was designed according to the same rigorous stylistic principles. The Werkstätte designed furniture and had studios for works in gold and silver, metalwork, bookbinding, toys and leatherware, as well as for carpentry and lacquerware. Much of the furniture was bentwood and inexpensively massproduced by the firms of the Thonet Brothers and J. & J. Kohn to designs by Hoffmann, Wagner, Gustav Siegel and Marcel Kammerer, making the 'avant-garde' accessible to all, and thereby achieving William Morris's dream.

In 1899 Joseph Maria Olbrich left Vienna and was appointed to a post in Darmstadt by the Grand Duke Ernest Ludwig; his Viennese origins were to have a visible effect on German modernism, the core of which was in and around Darmstadt. The influence of The Studio had already been felt, and had led to the launching of two important magazines in Germany in 1897, *Dekorative Kunst* and *Deutsche Kunst und Dekoration*. The message contained in these journals was simply: 'Everything is art, and nothing made by man should not be considered so.' The art of living, according to modernist German thinking, affected every aspect of daily life, from having a bath to contemplating art, and it was this all-embracing attitude towards the arts that characterized modern interior design in Germany.

Many of these ideas came directly from Great Britain and the followers of Ruskin, and it is worth noting the family link between Darmstadt and London at this time. Grand Duke Ernest Ludwig of Hesse was married to Queen Victoria's favourite daughter Alice. England was his second home, and he went there for visits almost every year. Like his father-in-law Prince Albert, he was an untiring patron of the arts, and together with Alexander Koch, the editor of *Deutsche Kunst und Dekoration*, worked to reform the state of the arts in Germany. Under the patronage of the Grand Duke an artist's co-operative or 'Künstlerkolonie' was formed in Darmstadt in 1898, and the first Darmstadt exhibition bears the stamp of Alexander Koch, whose philosophy was that 'there is only one kind of art. Architecture, sculpture, painting, and the applied arts, make the same universal statement, all influencing and working upon each other.' It was in this spirit that the products of the German avant-garde, dominated by figures such as Peter Behrens, August Endell, Joseph Maria Olbrich and Richard Riemerschmid, were seen together for the first time, alongside the works of their European and British counterparts. Further exhibitions were held in Darmstadt in 1901, 1904, 1908, 1911 and 1914.

In Belgium and Holland too, architects and designers felt the need to break with nineteenth-century traditions and to forge ahead. As in all other European countries there emerged a clear division between a rectilinear avant-garde style preoccupied with functionalism, and the curvilinear exaggeration of a new decorative language that came to be called 'Art Nouveau'. In Belgium these avant-garde extremes were expressed most clearly on the one hand in the furniture of Gustave Serrurier Bovy and the economical designs of Henry van de Velde, and on the other hand in the extravagant whiplash fantasies of Victor Horta. In Holland the same extremes coexisted, with the restraint of Jan Eisenloeffel alongside the exoticism of decorators like Schellink and Hartring for the Rozenburg porcelain factory. Although for a while the two extremes remained poles apart, during the last decade of the century Arts and Crafts became less strict and unyielding, giving way eventually to the more obvious decorative appeal of Art Nouveau.

1

2

The American Arts and Crafts designers looked principally to their British counterparts for inspiration, with the exception of Louis Comfort Tiffany who after studying painting in Paris returned to America and became an interior designer with considerable influence. He was known above all for his imaginative use of stained glass in windows and in particular in a wide range of colourful lamps with leaded glass shades and decorative bronze bases. As always with architects, the best of them (like Frank Lloyd Wright) were the thinking men of the design world with new ideas for interior design with which to adorn their buildings.

1.   A large spherical copper urn, designed by Frank Lloyd Wright, probably executed by James A. Miller for the Edward C. Waller House, Riverforest, Illinois, circa 1899, set on a four part foot and with galvanized tin liner; 46 cm. high.

2.   A photograph of the entrance hall of the Edward C. Waller House, Riverforest, Illinois, circa 1899, showing the copper urn in situ.

3.   A fine pair of leaded glass landscape windows by Tiffany Studios, commissioned circa 1900; both 146.7 × 80.6 cm. including wood frames.

3

1

2

3

4

Designers of the British Arts and Crafts movement expressed their dissatisfaction with accepted Victorian tradition, and thought deeply about structure and decoration alike. Dr Christopher Dresser, in his search for basic functionalism, is now considered to be the one designer whose ideas pointed the way most clearly out of the muddle of Victorian design and towards the twentieth century.

1. A pottery vase designed by Christopher Dresser, the shoulders modelled with four grotesque masks, handles extending from their mouths. 32 cm. high. Impressed Chr. Dresser, facsimile signature.

2. A rare electroplated claret jug designed by Christopher Dresser and executed by Elkington & Co. 21.2 cm. high. Stamped Elkington marks RD22871 for 1885.

3. A selection of metalwares designed by Christopher Dresser, showing the clean lines of his designs, circa 1880–1890. Brass kettle, upper right 24.5 cm. high.

4. A Hukin and Heath electroplated and glass claret jug, an electroplated and Royal Doulton claret jug, and an electroplated soup tureen and cover, all designed by Christopher Dresser; jug on left, 23.7 cm. high, dated 1897.

5. A large Minton 'moon flask' pottery vase with colourful hand-painted decoration in the Aesthetic manner, enriched with gilding, circa 1890. 43.2 cm. high. Impressed Minton 8671, artist's monogram DJ. Printed Mintons Art Pottery Studios, Kensington Gore.

6. A Minton Aesthetic Movement hand-painted wall charger by Annie Cole after a design by W.S. Coleman. 48.5 cm. diam. Impressed Minton and with Annie Cole's hand-painted signature, 1885.

7.   A white metal waist clasp designed by Alexander Fisher, set with opals and polychrome enamel, inscribed with the words Tristan, Isolde, the oval enamel panels relating to this legend; 19.2cm. wide, signed Alex. Fisher and monogram F.D.

8.   Part of a set of William Morris curtains of woollen tissue woven with the peacock and dragon pattern. Each of four curtains approx. 274 × 152cm.

9.   An open armchair attributed to George Walton. The move to simplicity of design can be seen here.

10.   A mahogany, ebonized and marquetry plant stand in the style of Charles Bevan, with zinc liner; 77.6cm. high.

5

6

7

8

9

10

Although harking back to medievalism, the Guilds and Societies of Craftsmen were a feature of the struggle at the end of the nineteenth century towards a more rational approach to design through skilled craftsmanship. It was as much as anything a reaction against the over-industrialization of design during the first part of the century when machined decoration took over and was popular mainly because of its novelty. Those who formed themselves into guilds wished to revive traditions of honest craftsmanship in all areas of the decorative arts. The Guild of Handicrafts was known principally for jewellery and metalwork.

1

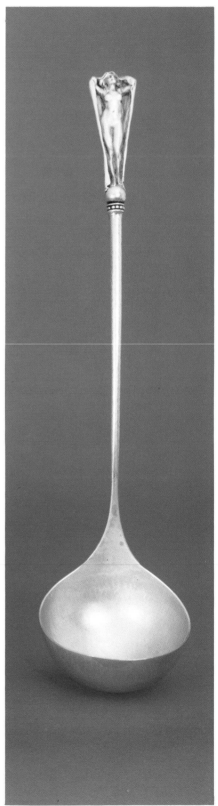

2

1. An Arts and Crafts pendant and chain, signed by Edgar Simpson, white metal set with moss-agate cabochons.

2. A Guild of Handicrafts hammered silver ladle designed by Charles Robert Ashbee and modelled by Alec Miller, the finial cast with the cloaked figure of Aphrodite; 38.3 cm. high, stamped G. of H. Ltd. London 1903 (12 oz.).

3. A silver porringer, a silver and green glass decanter and a silver muffin dish and cover, designed by C.R. Ashbee for the Guild of Handicrafts, 1905, 1903 and 1900. The clean, functional lines are well illustrated here. Decanter 22.5 cm. high.

4. A Guild of Handicrafts white metal and enamelled inkwell, attributed to C.R. Ashbee; 10.5 cm. high.

3

4

1

British Studio Pottery enjoyed a revival during the last two decades of the nineteenth century. There were a number of individual artist-potters who opened small studios developing their styles. Among these smaller firms William De Morgan and the Martin Brothers are the best known. De Morgan was known for his Persian-style wares which were made both in lustre and matt glazes decorated with mythical beasts or floral patterns. The Martin Brothers made vases, often with incised decoration, but are remembered particularly for their amusing character jugs and tobacco jars modelled as birds (which were in fact caricatures of famous politicians).

1. Four William De Morgan tiles in ruby lustre on a cream ground, circa 1880, 15cm. square.

2. A William De Morgan ruby lustre charger painted with a peacock with spread plumage, circa 1900, 36cm. diam. The peacock was one of the popular symbols of the period.

3. A William De Morgan ruby lustre pottery vase painted with lions on a ground of looping scrolls, 17cm. high. Painted on base de Morgan Ware 1898.

4. A selection of stoneware Martin Brothers grotesque double face jugs, incised and modelled with puckish faces, circa 1900–1903, jug at left 17cm. high.

2

3

4

5.   A large Martin Brothers stoneware vase, incised with scrolling flowers and foliage in shades of blue on a pitted biscuit coloured ground.

6.   A Doulton stoneware menu card holder modelled by George Tinworth, 12 cm. high. Marked H. Doulton Lambeth, incised Tinworth and assistant's monogram, circa 1885.

7.   Three stoneware bird tobacco jars and covers by Martin Brothers. L. to R. 28 cm., 22.5 cm. and 17 cm. high. Incised signatures London & Southall 1903 and 1914.

8.   'The Sixth Day of Creation', a ceramic rectangular plaque after Sir Edward Burne-Jones decorated by Alice Louise Jones for Della Robbia, 57 × 23.3 cm. Incised galleon mark and DR 1906. Painted decorator's initials.

5

6

7

8

The British architect-designers at the turn of the century had worldwide influence. Their thinking owed much to the design philosophy of William Morris, John Ruskin and their followers. It was above all their simplicity and sparing use of decoration that attracted attention.

1. A dark stained pine dresser designed by Charles Rennie Mackintosh, probably for the Dutch Kitchen, Argyle St. Tea Rooms, Glasgow; the two upper side cupboards inlaid with chequered squares of mother-of-pearl, the drawers fitted with brass handles; 160.4 cm. high, 146.1 cm. wide, 22.5 cm. deep; circa 1898.

1

2. An important C.F.A.
Voysey oak music cabinet on
stand, designed for W. Ward
Higgs 1898, with brass hinges
and heart shaped lock plate;
144 cm. high, 104 cm. wide.

2

The British Arts and Crafts movement was made up of craftsmen and designers who had grown weary of muddled Victorian standards. Their aim was to redefine and rediscover honesty in design which involved a process of stripping it of the clutter of random decoration that was becoming more and more the design tradition in Victorian England.

1. A silver and green glass two-handled cup by James Powell and Son, the hammered silver cast with a pattern of fruiting vines; 22.8 cm. high. Stamped makers mark JP & S and London hallmarks for 1909.

2. Two De Morgan wall-plates, one painted by Fred Passanger with a galleon, covered in ruby and ochre lustres, the other with a winged double-headed putto in pink and ruby lustres; Galleon dish 37.5 cm. diam., and with painted initials FP.

3. An earthenware circular wall plaque and two saucer-shaped dishes by Della Robbia, the central plaque painted by Cassandra Annie Walker and 36.5 cm. diam. Incised DR and galleon mark and painted with artist's initials, circa 1905.

4. Part of a Foley Art China coffee set designed by George Logan, the printed rose motif and diamond shapes typical of Glasgow school design, green and lilac on a white ground. Printed mark Foley Art China Peacock Pottery.

1

2

3

4

5

5. Three items of pottery designed by Christopher Dresser. His designs ranged over a wide variety of domestic objects in ceramics, glass, furniture and metalware showing his great versatility. Linthorpe teapot, centre, 21.3 cm. high.

6. One of a pair of massive Burmantofts Faience jardinieres on stands, incised and painted in blues, green and brown with the popular subject of peacocks in a garden and with foliate base; jardiniere 53.5 cm. diam. stand 51 cm. high; impressed BF monogram.

7. A rosewood octagonal centre table designed by E.W. Godwin, circa 1880. 92 cm. diam., 73.7 cm. high. Branded Collinson & Lock London 1053.

8. A Lamb of Manchester dark stained beechwood davenport, carved on the sides with gothic roundels, initials and the date 1879; 63 cm. wide. Stamped 'Lamb Manchester 40921'.

9. A Wylie and Lochhead mahogany display cabinet designed by E.A. Taylor with leaded glass cupboard doors, the doors of the lower section inlaid with brass, pewter and mother-of-pearl; 176.7 cm. high, 88 cm. wide.

10. A Liberty & Co. oak dressing table probably designed by Leonard F. Wyburd, circa 1899. The rail above the mirror inlaid with three bell-shaped foliate motifs in pewter; 98.5 cm. wide.

6

7

9

8

10

The Wiener Werkstätte (or Vienna Workshops) showed Austria's modernist response by architect-designers to the new century. They formed themselves into a reactionary co-operative, and the style developed by them is also known as 'Secession' style alluding to the fact that their ideas were fundamentally different and new. From 1901 onwards an annual exhibition was held in a building in Vienna designed specially for this purpose, and there was also a yearly publication called 'Ver Sacrum' devoted mainly to graphic arts.

1. 'Sitzmachine', a mahogany stained beechwood armchair designed by Josef Hoffman for J. & J. Kohn, with adjustable back; 110 cm. high, marked J. & J. Kohn, circa 1905.

2. Part of a 96 piece silver flatware service designed by Josef Hoffman for the Wiener Werkstätte, circa 1905. The knives with stainless steel blades, all with stamped JH monogram, WW monogram, 900 standard and control mark. 149.5 troy ozs. gross.

1

2

3.   A pink glass bowl with blue overlay designed by Koloman Moser for Loetz, circa 1905; 23 cm. diam.

4.   A mahogany stained beechwood cabinet designed by Prof. Kolo Moser for J. & J. Kohn circa 1901, with glazed cupboard doors and brass feet and handles; 138 cm. high.

5.   A fine hammered silver plated table lamp designed by Josef Hoffman, executed by the Wiener Werkstätte, circa 1905, with glass balls suspended from the domed shade; 43.5 cm. high, impressed Wiener Werkstätte.

3

4

5

The Modernism of the Glasgow School was more enthusiastically received in Germany and Austria than in Britain. The work of Mackintosh was published in Studio magazine, which was widely read in these countries. Josef Hoffman openly recognized his debt to Mackintosh and British designers generally, who were invited to show their work at the Secession exhibitions in Vienna.

1. A silvered copper ewer and bowl designed by C.R. Mackintosh, the hammered surfaced ewer with curved riveted handle, the oval bowl with everted rim; ewer 28 cm. high, bowl 39.8 cm. wide, circa 1904.

2. A brownish black ebonised oak ladderback side chair with rush seat, designed by Charles Rennie Mackintosh for Miss Cranston's Willow Tea Rooms, Glasgow, 1903; 104.5 cm. high, 45.5 cm. wide.

3. A mahogany desk designed by Josef Hoffman for J. & J. Kohn circa 1905; 107 cm. wide, 95 cm. high. Linear, geometric forms are dominant.

4. A metal and glass hall lantern by Charles Rennie Mackintosh, designed for William Davidson Jr., Windyhill, Kilmalcolm 1901, the upper small square apertures on opposite sides backed by yellow opalescent cased glass panes; 25.5 × 20 cm.

2

1

3

4

5.   A Koloman Moser letter rack and matching inkwell for Franz Hiess and Söhne, Vienna circa 1900, mother-of-pearl applied on wood overlaid with silver and set with glass stones; rack, 14.3 cm. wide, stamped makers mark. Although design was restrained, materials used were always of the highest quality.

6.   A mahogany cabinet by Josef Hoffman for J.J. Kohn 1904, of demi-lune form with silvered metal feet; 195 cm. high, 79.5 cm. wide.

7.   A 'Purkersdorf' beechwood side chair with red leather upholstered seat designed by Josef Hoffman, executed by J. & J. Kohn 1903–1905; 99 cm. high. (Reputedly one of forty two examples executed for the Purkersdorf Sanitorium.)

8.   A bentwood 'Fledermaus' armchair designed by Josef Hoffman in 1907 for the Fledermaus Café in Vienna, executed by Thonet; 73.5 cm. high.

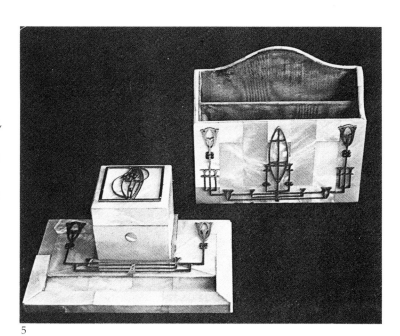

5

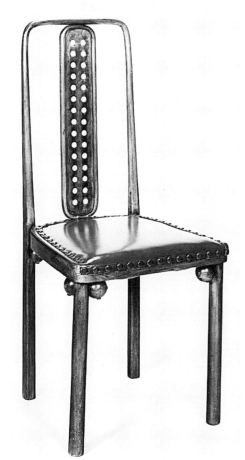

8

7

1

The Artists' Colony at Darmstadt also held exhibitions of modern design at the turn of the century and was particularly fortunate in being able to enjoy the generous patronage of the Grand Duke of Hesse, whose own palace was decorated partly in the contemporary style with designs by British as well as German architect designers. His patronage of such British designers as Mackintosh and Baillie-Scott started a craze in Germany for British Arts and Crafts design.

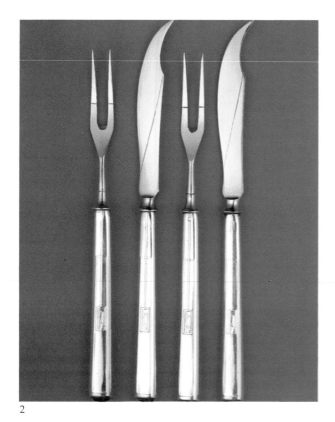

2

3

1. A hammered copper plant stand designed by Josef Maria Olbrich circa 1898; 74 cm. high. Olbrich moved to Darmstadt in 1899.

2. A parcel gilt cheese service by Josef Maria Olbrich (four pieces from a set for twelve people illustrated), the embossed handles with artist's monogram incorporated in the design, circa 1900; 16.5 cm. length of knife; stamped French import marks.

3. A brass mounted iridescent glass vase attributed to Loetz, the design in the manner of Hans Christiansen, circa 1900; 37 cm. high.

4. A pair of twin branch pewter candlesticks designed by Josef Maria Olbrich, executed by Eduard Hueck, circa 1902, cast with a curvilinear motif; 36 cm. high; stamped Silberzinn 1819E Hueck and with Olbrich's mark.

4

1

2

3

Charles Rennie Mackintosh was the leader among a small group of Scottish architects and designers who formed the Glasgow School. Those most closely associated with Mackintosh were Herbert MacNair and the Mac-Donald sisters, one of whom married Mackintosh the other MacNair. All of them were young and expressed themselves in a language of stylish geometric ornament that was highly original and extremely modern in concept. Mackintosh did his studies at the Glasgow School of Art where he was encouraged in his avant-garde ideas by the principal. Although the Glasgow style was much copied, no other designers ever could compete with its combined curvilinear, daring and 'spooky' imaginery.

1.   A Wylie and Lochead oak and marquetry settle designed by John Ednie, with green leather seat and back panels; 155 cm. high, 137.8 cm. wide. This settle is one of a pair designed by John Ednie for the Wylie and Lochead pavilion in the Glasgow Exhibition of 1901.

2.   An ebonized oak chair designed by Charles Rennie Mackintosh for Miss Cranston's Willow Tea Rooms, Glasgow, which opened in 1904. These chairs were used in The Gallery and The Front Salon; 104 cm high (cf. p. 36, no.2).

3.   A pair of ebonized wood and silver candlesticks, designed by Charles Rennie Macintosh, the tapering elliptical uprights supporting a brass ring to hold the hammered silver bowl with candle spike; silver stamped D.W.H. for David W. Hislop, and hallmarks for Glasgow 1904; 31 cm. high.

4.   An ebonized wood and marquetry pen box and cover designed by Charles Rennie Mackintosh, the sides inlaid with walnut in a chequered pattern, the cover and finial inlaid with mother-of-pearl 'petals', the interior with a removeable pen tray and glass inkwell, circa 1904; 10.5 × 24.7 cm.

4

5. A beaten pewter rectangular wall mirror, designed and executed by Margaret and Frances Macdonald, embossed with butterflies, sunflowers and curving, elongated stems; with ebonized wood back; 69 × 60.5 cm; impressed Margaret Macdonald, Frances Macdonald 1897.

The sisters opened their own studio in Glasgow in 1894, devoting themselves to the applied arts. The studio closed when Frances married Herbert MacNair in 1899, and subsequently Margaret married Charles Rennie Mackintosh in 1900.

6. A Liberty pendant and chain designed by Jessie M. King in silver and turquoise enamel, stamped L & Co.

7. A cast iron fire grate, the design attributed to George Walton; 39.6 cm high.

8. A Glasgow School white metal ink stand, the cover inset with a blue and green enamel plaque; circa 1900, 12 cm. high. This style follows that of Charles Rennie Mackintosh and is rather similar to a jewellery case designed by Mackintosh for Jessie Keppie, now in the Victoria and Albert Museum.

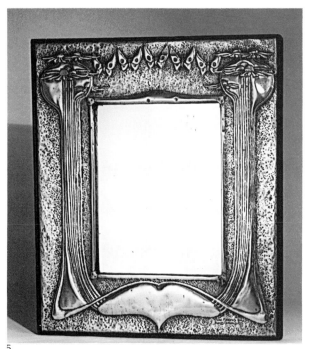

5

6

7

8

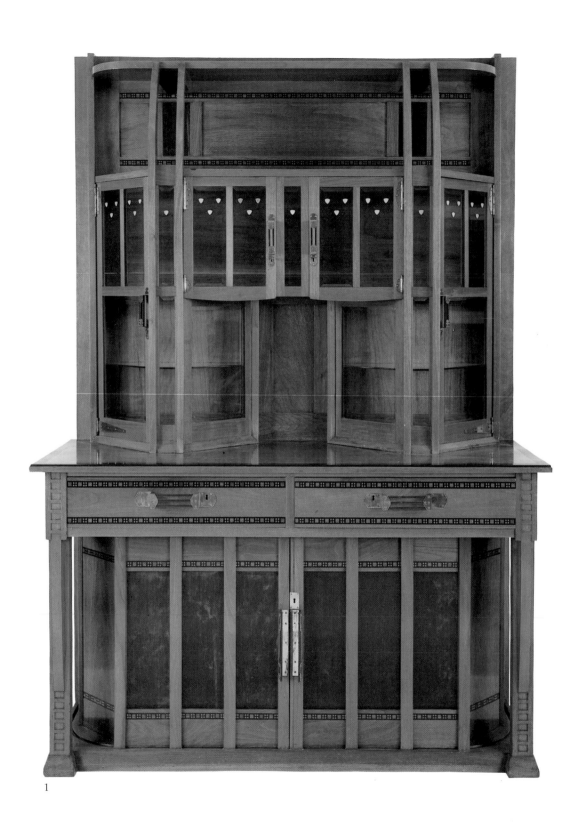

1

Each country developed its own brand of Art Nouveau, and in each country there were extremes within this style with pure geometry at one extreme and a labyrinth of whiplash lines at the other. The geometrical approach was the more forward-looking of the two and would eventually be developed by a new generation of designers to become 'Art Deco'.

1. A breakfront Cuban mahogany dresser by Gustave Serrurier-Bovy, inlaid with brass and ebony and mounted with geometric brass and steel handles; 224cm. high, 158.5cm. wide; applied with maker's label circa 1908.

2. A Patriz Huber liqueur set comprising a decanter and six cups in white metal and glass; decanter 18.4cm high; stamped 935 German silver mark and artist's monogram P.H. circa 1900.

3. A porcelain part dinner service designed by Peter Behrens 1901, manufactured by Gebr. Bauscher, Weiden. The delicate linear designs are typical of this period.

2

3

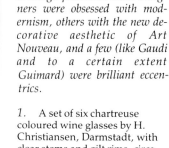

1

2

3

4

5

6

There was a wealth of new imagery for designers to work with at the turn of the century and many new solutions were found to design problems. Some designers were obsessed with modernism, others with the new decorative aesthetic of Art Nouveau, and a few (like Gaudi and to a certain extent Guimard) were brilliant eccentrics.

1.   A set of six chartreuse coloured wine glasses by H. Christiansen, Darmstadt, with clear stems and gilt rims, circa 1906, 20.5 cm. high.

2.   A two-handled stoneware vase designed by Hugo Leven for Reinhold Merkelbach, decorated in relief with a band of Jugendstil motifs; 23 cm. high, marked with HL monogram circa 1905.

3.   A glass and silvered bronze centrepiece by Baccarat, the clear glass bowl cut and moulded with geese in flight, the four footed mount cast with birds amidst branches; 35.3 cm. wide; stamped circular Baccarat mark.

4.   A dessert server and two of twelve sorbet spoons, designed by Peter Behrens and manufactured by Franz Mosgau, Berlin, the bowls of parcel gilt; server 22.4 cm; stamped FZM monogram and marks (8 ozs 15 dwts).

5.   A brass and copper lamp by Henri van de Velde; 48 cm. high.

6.   A carved pearwood sidechair by Hector Guimard, circa 1905, 110.5 cm. high, 47 cm. wide; a carved oak pedestal, 102 cm high, supporting a bronze vase 26 cm. high, both also by Guimard.

7.   A German Arts & Crafts stained walnut single bed and dressing table from a suite of bedroom furniture; bed 105.5 cm. wide; dressing table 171.5 cm. high.

8.   A dining chair from an oak dining room suite designed by Peter Behrens in 1902.

9.   A mahogany, bronze mounted coiffeuse by Gustave Serrurier Bovy; 188 cm. high, 129 cm. wide; branded maker's marks. This piece was exhibited at the Exposition Universelle, Paris, 1900.

10.   An 'Uccle' padouk wood side chair with rush seat by Henri van de Velde, designed circa 1895, executed circa 1896–98; 94 cm. high.

11.   A Serrurier–Bovy 'Silex' dismantling mahogany chair, upholstered in green velvet, constructed with dowelling and four screws with backplates for easy dismantling, circa 1905.

7

8

9

10

11

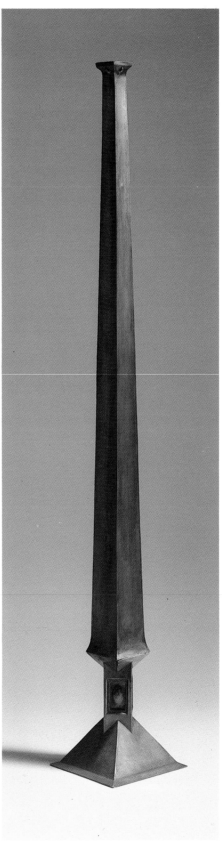

Frank Lloyd Wright was born in 1869 in Richland Center, Wisconsin, and died in Phoenix, Arizona in 1959, working his whole life as an architect and designer. His early commissions are considered by some to have been the most important and most influential. To a certain extent they predate the rectilinear style of avant-garde Dutch designers, like Gerrit Rietveld, during the second decade of the twentieth century. These commissions include a number of private houses like the Darwin Martin and Bradley Houses and some office buildings, the most interesting of which was the Larkin Building – as remarkable for its architecture as for its interior, with a series of simple metal desks with attached swivel chairs which still look modern today.

1. A fine leaded glass interior window designed by Frank Lloyd Wright for the Darwin D. Martin House, Buffalo, N.Y. 1904, executed by Linden Glass Company, in original pine backed oak frame; 86.5 × 40.5 cm.

2. An important copper 'weed' vase by Frank Lloyd Wright, circa 1890–1900; 74 cm. high. This shows the spare, clean lines of new design.

3. Two leaded glass skylights designed by Frank Lloyd Wright for the B. Harley Bradley House, Kankakee, Illinois, circa 1900, elaborately and variously leaded within a stylized American Indian motif, in their original frames; 94.5 × 53 cm.

1

2

3

Frank Lloyd Wright was the first of the American architect designers to occupy himself with all aspects of the decorative arts appertaining to the interior design of his buildings. His style of interior design was in keeping with the American Arts and Crafts Movements as disseminated in publications like Owen Jones's Grammar of Ornament, *Christopher Dresser's* Principles of Decorative Design *and Charles Eastlake's* Hints on Household Taste in Furniture, Upholstery and Other Details, *and later made popular by Gustav Stickley with his simply designed oak furniture.*

1.   A view of the Bradley living room showing an example of the window and the wall sconces in situ.

2.   One of a pair of brass wall sconces with opalescent glass globular shades designed by Frank Lloyd Wright for the B.H. Bradley House, Kankakee, Illinois, 1900. 45.5 cm. high overall.

1

2

3

3. A rare leaded glass table lamp designed by Frank Lloyd Wright, circa 1904, the cantilevered, semi-opaque glass shade on an adjustable arm; shade 27.3 cm. square, lamp 43.8 cm. high.

4. A reproduction of the 1902 catalogue cover of the Chicago Architectural Club exhibition at the Art Institute of Chicago, showing the 'weed' vases flanking the 'first modern chair'.

5. A pair of oak side chairs designed by Frank Lloyd Wright for the Hillside Home School, Spring Green, Wisconsin, circa 1887–1903; 101 cm. high.

4

5

CHAPTER 2

Art Nouveau

Art Nouveau was the phrase coined in 1895 by Samuel Bing, a German-born Parisian dealer, for a new style of merchandise seen for the first time at his store which was called 'La Maison de l'Art Nouveau'. It has come to be accepted internationally as a loose term to cover almost all turn-of-the-century styles and has led to a good deal of confusion. As usually happens with a fashion trend, Art Nouveau was discarded and forgotten for almost half a century after its heyday, only to be rediscovered in the late 1960s (almost simultaneously with Art Deco). At the turn of the century Paris led the world in fashion, and as a direct consequence it was in French Art Nouveau that the new fashionable style of decoration found its first and fullest expression. But at the time it was also known by many other names. In Italy it was called 'Il Stile Liberty' after Arthur Lasenby Liberty's London store. In Germany it was Jugendstil (youth style), and in Vienna it was known as Secession style after the Secessionists. In France it was also known as 'style nouille' (spaghetti style) or 'style métro' after Hector Guimard's extravagant designs for the Paris underground.

Unlike the avant-garde trends described in the last chapter, French Art Nouveau was pure decoration inspired by the sinuous shapes found in plant forms. It was as emotional as the avant-garde was practical, caring deeply about poetry and the force of nature rather than form and function. And yet this style was also a

reaction against Victorian tradition, in particular the tradition of slavish and accurate imitation of nature. Art Nouveau at its most extravagant went to ridiculous lengths of distortion, with long streaming hairstyles on youthful maidens winding their way to decorative lunacy. And yet many of the sources for the decorative 'revolution' were the same as those for the avant-garde functionalists. Both found their inspiration in a close study of nature, but with different responses. Owen Jones, author of what became a standard text-book for designers called *The Grammar of Ornament*, wrote: 'The beauty of form is produced by lines born out of each other in gradual undulations.' These 'undulations' became a sort of leitmotiv for Art Nouveau decoration, and were in essence a revolt against academic art and naturalism. 'The most obvious stylistic traits of Art Nouveau are fluid forms and twisting, interlacing lines, which were intended to represent the endless process of natural creativity. The result was the organic, biomorphic and phytomorphic forms that are so immediately striking in Art Nouveau works, whether in architecture, furniture, ceramics or poster advertising.'

Before Art Nouveau burst in on the Paris scene in the mid-1890s, late nineteenth-century French design had gone through a dull period, paying little heed to modern trends or the teachings of Ruskin and Morris. In the early 1890s craftsmen were still reproducing pastiches of earlier decorative styles, but Bing saw a need for new ideas when he opened his shop in 1895. He had already been living in Paris for nearly 25 years, dealing mainly in Japanese art, but felt impelled to provide an outlet for the young talent he saw around him in Paris. His shop became the centre for this altogether unexpected decorative style, inspired chiefly by the work of Hector Guimard in Paris and Victor Horta in Brussels. The

(*Above*)   A Loetz goose-neck iridescent glass vase with combed iridescent silver and purple feather design over green glass, circa 1900; 27.1 cm. high.

(*Left*).   A blue Jack-in-the-Pulpit Favrile glass vase by Tiffany Studios; 54 cm. high, foot inscribed 6119E L.C. Tiffany-Favrile.

impact of Bing's venture on European decorative arts was enormous. Designers from all over Europe and some Americans too were shown at 'La Maison de l'Art Nouveau', but the emphasis was on French design, with furniture by Georges de Feure and Eugène Gaillard, pottery by Eugène Colonna, glass by Emile Gallé and jewellery by René Lalique. The work of these artists also dominated the 1900 Paris Exhibition, eclipsing for the first time in several decades the German and British designers.

Hector Guimard was the first and for a long time the leading exponent of French Art Nouveau, expressing himself principally as an architect, but one who was concerned equally with the interior decoration of his buildings. For him an interior had to be the continuation of the exterior, achieving unity and harmony without interruption of design. His earliest work in Art Nouveau was the Castel Beranger (1894-8), but it was the Métro stations in Paris (1899-1900) which really made him famous. 'In these charming buildings, a cross between pagoda and pavilion, and executed in glass and iron, he gave full reign to his imagination. Light bulbs appear to sprout from their holders like buds in spring; crustaceans from the ocean depths seem to have scattered their spiky shields along the balustrades. And yet every detail is subordinated to a stylistic common denominator 'Art Nouveau'.' It is this subordination to a decorative language that is the essence of Art Nouveau; practicality was secondary to stylistic trend so that objects were virtually in disguise, a Raoul Larche lamp transformed into Loïe Fuller doing the scarf dance, or an architectural fitting masquerading as a complex web of whiplash lines.

Samuel Bing's decision to change from Japanese art and artefacts was in some ways a practical one. Japanese art had been overexposed and its novelty had worn off in Europe; also collectors were losing interest because it had become too expensive, and so Bing was impelled to look for something new to deal in. He became interested in contemporary art, and after several successful exhibitions decided to open a gallery with a permanent display of modern decorative art in conjunction with exhibitions of paintings. The artists he chose were on the whole decorative painters, and the paintings of George de Feure in particular fitted into the scheme of things and harmonized with the surroundings of 'La Maison de l'Art Nouveau'. During the 1890s de Feure, already known as a painter, became highly regarded as a designer of textiles, furniture, porcelain, wallpapers and posters; in a sense this variety of talents was forced upon him, as from a very early age he had been compelled to earn a living, drifting from one job to another and eventually deciding to channel his ideas in the direction of drawing and designing. The subjects he chose were women and flowers, often combining the two in his designs, the woman sometimes becoming the flower she symbolizes as in his series of drawings called 'Feminiflores'. One commentator remarked that George de Feure's work was 'a hymn to the beauty of women'.

De Feure also contributed to another gallery of contemporary decorative arts opened in Paris by Julius Meier-Grafe in 1898 and called 'La Maison Moderne'. Pursuing the ideals of William Morris, Meier-Grafe advocated 'equality in the arts'. The façade of 'La Maison Moderne' and the showrooms were designed by Henry van de Velde, and Maurice Dufrène was responsible for much of the interior detail.

The French Art Nouveau designers created interiors full of exoticism and mystique, and in their search for a totally new look imposed new artistic criteria on the few rich clients they had, many of them involved in the world of the theatre and the arts. Robert Montesquiou, the poet, for example, was one of Gallé's most important patrons, and René Lalique made many of his most elaborate pieces of jewellery for the legendary actress Sarah Bernhardt. This sort of clientele dictated a degree of excellence which marked the early years of Art Nouveau before it became popular and commercialized as a result of its great success at the 1900 Exhibition. Furniture was hand-carved, inlaid and made of exotic woods to intricate original designs. In his jewellery, Lalique preferred intricate workmanship to gems, choosing to combine semi-precious stones with materials such as ivory, glass and enamel. He was first noticed in 1893 when he exhibited at the Société des Artistes Français the jewellery he had designed for Sarah Bernhardt, a collection considered to be more works of art than jewellery.

Lalique's new approach to precious metals and gemstones was copied by other jewellers of the time like Eugène Gaillard, Charles Boutet de Monvel, Henri Vever and Georges Fouquet. Lalique combined detailed precision and elaborate craftsmanship with a fertile imagination; artistically he was very taken with the current decorative language of flowers, insects and long flowing hair. As Martin Battersby says, 'artists were obsessed to the point of fetishism with women's hair, which seems to have, as they depicted it, a separate life of its own, not agitated by the wind, but curling in arabesques like the tendrils of a plant seeking to entwine itself around a support or a victim.' This obsession is perhaps best seen in the work of the Czech-born designer Alphons Mucha, who is remembered chiefly for his elaborate poster designs, executed in a highly personal style, some of the best-known of which were for Bières de la Meuse and Moët & Chandon. His style was too individual to be copied, although it has continued to have an effect on graphic design even up to the present day. The poster generally underwent a metamorphosis during the Art Nouveau period, partly because poster advertising, particularly on hoardings, was a new idea attracting more public attention than before and tempting artists to work in that field. In the 1890s the masters of the genre were almost all French, with Ernest Grasset, Jules Chéret and Théophile Alexandre Steinlen dominating the field, though by 1900 each country was discovering an easily discernible style of its own.

A white-painted and inlaid Shapland and Petter writing desk, inset with a leaded glass panel and with leather-lined top, the panels inlaid in fruitwoods with poppyheads and sinuous stems; 100 cm. high, 108.7 cm. wide.

This combination of a style full of poetry, exoticism and sheer luxury reached its peak at the 1900 Paris Exhibition with Samuel Bing's pavilion, a low, one-storey building designed by Georges de Feure. There was furniture by Gaillard and Colonna, and the walls were hung with paintings by a yet unknown artists, José Maria Sert. From the point of view of luxury, skill and craftsmanship it was one of the finest ensembles ever achieved in this style. But it also marked a turning-point, for it coincided with the popularization of Art Nouveau. After 1900 the style became commercialized, with machine-made artefacts, a lower standard of workmanship, and a less discerning clientele.

It was in Nancy, however, a small town just 200 miles south-east of Paris, that French Art Nouveau found its highest expression in the work of the glassmakers Emile Gallé and the Daum brothers, as well as in the furniture of Louis Majorelle. This group of artists with some others, such as Eugène Vallin and Jaques Gruber, formed L'Ecole de Nancy, Alliance Provinciale des Industries d'Art. The influences seen in their work were

threefold, made up of a blend of Japonisme, the visual and emotional forces of nature, both of which were common to nearly all Art Nouveau, and a third element peculiar to their style, the influence of Baroque and Rococo as seen at their very best in their native town. The main square of Nancy is one of the most perfect examples of these styles in France. L'Ecole de Nancy was not formed until 1896, but the work of its chief exponent, Emile Gallé, was already well-known throughout the 1890s, having been seen at the major industrial exhibitions. Gallé can only be described as a poet-industrialist, a genius who was preoccupied equally with both aspects of that title. Above his studio was inscribed the legend 'Ma Racine est au fond des Bois' (My Roots lie in the heart of the Forest); for him nature was an emotional force, full of poetry, lines of which often found their way into the artistic composition of his work. By 1900 his workshop had 300 employees, and had become a highly successful business enterprise.

Gallé is best known for his revitalization of the cameo and carved glass techniques, with which he created a

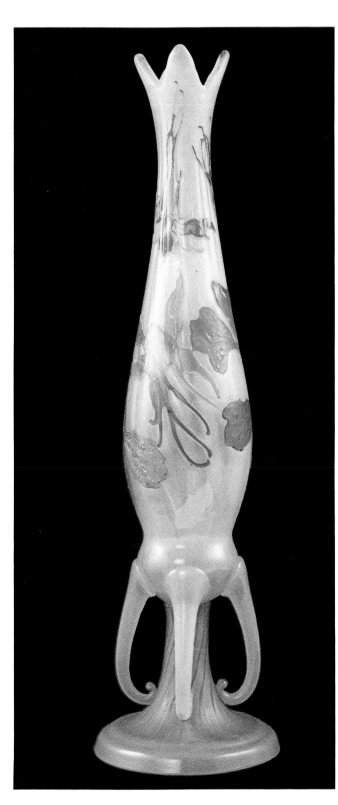

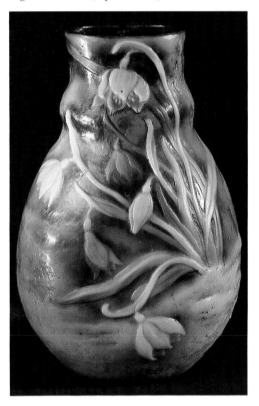

(*Left*) A Gallé marqueterie de verre, engraved and applied glass vase; 43.2 cm. high, engraved and gilt Gallé.

(*Below*) An overlay, engraved and verrerie parlante glass vase, carved with snowdrops and inscribed 'Il faut si peu de chose pour réveiller les anges endormis, Maeterlinck'; 16.6 cm. high, engraved E. Gallé (repair to neck).

very personal style of decoration that is synonymous with Art Nouveau. His work falls into two main categories, the simpler pieces produced as industrial glass to be sold as widely as possible, and the complicated and meticulously worked unique pieces, intended as works of art. His chief rivals, the Daum brothers, had a somewhat different approach; apart from various techniques discovered and used almost exclusively by them, their attitude was less lyrical, and more matter of fact. They too worked in cameo techniques, with interesting extra effects such as the inclusion of gold foil and decoration between the layers of glass, producing atmospheric effects like rain and snow, a technique known as 'intercalaire'.

As for the furniture made by artists of the Nancy School, it too had a special style. In adition to glass and some faience, Gallé also produced some furniture, mostly with marquetry decoration, but it was Louis Majorelle who was the most successful of the furniture designers. At his workshop, which employed 30 hands, the pieces made were on the whole in earlier French styles, with large cupboards in the Renaissance style, desks mainly in Louis XV and chairs in Louis XVI style. 'But a common feature of almost all of them, especially

(*Opposite*) A gold, mother-of-pearl, pearl and tortoise-shell hair comb by Georges Fouquet; 14 cm. high, signed G. Fouquet.
An opal, gold and silver belt buckle by Lucien Gaillard; 10 cm. wide, signed L. Gaillard.
A horn, ivory, gold and glass paper knife by René Lalique; 32.5 cm. long, inscribed Lalique.
An ivory, enamel and gold parasol handle by René Lalique; 19.5 cm. high, inscribed R. Lalique.

the smaller pieces, is that the constructive elements – the actual structure – are transformed into stalks of branches springing out from the constructive points. The decoration – both the inlay work and carving – is floral in character, blossoming freely all over the surface.'

English Art Nouveau was far less flamboyant in character and showed considerable restraint, while still being a revolt against mid-Victorian taste and style. The reason for this was probably that whereas in France Art Nouveau made a sudden dramatic appearance, in England it evolved quite naturally, and even the sensationalism of Aubrey Beardsley's drawings showed formality and a deep sense of order. They grew out of the Japanese taste that dominated Aesthetic Movement design. Beardsley was in fact as near as England got to pure Art Nouveau, and perhaps his influence would have changed the face of Art Nouveau in England had he lived beyond an untimely death at the age of 26. In England there were no traces of the Rococo elements which influenced the continental style.

The best of English Art Nouveau is seen in some of the wallpaper and carpet designs of Charles Annesley Voysey, as well as in the more elaborate pieces of Ashbee silver and jewellery. But once again it was a retail store that popularized the fashion in England at the turn of the century. Arthur Lasenby Liberty had opened his shop on Regent Street as early as 1875 for the sale of silks from the East, but in the 1890s and more particularly in the first decade of the twentieth century, the best Liberty products also constituted what was best in Art Nouveau in England, including furniture, textiles, silver, pewter and jewellery. Arthur Liberty, as he said in a paper delivered in 1904 entitled 'Pewter and the Revival of its Use', was scornful about 'the fantastic motif which it pleases our Continental friends to worship as L'Art Nouveau'. At Liberty's one found elegance without flamboyance. Because its records were destroyed by fire, little is known about the history of the company, beyond the fact that certain independent designers worked for the firm and that it also had its own design studio.

The most original ranges produced by Liberty were 'Tudric' and 'Cymric', the names given to their pewter and silverware. The Cymric range was started in the last two years of the 1800s, and the pieces were made in conjunction with the Birmingham manufacturer W. H. Haseler, to designs by Oliver Baker, Rex Silver and Archibald Knox. The most prolific of these was Knox, a Manxman steeped in Celtic art who came to London in the mid-1890s. His designs, often incorporating Celtic motifs, are strong but controlled, often using semiprecious stones like turquoise matrix set into metal. The firm of Murle Bennett also produced some of his designs. Most of the best Tudric designs were also by Knox and worked particularly well in a new blend of pewter with a high silver content as manufactured by Liberty. The best Tudric and Cymric at their most stylish typify the later English Art Nouveau style. Among independent furniture designers the best-known were Voysey and George Walton, a Scottish designer who along with

E. A. Taylor designed some of the most stylish Art Nouveau furniture produced in Britain. E. G. Punnett, who worked for Birch of High Wycombe, also designed for Liberty. Another furniture designer, whose work is very typical of English Art Nouveau, is J. S. Henry, whose pieces were sparingly inlaid with coloured woods and metals.

In each of the European countries Art Nouveau developed national characteristics, but France was regarded the undisputed leader of the style. The distinguishing features in each country were either determined by the genius of a particular artist with an unmistakable individual style, or by a successful industrial venture like the Württembergerische Metal Fabrik (WMF) or Loetz. In some instances this success was due to a small group of talented designers working anonymously for a particular firm. Outside Britain and France, the most remarkable individual talents were Antonio Gaudí in Spain and Horta in Belgium. Gaudí lived and worked in Barcelona where his eccentric and remarkable Church of the Sagrada Familia still dominates the city despite the fact that it was never completed, though under continuous construction from 1883 to 1926. It is so strange and mannered a building as to defy description, being full of mysticism and symbolism derived from a variety of influences ranging from Ruskin and the French neo-Gothic architect Viollet-le-Duc to Wagner. Elsewhere in Barcelona there are buildings by Gaudí full of the mystic symbolism which he felt should inhabit architecture, each one an integrated whole with every detail designed by himself. Both he and Horta were pioneers whose highly individual genius extended beyond the boundaries of architecture and decorative design, creating new ideas in the 1890s before French Art Nouveau erupted into the world, reached its peak very quickly and sank into a rapid decline. Horta's first commission, the Maison Tassel in Brussels, was completed in 1893, and in this and later buildings (the most famous of which is possibly the Maison Solvay also in Brussels) architecture found a rhythm that rapidly gained momentum as it influenced architecture and designers from Guimard to Jan Toorop.

Toorop was in fact exceptional in Holland, for Art Nouveau in that country was on the whole even more restrained than in Britain. But Toorop, whose connection with Art Nouveau was mainly through his graphic work, developed a mystic style with labyrinthine, curvilinear patterns in which one feels that sinuous ornament dictates the character of an image, with heads and limbs bobbing up almost as an afterthought. His best-known work is probably the poster for salad oil, or 'Delftsche Slaolie'. At the other extreme of Dutch Art Nouveau is Hendrik Berlage's Amsterdam Stock Exchange, built between 1898 and 1903, with clean and firm lines, free of all unnecessary ornament. Again and again one is struck by the extremes of Art Nouveau, with exaggerated curves at one end and stark rectilinear simplicity at the other. On occasion the two combined very successfully, with many of the Wiener Werkstätte designs illustrating the best examples of this fusion, and leading the way to the formal geometry of Art Deco. Apart from what has already been described there was very little other pure whiplash design in Europe, except perhaps for the furniture of Carlo Zen and Eugenio Quarti in Italy, the European country least affected by the craze for Art Nouveau.

In Germany and the Scandinavian countries Art Nouveau was never an extreme style. All elements of its decorative language were absorbed and developed with a characteristic academicism. In Germany there was both figurative and abstract 'Jugendstil'. The earlier German style (before 1900), as seen in the embroideries of Hermann Obrist, was influenced chiefly by the floral wallpaper and textile designs of William Morris, and was referred to in Germany as 'Kunstgewerbliche Anglomanie' (decorative Anglomania); but after the turn of the century the stylization became more abstract. Many designs were those of architect-designers executing commissions for public or private buildings, and there was plenty for them to do as it was a period of industrial development with funds available both in the public and the private sectors.

In the decorative arts the glass, ceramics, metalwork and furniture industries all encouraged contemporary design, and some of the highest-quality European Art Nouveau was produced by German factories such as Meissen and Nymphenburg. A few companies devoted almost their entire output to the new style; the Württembergische Metal Fabrik (WMF), for instance, produced Art Nouveau artefacts almost exclusively during the first decade of the twentieth century, catering for a mass market which necessitated a middle-brow interpretation of Art Nouveau that borders on kitsch, with a wide range of decanters, sweetmeat dishes and silvered pewter bowls overdecorated with winged maidens and floral ornamentation. Other metal firms, like Kayserzinn and Hueck, employing such designers as Albin Mueller and Olbrich and Hugo Leven, produced more interesting work, including some classic pieces like the Olbrich candlesticks. At Meissen the new porcelain was designed by George Hoentschel, Peter Behrens, and perhaps most important of all, the Belgian designer Henry van de Velde whose work was one of the main influences on the later German Art Nouveau style.

German Art Nouveau centred around Munich, partly because four decorative arts journal were launched in the area, all in 1897, partly also because of the important patronage of Grand Duke Ernest Ludwig of Hesse. Outstanding among the German designers were Richard Riemerschmid, Hans Christiansen, Patriz Huber and Bernhard Pankok, all of whom designed complete interiors and were interested in all aspects of the decorative arts. Art Nouveau lasted for a comparatively short time in Germany and never became a homogeneous style as in France, although there were many distinguished individual designers in all branches of the decorative arts from furniture to jewellery. The reason for its short lifespan was that it arrived in Germany late, the first Japanese exhibition not being organized until 1882 in Berlin, long after the rest of Europe had been

One of a pair of WMF electroplated comportes, the stem modelled as Art Nouveau maiden, the bowl pierced and embossed with berried foliage; 40.8 cm. high, stamped WMF.

influenced by the Orient.

In the Scandinavian countries, the most interesting Art Nouveau was in Finland, particularly in some of the tapestries and furniture that were produced there. There was no real Scandinavian 'School' of Art Nouveau apart from this, although there was interesting porcelain at the Rørstrand factory in Sweden and at the Royal Copenhagen and Bing and Grøndahl factories in Denmark. The Danish silversmith Georg Jensen also executed some of the earliest designs of his career in this style.

In Austria, apart from the famous Wiener Werkstätte designers, the one oustanding contribution to Art Nouveau was the glass produced by the firm of Johann Loetz Witwe under the direction of Max Ritter von Spaun, who was artistic director from 1879 until his death in 1909. Loetz carried out a number of designs for the Wiener Werkstätte, but the major part of their output during this period was a variety of iridescent glass in organic shapes, made according to complex technical formulas which they patented. The glass was of excellent quality and original in design, providing some of the most stylized mass-produced Art Nouveau articles of any European country. Loetz openly acknowledged their debt to Tiffany, actually calling some of their early iridescent ware 'Gläser à la Tiffany'.

This is a rare exception, for on the whole American Art Nouveau depended heavily on the European style. Even Louis Comfort Tiffany, while he was an innovator in one sense, was much more an artist who felt a close affinity to Art Nouveau and was happy to give his own account of the style without any progressive artistic statements. His originality lay more in a highly unorthodox approach to glass techniques, which he used first for stained glass. Later he extended these techniques and developed an entirely new method of

A marqueterie de verre and wheel-carved dragonfly
coupe by Emile Gallé, 1903; 19 cm. high, 20.5 cm. diam.

making the leaded glass lampshades with which his
name is most readily associated. His experiments
resulted in a very wide range of glass, some of it almost
jewel-like, and in the most complicated of his lamps like
the magnolia, wisteria, or dragonfly lamps, the different
varieties and colours were used to magical effects. As
with Tiffany stained glass, the effect was achieved by
combining a variety of textures and thicknesses of glass
in the same piece as well as by colour and design. The
weak electric bulbs which lit the shades provided a
glowing effect which was completely new at the time,
and was probably the most original early artistic use of
electricity. There was also a range of Tiffany studio glass
made for artistic rather than practical purposes, for
which the trade name Favrile glass was used.

Tiffany was one of the very few American artists who
worked in the Art Nouveau style, which was in part due
to his early studies as a painter in Paris. On the whole,
American design at this period was more oriented
towards a much earlier British Arts and Crafts tradition,
with one other notable exception in the Chicago architect Louis Sullivan, who created an Art Nouveau style
completely separate from that of Tiffany in New York.
Sullivan too had studied in Paris at the Ecole des Beaux-
Arts before settling in Chicago at the age of 23; he practised there as an architect for the rest of his life, but some
of his greatest work was built during the Art Nouveau
period with the department store Carson Pirie Scott
being perhaps the most spectacular of these. He too
developed a personal style which is easily recognizable.
It was in Chicago too that the periodical, the *Chap-Book*,
was published, with illustrations by William Bradley
whose work is reminiscent of Beardsley, but has a dis-
tinct style of its own, as seen in his illustration entitled
'The Serpentine Dancer', an almost abstract image of the
American dancer Loïe Fuller, the legendary figure
whose extraordinary scarf dances were almost the
embodiment of Art Nouveau.

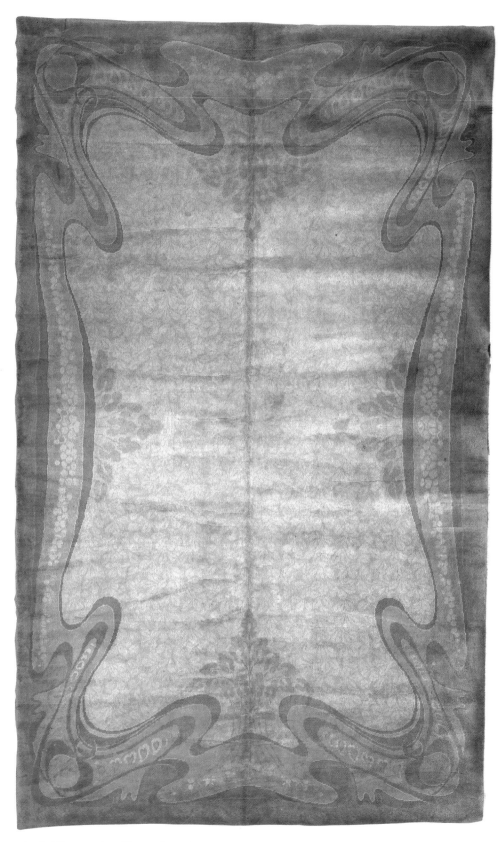

An Art Nouveau hand-knotted wool carpet, the design attributed to
Edward Colonna, circa 1900; 567 cm. × 342 cm.

The curvilinear designs of European Art Nouveau have earned it, among other descriptions, the name Spaghetti Style. When used with flair as in the designs of Hector Guimard in France and Victor Horta in Belgium it has rhythm and a strong dramatic impact. It was also used to great effect by a few of the Italian designers (Carlo Zen, Alessandro Mazucotelli) and by the Czech artist Alphonse Mucha.

1. An Italian mahogany extending dining table by Eugenio Quarti; 134.5 cm. wide. Together with Zen, Quarti was the best-known Italian designer at work during the Art Nouveau period.

2. A rare ormolu mounted chandelier by Hector Guimard circa 1900, opaline glass panels alternating with beaded glass tubes and gilt bronze rods; 44 cm. high, unsigned.

6

3. A nest of three oak marquetry tables by Emile Gallé, the rectangular tops inlaid in various woods with landscapes, flora and animals; largest table, 68 cm. high, 37.5 × 57 cm. signed in the marquetry. Gallé furniture differed greatly in its quality, and that illustrated here falls into a medium-priced comercially produced range.

4. A pair of pewter two-branch candelabra designed by Albert Reimann, 38.2 cm. high. This is an example of geometry as opposed to the random curvilinear Art Nouveau style.

5. Two from a set of six Italian mahogany armchairs by Carlo Zen, the foremost Italian furniture designer at this period.

6. A shield-shaped cast iron balustrade with green patina, from the Paris Métro, designed by Hector Guimard, circa 1900, 75 cm. high, unsigned.

7. A William Hutton & Sons silver cup and cover with wirework handles of whiplash design, and the finial modelled as a naked female figure; 29.5 cm. high, London hallmarks for 1903 and maker's monogram WH&S (13 oz. 17 dwt.).

8. A Gustave Gurschner bronze and Loetz glass table lamp; 58 cm. high, base inscribed Wien Gurschner Deposé.

9. A satinwood and marquetry coiffeuse inlaid with fruitwoods, by Jacques Gruber; 126 cm. high, 97 cm. wide, signed in the marquetry J. Gruber. Note the combination of different exotic woods in this piece.

10. A cast iron umbrella and cane stand by Hector Guimard, the scalloped base cast with sinuous flowers and stems; 87.5 cm. high.

7

8

9

10

Once they discovered whiplash design, the French designers revelled in the decorative possibilities it offered. The main source of inspiration for their designs came from the botanical world and in particular the tortuous nature of roots and the unending patterns of their growth. Throughout his life Emile Gallé studied natural forms, which always ended up being the subject of his decoration on furniture and glass. But nature was for Gallé merely the basis for his rich poetic imagination to work on. He exaggerated its realities to create a new decorative style full of poetic images which were at once realistic and full of licence.

1

2

1. A fine inlaid and carved bureau-de-dame in the 'umbel' pattern by Emile Gallé; 85 cm. high, 96.5 cm. wide; signed Gallé in marquetry.

2. A walnut and fruitwood marquetry ormolu-mounted étagère by Emile Gallé; 92 cm. wide; signed in the marquetry Gallé Expos 1900.

3. 'Nénuphars', a mahogany, burr walnut and ormolu guéridon by Louis Majorelle, the ormolu mounts cast with lily leaves and flowers, circa 1900; 74.8 cm. diam.

4. An inlaid mahogany vitrine by Emile Gallé, with bevelled glass cupboard doors above open shelves; 159 cm. high.

4

3

Insects, flora, fauna and marine life formed the decorative world of the two great glass designers of the Art Nouveau period, Emile Gallé and Antonin Daum. Their approach to nature was different. There is no doubt that Gallé was the great innovator and that Daum followed his lead, capitalizing on a style that Gallé had made popular. Gallé's response to nature was highly individual and deeply emotional. Carved above his studio was the legend 'Ma Racine est au fond des bois' (My Roots lie in the heart of the forest). Daum's response to nature was more matter-of-fact and purely imitative.

1.   A double overlay glass and bronze mounted miniature lamp by Emile Gallé; 16 cm. high, relief signature.

2. A Daum double overlay glass vase, the opalescent martelé ground overlaid in pale purple and green and wheel carved with purple croci; 17 cm. high, etched and gilded signature Daum Nancy and the Cross of Lorraine.

3. A Daum blowout vase, with moulded and carved relief decoration, circa 1900; 29.8 cm. high, incised Daum Nancy.

4. A Daum cameo glass vase, with carved and acid-etched decoration, circa 1900; 35.5 cm. high, cameo signature Daum Nancy with Cross of Lorraine.

5. A Gallé cameo glass vase, with carved and acid-etched decoration of leaves and berries; 34.4 cm. high, cameo signature Gallé.

6. A Gallé double overlay solifleur vase with carved, acid-etched and fire-polished decoration of clematis; 79.5 cm. high, pontil etched Gallé déposé.

7. A double overlay glass vase etched with poppies, by Muller; 40.5 cm. high, cameo signature.

8. A cameo glass vase by Emile Gallé etched with sprays of honeysuckle; 22.9 cm. high, cameo signature Gallé.

9. 'Les Coprins', a wrought iron mounted, triple overlay, internally decorated and engraved glass table lamp by Emile Gallé, designed as three fungi resting on a black patinated and foliate wrought iron base; 83 cm. high, medium shade engraved Gallé. This lamp almost goes beyond poetry into surrealism.

10. A Harant-Guignard applied and cameo glass marine baluster vase; 14.7 cm. high, engraved HG monogram and retailer's inscription Le Rosay, Paris.

7

8

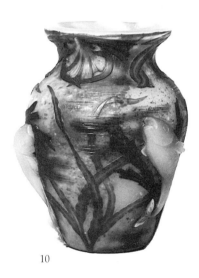

10

9

Electricity was still a comparative novelty at the turn of the century, and the possibilities it offered were a challenge to glassmakers above all. Of all materials glass is transformed most by light, and in particular cameo glass where the intensity of light varies with the thickness of the glass, creating a sculptural three-dimensional effect when a lamp is lit. The all-glass lamps of Daum and Gallé had concealed lighting in the base as well. Lit from within, the imagery of these lamps takes on a warm glow.

1. A large double overlay landscape lamp by Daum; 86.5cm. high; shade signed Daum, Nancy, the base with Daum monogram.

2. An Emile Gallé triple overlay glass nasturtium lamp and shade; 40cm. high; shade and base with Gallé cameo signature.

3. A triple overlay glass table lamp by Emile Gallé; 79cm. high, with cameo signatures Gallé on base and shade.

1

2

1

2

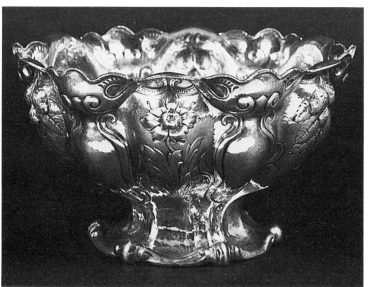

3

4

5

Some of the most popular symbols of Art Nouveau are seen in the imagery of those objects illustrated here, the peacock, the orchid and the dragonfly. They appeared on furniture, glass, ceramics and jewellery. The dragonfly with its brilliantly coloured translucent wings was a favourite subject for jewellers working in plique-à-jour (or transparent enamels), and appears repeatedly in Lalique jewellery of the Art Nouveau period. The peacock's tail was also a challenge to the enameller's art, and peacock blue together with turquoise and the other exotic colours to be found in peacock feathers are very typical of Art Nouveau colouring.

1.   A glass and silver chalice by René Lalique, the reticulated silver mount of pine cones and needles blown with opalescent glass; 19 cm. high, impressed Lalique 7 (minor restorations).

2.   A silver vase of petal form by Philippe Wolfers; 10 cm. high, impressed Wolfers Frères 800; 22 troy ozs. (with glass liner).

3.   An enamelled silver, wood and bronze wall mirror by Henri Vever, the bronze frame surmounted by an enamelled peacock; 60.5 cm. diam., impressed Vever (some restoration to peacock).

4.   An inlaid mahogany
secretaire by Louis Majorelle,
the fall front finely inlaid with
flower-laden vines; 159 cm.
high, 64.7 cm. wide.

5.   A hammered silver
punchbowl by Gorham, circa
1900, repoussé with a design of
flowers and scrolls; 25 cm.
diam., impressed firm's
hallmarks (46 troy ozs.).

6.   A silver and gold belt
buckle by René Lalique, a Lady's
Slipper orchid incorporated in
the design; 9.5 cm. diam.,
stamped Lalique.

7.   A pearl and horn hair comb
by Lucien Gaillard circa 1900;
16 cm. high, inscribed
L. Gaillard.

8.   Three Bonté openwork
horn pendants suspended on
silk cords interspersed with
glass beads; 7.5, 10 and 7 cm.
high, all with incised signatures.
Carved horn was popular for
jewellery especially hair
ornaments.

9.   A nest of inlaid walnut
tables by Emile Gallé, the four
graduating rectangular tops
inlaid with woodland and rural
scenes; largest table 71 cm. high,
top 62 × 42.5 cm. Marquetry
signature on each table.

6

7

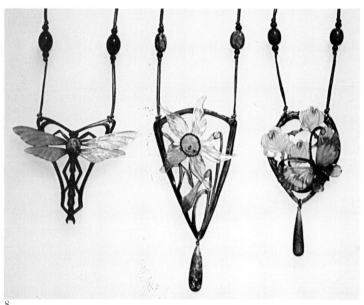

8

9

By 1900 the art of cameo glass had become widely popular in France. At the height of his career Emile Gallé was able to employ several hundred craftsmen to work for him in this laborious technique in which layers of glass are cut away by repeated treatment with acid. The simpler designs were executed in large editions with the minimum artistic supervision, but Gallé's masterpieces, as seen here, were as brilliant and inventive technically as they were artistically. In addition to cameo cutting they also had applied and marquetry (or inlaid) decoration, and each piece was unique.

1

2

1. 'Roses De France', a silver mounted, applied and triple overlay glass scent bottle and stopper by Emile Gallé; 10.8cm. high, engraved Gallé and applied with firm's original paper label.

2. A Gallé marqueterie-sur-verre, marqueterie intercalaire, engraved and verrerie parlante glass vase, engraved and hammered "Il vit que la lumière était belle, et l'aima" around the rim; 13.5cm. high, engraved Gallé.

3. An important marqueterie-de-verre and wheel-carved dragonfly coupe by Emile Gallé, 1903; 19cm. high, 20.5cm. diam.

4. 'Feuille De Chou', an applied and martelé coupe by Emile Gallé, the marbled glass applied with white veins; 15cm. high, cameo signature Gallé.

5. A mould-blown, overlay, martelé, intercalaire, applied and engraved glass vase of inverted helmet shape, applied with a shell and jellyfish; engraved Gallé.

3

4

5

1

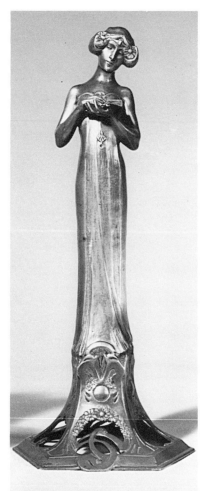

2

Art Nouveau maidens were either scantily or exotically clad, wore flowers in their hair, which was long and flowing, and were as often as not depicted doing an elaborate dance involving folds of drapery. The most famous dancer of the period was Loïe Fuller, whose costumes were of pleated gossamer silk featuring a long trailing scarf which was unfurled like a banner when she danced.

1. 'Le sommeil, femme aux pavots', a gilt bronze bust cast from a model by Maurice Bouval, on marble base; 43 cm. high, inscribed M. Bouval, stamped E Colin & Cie Paris.

2. A gilt bronze female figure cast from a model by Charles Korschann; 36.5 cm. high, inscribed Ch. Korschann Paris.

3. 'Troublante Comme L'Onde' a parcel gilt bronze group of an exotic dancer with an octopus, cast from a model by Louis Chalon; 53.7 cm. high, inscribed L. Chalon and Louchet. Voluminous drapery is used to dramatic effect here.

3

4

5

6

7

8

4. A Koening & Lengsfeld ceramic figure of a young woman gazing into an oval mirror; 70 cm. high, impressed Koening & Lengsfeld Köln Lindenthal 2687. There were many versions of this idea, often in pewter or another metal.

5. 'L'Idée', a bronze female nude figure cast from a model by Raoul-François Larche, the bronze rock base cast as an inkstand, the enclosed inkwell with hinged cover; 48.9 cm. high, inscribed Raoul Larche, stamped L576 and impressed with the Siot-Decauville foundry seal.

6. A Heubach biscuit porcelain figure in the style of Loïe Fuller, modelled by Agathon Leonard; 31.5 cm. high, impressed marks. Similar figures were made by the Sèvres porcelain manufactory, and were also cast in bronze, sometimes in combination with ivory.

7. 'Carthage', a gilt bronze group cast from a model by Théodore Rivière, inspired by Sarah Bernhardt and depicting Mathô embracing the feet of Salammbô; 41 cm. high, inscribed Theodore Rivière, Carthage 1892, founder's seal Susse Frères Editeurs Paris.

8. A bronze figural lamp cast from a model by Auguste Moreau, the flowering branch containing light fittings, circa 1900; 100 cm. high, inscribed Aug. Moreau.

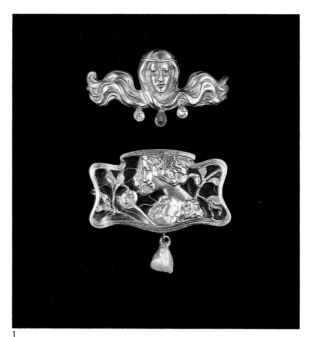

1

2

Hair in Art Nouveau imagery, like botanical roots, was cherished for its sinuous curvilinear flow, and in the elaboration of whiplash design the two sometimes become one; a maiden's hair winds itself in complicated tendrils until it disappears beneath her feet. Both in literature and in the visual arts at this period hair or 'La Chevelure' (as it becomes in the more picturesque French translation) features heavily. The story of Mélisande letting her hair cascade from a tower to envelop her lover Pelleas is the source of much Art Nouveau imagery in writing as well as design.

3

4

1.   (*Top*) An Art Nouveau
female head brooch designed by
A.G. Sandoz, signed circa 1900.
(*Bottom*) An Art Nouveau
shaped rectangular brooch,
centred with a maiden's head
and shoulders on a plique-à-jour
ground, circa 1900.

2.   A sapphire and plique-à-
jour pendant by Luis Masriera
(five sapphires missing.) Plique-
à-jour was a transparent vitrified
enamel popular among Art
Nouveau jewellery designers.

3.   'Femme Chauve-Souris', a
polychrome bronze figure of a
bat woman cast from a model by
Agathon Léonard, circa 1900;
33.6 cm. high, signed.

4.   A bronze figural lamp cast
from a model by Gustave
Gurschner, cast as a male and
two female figures clinging to
flowing drapery, one figure
holding the glass shade
attributed to Loetz; 51.7 cm.
overall height, bronze inscribed
Gurschner Deposé (wired for
electricity).

5.   Two pieces of jewellery by
René Lalique; a chalcedony,
enamel and gold brooch
suspending a baroque pearl;
6.5 cm. long, impressed Lalique;
and an enamelled gold pendant
cast with four priestesses, on an
enamelled ring and bar chain;
pendant 9.5 cm. long, stamped
Lalique.

Maidens appear again and again in Art Nouveau, and no idea involving a maiden seems to have been considered too far-fetched. Mermaids were popular in a visual language that dealt with transformation. They were also a convenient excuse for introducing mother of peal, which was very popular at this period. The idea of a mermaid holding a conch shell was particularly popular as it made a decorative lamp with the mermaid supporting the shell in which a bulb could be concealed. There are many versions of this idea.

1.   A dark brown patinated bronze figural candlestick cast from a model by Gustave Gurschner; 28.6 cm. high, inscribed Gurschner.

2.   A WMF white metal dish on stand cast as a winged maiden standing before lily pads on scroll support; 21 cm. high, stamped marks.

3.   A leaded glass nautilus lamp by Tiffany Studios with bronze mermaid base; 43 cm. high, impressed Tiffany Studios New York 28631 and Gudebrod.

6

4.   A parcel gilt bronze equestrian group of a Valkyrie cast from a model by Louis Chalon, on green marble plinth; 56.2 cm. high, inscribed L. Chalon and stamped CA9.

5.   A bronze casket cast from a model by Gustave Gurschner, with a high rich dark brown patina; 17.8 cm. high, inscribed Gurschner Deposé.

6.   An electroplated pewter mirror frame attributed to WMF, the rectangular shape broken by whiplash foliage and a female figure; 50 cm. high, circa 1900.

7.   A gilt-bronze figural lamp cast from a model by Louis Chalon, the young woman wearing only an elaborate foliate head dress; 61 cm. high, inscribed L. Chalon.

8.   A pair of asymmetrical, electroplated pewter two-branch figural candlesticks; 33 cm. high.

9.   'La Fille des Glaces', a metal and glass figure of an ice maiden, the bronze cast from a model by Julien Caussé, the opalescent glass base from a mould by Eugene Rousseau, adapted as a luminaire; 59.7 cm. high, inscribed Caussé.

7

8

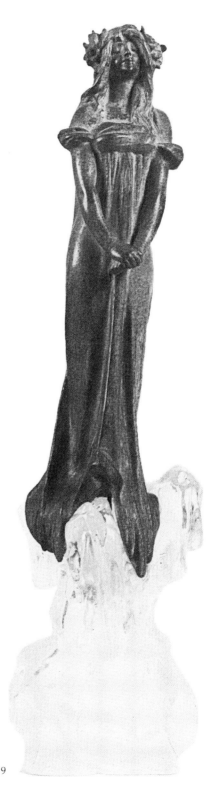

9

1

2

The French Art Nouveau jewellers had a preference for semi-precious stones masterfully set in precious metals. Baroque pearls, opals, transparent enamels and solid enamels are the most typical features of Art Nouveau jewellery. These examples show how Lalique used subjects from nature to inspire his designs.

1.   A diamond, gold and plique-à-jour enamel dragonfly brooch by René Lalique; 9.5cm. wide, inscribed Lalique Em. Anssart.

2.   A diamond, tourmaline and plique-à-jour dragonfly pendant brooch by René Lalique; signed.

3.   A diamond-set, enamelled gold and glass hair band by René Lalique, circa 1898, set with moulded glass pansies; stamped Lalique. After crafting exquisite jewellery for several years, incorporating the use of moulded glass, Lalique turned to the development of moulded glass to create good quality decorative items available to a more general public.

4.   A natural pearl, diamond, enamel and gold collar by René Lalique, circa 1900, signed Lalique.

5.   (*Left*) An enamel, pearl and gold pendant by René Lalique cast with female profiles with waving hair and enamelled swallows; signed.
(*Lower centre*) A hardstone, pearl, enamel and silver brooch by Lalique, a central hardstone head with silver swan helmet flanked by enamelled peacock wings; signed.

3

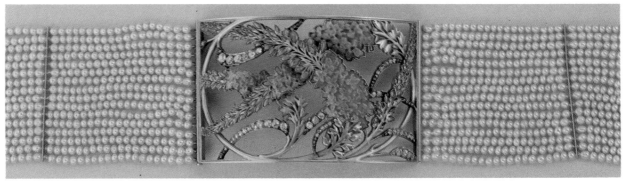

4

(*Top centre*) A pearl, diamond,
plique-à-jour enamel and gold
pendant, designed as two
dragonflies by Lalique; signed.
(*Right*) An enamel, pearl and
gold pendant by Lalique cast
with an openwork design of
pine cones and needles; signed.

1

3

2

Art Nouveau pottery used the whiplash imagery a little more sparingly mainly because it was more difficult to use successfully in this medium. Studio potters in Europe and in England either set up their own businesses or worked as designers in the industry. Many of the leading manufacturers followed the example of Royal Doulton and Minton in England and set up special studio departments employing designers and decorators. At Minton their Secessionist ware was the range of pottery in England that best captured the spirit of Art Nouveau, though, as with all British Art Nouveau, it was more restrained than its French counterpart.

1.   A bronze-mounted porcelain vase by Charles Korschann and Louchet, the gilt bronze openwork handles and domed foot cast with freesias; 67.5 cm. high, impressed Ch. Korschann Paris and Louchet.

2.   A massive ceramic vase in the Germanic manner painted in naturalistic colours, with two-handled gilt metal mount; 74.5 cm. high.

4

3. Part of a Maison Moderne tea-set designed by Maurice Dufrène, circa 1900. Printed monogram LMM, La Maison Moderne, teapot with underglaze painted signature M. Dufrène.

4. One of a pair of porcelain jugs designed by Georges de Feure, for Haviland, Limoges, circa 1905, signed de Feure and Ch. Field Haviland Limoges, GDA France.

5. A Minton 'Secessionist' jardiniere and stand, the foliage and linear decoration outlined in slip; 103.5 cm. high, impressed marks Minton Ltd, circa 1910.

6. A large Sèvres porcelain vase on bronze base, hand-painted with an allover pattern of flowers and foliage; 98 cm. high, base with printed marks Manufacture Nationale. Décoré à Sèvres. 1905.

7. A circular lustre pottery plaque by Clément Massier, painted with iris blooms; 42 cm. diam., signed M. Clément Massier Golfe Juan (Alpes Maritimes), engraved MCM 1901.

8. A lustre pottery cache-pot by Clément Massier with stylized bat-wing handles; 34 cm. wide, painted marks CM Golfe Juan.

5

6

7

8

Dutch Art Nouveau had a highly individual style in which batik and the decorative influence of the Dutch East Indies could be felt. The eggshell ware produced by the Royal Rozenburg factory at the Hague is some of the most prized porcelain among collectors of Art Nouveau today. Because of its extreme fragility very little survives. Rozenburg produced pottery as well as porcelain. In Hungary the principal manufactures of pottery were Zsolnay, who made iridescent ware which in this field of pottery was among the most successful anywhere in Europe at incorporating typical Art Nouveau imagery with stylized plant forms in relief.

1.   A Zsolnay monumental lustre pottery cache-pot on trailing tulip feet; 29 cm. high, signed with firm's medallion mark (rim repaired).

2.   A stoneware vase by Zsolnay with stylized decoration of gnarled root, circa 1900; 81 cm. high.

3.   Four Zsolnay polychrome pottery vases, slender vase at left, 40 cm. high, all signed with firm's medallion marks on base.

1

2

3

4.   A two-handled porcelain vase by Rozenburg, 1900; 22 cm. high, painted Rozenburg den Haag 1720 V with a stork and a bee.

5.   A Rozenburg earthenware mantel clock painted with a sinuous serpent amidst stylized foliage; 35.5 cm. wide, painted Rozenburg mark.

6.   A pair of Rozenburg eggshell porcelain cups and saucers decorated by J. Schellink, 8 cm. high; a similar vase decorated by Hartgring, 16.5 cm. high, all signed with 1904 year mark.

7.   An eggshell porcelain vase by Rozenburg, The Hague, circa 1900; 18 cm. high, stencilled firm's marks, painted 991, with an insect and artist's initials.

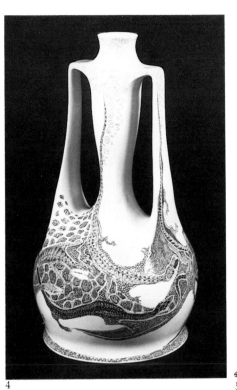

4

5

6

7

1

It is remarkable how insidious the Art Nouveau style became; no fashionable designer of the period was able to resist its appeal. No doubt this was partly due to its extreme popularity. The advantage of its 'insidiousness' from a commercial point of view was that one piece of Art Nouveau demanded another, so that eventually it became a total look with which it was difficult to mix other styles.

1. A bronze 'scarab' vase cast from a model by Gustave Gurschner; 18 cm. high, stamped Gurschner. The highly decorative frieze of circular motifs was used frequently in early 20th-century Austrian design.

2. A silver and glass wall mirror by William Comyns, the silver frame with a repoussé floral design; 38 × 51 cm, impressed with firm's marks and hallmarked for 1904.

3. A silvered pewter and nautilus shell desk lamp, cast from a model by Max Klinger, executed by H. Gladenbeck & Son, Berlin; 28 cm. high, stamped marks and incised MK.

4. A gilt bronze table lamp cast as a wood nymph resting in the boughs of a tree, from a model by E. Thomasson, Sweden; 28.5 cm. high, signed.

5. A WMF pewter and green glass claret jug, the whiplash handle and stopper pierced and cast with berried sprays; 38 cm. high, stamped marks.

2

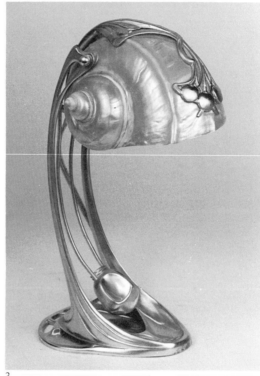

3

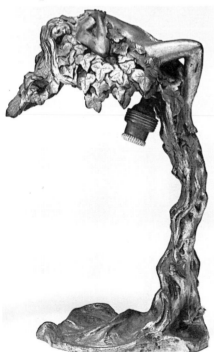

4

5

6

6. An electroplated and clear glass claret jug by WMF; 35.1 cm. high, stamped marks. Foliage is used to good effect here to soften the severity of the upper section.

7. A WMF electroplated pewter drinking set cast with a whiplash and hollyleaf design; tray – 48 × 34 cm. stamped marks circa 1900.

8. A mahogany inlaid vitrine with glazed cupboard door in the style of Wylie and Lochead, Glasgow; 171 cm. high, 121 cm. wide.

9. A mahogany display cabinet inlaid with stained woods and mother-of-pearl; 135 cm. wide, 202 cm. high.

10. A mahogany extending dining table by Jacques Gruber; 129.5 cm. long.

11. A dark patinated wooden settee, inlaid with fruitwood and mother-of-pearl, with Jugendstil patterned woven upholstery, part of a suite comprising a settee, two armchairs and two sidechairs, circa 1910; settee 107 cm. wide.

7

8

9

10

11

1

Carlo Bugatti was one of the designers of this period whose inspiration came from the Middle-East. Middle-Eastern influence was not uncommon, but nowhere as pronounced as in the designs of Bugatti. But these eccentric and often uncomfortable pieces of furniture are at the same time closely related to typical Italian Art Nouveau design of the period as seen in the inlaid furniture of Zen and Quarti.

1. An ebonized and rosewood gentleman's armchair by Carlo Bugatti, the back, sides and seat covered in painted vellum, the apron frieze with geometric metal inlay, circa 1900; 94 cm. high.

2. An ebonized and rosewood partners' desk by Carlo Bugatti, the vellum panels painted with stylized grasses and birds, the borders inlaid in pewter and brass with geometric dragonfly motifs, circa 1900; 140 cm. wide.
    The arches incorporated in the design give the desk a distinctly Moorish look, an effect frequently recognizable in Bugatti's work.

2

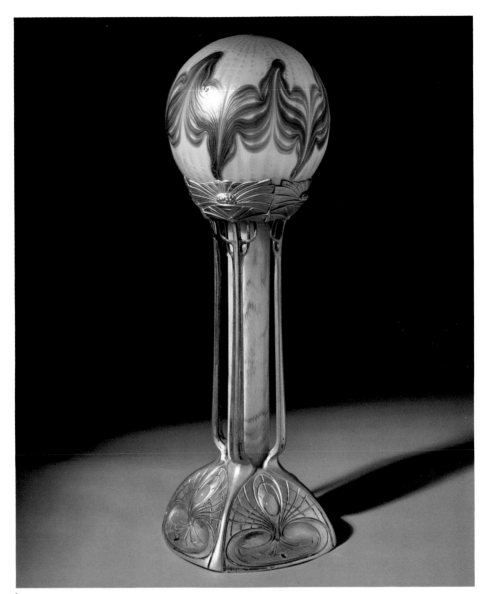

Apart from the Vienna Secessionist designs, Austria's main contribution to commercial Art Nouveau was the wide range of brilliantly coloured iridescent glass produced by the firm of Loetz, which was popular in America as well as Europe.

1. A glass and gilt metal table lamp by Loetz, with globular iridescent glass shade, the gilt metal base set with opalescent glass cabochons; 55.5 cm. high.

2. Five Loetz iridescent glass vases: wide-necked vase at left 15 cm. high, three engraved Loetz, Austria.

1

2

1

2

3

4

5

6

Liberty metalwork by a variety of designers, the most famous of whom was Archibald Knox, stands out as some of the most sophisticated English Art Nouveau. It was known under the two trade names of 'Tudric' (for pewter) and 'Cymric' (for silver), and was often set with enamel or semi-precious stones, the favourite of which was torquoise.

1.   A Liberty & Co. 'Cymric' enamelled silver and mother-of-pearl vase, probably designed by Archibald Knox; 19.5 cm. high, impressed Cymric 369138 and with firm's hallmarks circa 1900. 12.5 troy ozs. gross weight.

2.   A 'Tudric' polished pewter clock by Liberty & Co., the circular copper face enclosing a blue and green enamelled roundel, two blue enamelled roundels at the base; 20 cm. high, impressed Tudric 0370.

3.   A Liberty & Co. pewter clock, the copper face set at the centre with a turquoise enamel plaque; 33 cm. high, stamped Tudric 0150, circa 1900.

4.   A Liberty & Co. silver teaset, the design attributed to Archibald Knox, set with cabochon green hardstones. Each piece marked Cymric, L & Co. and Birmingham hallmarks for 1901.

5.   A Liberty 'Tudric' hammered pewter tea set, the teapot and hot water jug with cane covered handles; tray 48 cm. wide, stamped Tudric 0231 and other marks circa 1900.

6.   A Liberty 'Tudric' pewter and Powell green glass decanter, 30cm. high. A pair of Liberty 'Tudric' mugs designed by Archibald Knox with green glass liners by James Powell & Son; each 13cm. high, impressed marks, circa 1900.

7.   A 'Tudric' enamelled pewter inkwell a pewter biscuit box and cover designed by Archibald Knox and a small pewter cake dish, all made for Liberty & Co. circa 1903; dish 22.5cm. wide, stamped marks.

8.   A Liberty 'Tudric' pewter and 'Clutha' glass bowl on stand designed by Archibald Knox, circa 1900; 17cm. high, stamped Tudric 0276. 'Clutha' was a Glasgow glass-making factory frequently used by Libertys, Christopher Dresser and George Walton in the 1890s.

9.   A set of six silver pastry forks by Liberty & Co., the stems cast with stylized honesty; stamped maker's marks and hallmarks for 1913.

10.   A polished pewter photograph frame, the design attributed to Archibald Knox, with oak back; 18cm. high.

11.   A Liberty pewter bowl designed by Archibald Knox, fitted with a green glass liner; 20.3cm. diam., stamped Tudric 0320.

12.   A 'Cymric' silver, quartz and shagreen humidor by Liberty & Co. circa 1897, the quartz knop supported in a pierced silver mount, and with cedar lined interior; 20.5cm. high, 13cm. square; impressed hallmarks L. & Co. Cymric, 31.5 troy ozs. gross.

7

8

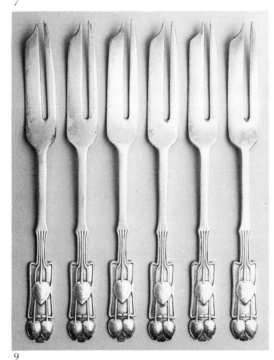

9

10

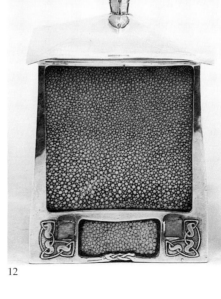

12

11

Plant form motifs, their stylization emphasizing the sinuous lines of tendrils and root formations, found their way into every aspect of decorative design during the Art Nouveau period. In the work of French furniture designers, particularly Gallé and Majorelle, the plants were accurately reproduced despite strong stylization. The Belgian designers, particularly Horta and Van de Velde, borrowed from the plant world but ended up with greater abstraction where shape was more important than botanical detail. In Germany plant forms were treated with geometric formality as seen in the furniture of Hans Christiannsen, where the wreaths of flowers are complimented by a starker geometry in the mother of pearl dots and carefully designed ribbons and bows.

1

2

1. A chair designed by
Georges De Feure in carved
mahogany of curvilinear design
upholstered in orange and gold
silk brocade.

2. A suite of furniture
designed by Hans Christiansen
in rosewood inlaid with pewter
and mother-of-pearl comprising
a cabinet and two side
cupboards; 165 cm. high, 87 cm.
wide (centre cabinet).

3. A mahogany billiard table
by Gustave Serrurier-Bovy, the
arched supports and gently
curving branched legs showing
more restrained aspects of the
Art Nouveau style, circa 1901;
239 × 133.5 cm.

4. A music cabinet designed
by Louis Majorelle in palisander
wood and mahogany, the door
and drawer inlaid with tulips,
butterflies and foliage; 146.5 cm.
high, 30.5 cm wide; signed L.
Majorelle in marquetry.

5. A display cabinet in
mahogany designed by Gaillard
with stylized curvilinear
decoration; 220 cm. high,
120 cm. wide.

3

4

5

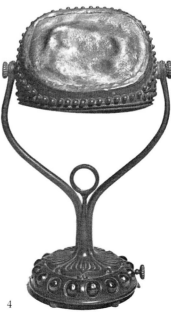

Louis Comfort Tiffany studied painting in Paris, but turned to interior decoration on returning to begin his professional life in America. He was undoubtedly the most successful of the American entrepreneurs in this field during the Art Nouveau period, and is best known for a vast range of leaded glass lamps with floral decoration. Apart from these there was experimental glass ware and pottery, and bronze wares including mirrors and desk sets. The bronze was usually heavy with moulded decoration, but many of the desk sets (and also some lamps) used a more delicate openwork design backed by marbelized green glass.

1. A glass and bronze water lily table mirror by Tiffany Studios; 49.5 cm. high, impressed with firm's logo and Tiffany Studios, New York 29238.

2. A twelve-light lily Favrile glass and bronze table lamp, the shades of iridescent yellow glass; 47 cm. high, shades inscribed L.C.T. Favrile, base stamped Tiffany Studios New York 21817.

3. A bronze and glass table mirror by Tiffany Studios, the arms and base cast as fern fronds and leaves; 54 cm. high, impressed marks.

1

2

3

4

4. A turtle-back tile and bronze desk lamp by Tiffany Studios, the shade inset with iridescent turtle-back tiles, the base set with a band of matching iridescent green glass cabochons; 35.7 cm. high, impressed Tiffany Studios New York D801, and with firm's logo.

5. A bronze inkstand in the form of three large scarabs with a hinged, domed cover by Tiffany Studios; 11 cm. high, impressed marks and firm's monogram.

6. A Cypriote Favrile glass and bronze box by Tiffany Studios, the cover and sides of iridescent glass, the bronze corner mounts cast with salamanders; 23.5 cm. long, unsigned (cover panel damaged).

7. A Cypriote Favrile glass vase by Tiffany Studios, 19.5 cm. high, inscribed Louis C. Tiffany, L.C.T. D140.

8. A curtain border leaded glass and bronze floor lamp by Tiffany Studios; 200 cm. high, including pig-tail finial; shade and base with impressed firm's marks.

9. A part desk set in etched metal and green marble glass by Tiffany Studios, in the pine needle design; width of utility box 17 cm., all stamped Tiffany Studios New York.

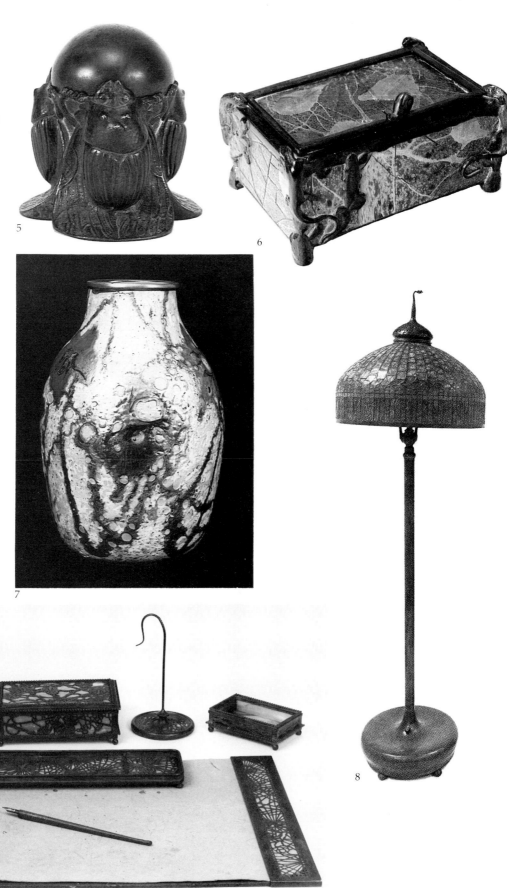

5

6

7

8

9

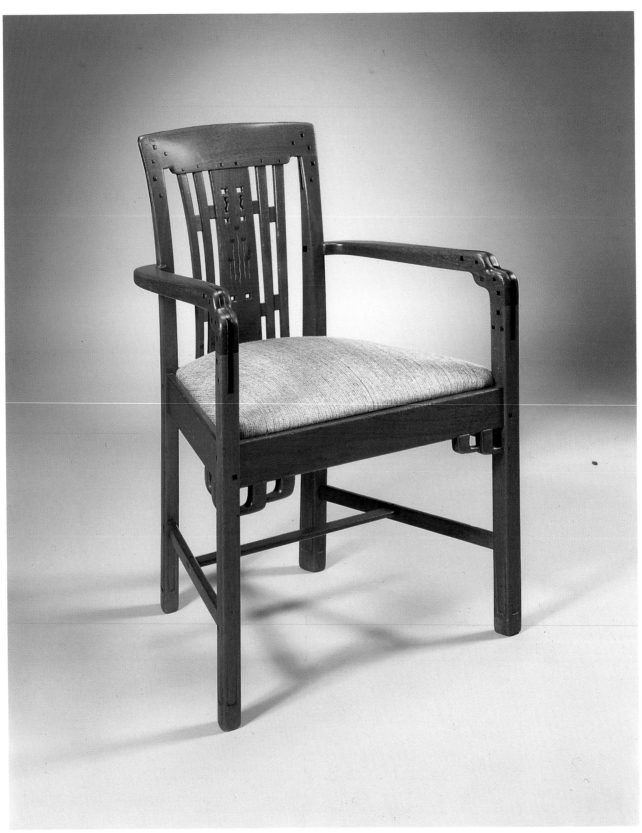

(*Above*)   An inlaid walnut and ebony armchair designed by Greene and Greene, executed in the workshop of Peter Hall for the living room of the Robert R. Blacker House, Pasadena, California, circa 1907; 85 cm. high, 61 cm. wide, stamped VII.

(*Opposite*)   A Moorcroft Macintyre 'Florian' ware vase with slip-trailed foliate decoration, circa 1900; 31 cm. high, green painted signature W. Moorcroft and printed mark Florian Ware. Jas. Macintyre & Co. Ltd. Burslem, England.

CHAPTER 3

Traditionalism

Whilst there have been a number of distinctive styles throughout the twentieth century with definite beginnings and ends, there has been a more gradual change in the traditional aspects of design in the decorative arts. Whilst the history of Art Nouveau, the Bauhaus, Art Deco and the 1950s style makes a colourful patchwork, the changes in a continuous Arts and Crafts tradition are less pronounced and there is a strong link between the work of today's artist-potters, glass and furniture makers and those who were working over half a century ago.

Twentieth-century design has been punctuated by a series of decorative fashions starting with Art Nouveau. Even though the style was at its height as early as 1900, its popularity continued, in commercial terms at any rate, almost throughout the first decade of the century. New stylistic developments were delayed somewhat by the outbreak of the First World War, which brought with it radical social change. It took some time for European society to settle down again in the aftermath of the war, with so many young men killed in the trenches, with women needed to fill some of the gaps left by this sad loss, and new frontiers resulting from victory and defeat. Not until 1925 did a definite new style emerge, a fashion trend in the true sense, for Art Deco was closely tied to sartorial elegance and the Paris couturiers, in a way that Art Nouveau had never been. As with Art Nouveau, its high point in 1925 was also the beginning of its decline, leading to a severer brand of modernism related to Bauhaus design in Germany. Again, in 1939, war, this time on a more devastating scale, brought about a second major interruption. The design industry virtually shut down and the break with tradition was far greater. When the world started up again in 1945, the changes were the most radical that had been seen in

twentieth-century decorative arts. Changes were also more frequent; whereas nearly a quarter of a century separates Art Nouveau and Art Deco, the great 1950s exhibitions, including the Festival of Britain Exhibition in 1951, and the Milano Triennale exhibitions and Expo 1958 in Brussels, each heralded new boundaries of change. The changes in this decade were far more complex and varied than before.

Art Nouveau and Art Deco have certainly dominated the history of design in this century, thereby overshadowing other areas which flourished alongside them without ever attracting the same publicity. Away from the glare of fashion, studio glass, pottery, well-crafted furniture and metalwork have evolved more conventionally, and it is only comparatively recently, in a period which has witnessed a renewed enthusiasm for craftsmanship, that the great craftsmen of the twentieth century have begun to be fully appreciated with the work of such men as Ernest Gimson, Peter Waals and Sidney Barnsley in England, Georg Jensen in Denmark, and Simon Gate and Edward Hald at Orrefors in Sweden. All these designers were very much of their time, but without paying too much attention to the dictates of fashion. In a sense they were also greater individualists, making it difficult to group them together under any one heading.

It was in England and America that the tradition of fine hand-crafted furniture was strongest during the first part of the century. The British tradition was centred in the Cotswolds with a group of craftsmen whose work has had a long-lasting effect on British furniture design. The work of Gimson, the Barnsleys (Sidney and his son Edward who is still alive today) and Peter Waals has been referred to as 'wonderful furniture of a commonplace kind'. It was distinguished by an

Two Ruskin high-fired pottery vases covered in mottled glazes; vase on left 21 cm. high, vase on right 23 cm. high, impressed Ruskin England 1933.
Centre: a Ruskin flambé vase with a speckled glaze; 17.4 cm. high, impressed Ruskin Pottery 1909.

honest approach to design, a regard for fine materials and above all pride in outstanding craftsmanship. Little time was wasted by these men on Ruskinian theory; their philosophy was self-evident in the quality of their work. Both the Barnsley brothers and Ernest Gimson were born in the 1860s and trained as architects. In 1901 Ernest Gimson and Ernest Barnsley went into partnership and they were joined in 1901 by a Dutchman Peter Waals who answered their advertisement for a foreman. High-quality furniture was produced in their workshop at Daneway House, a fourteenth-century manor house near Cirencester. In 1904 Sidney Barnsley wrote to the architect Philip Webb, 'I am still occupied principally in making good solid oak furniture with occasional pieces of more delicate kind as a rest and change.'

As the group became well-known they received a growing number of commissions for furniture. Gimson himself was not a furniture maker, but his designs, which survive in a large collection in Cheltenham Museum, show his architectural approach to furniture, which should be constructed rather than glued or screwed together. Even though it was not their intention, the furniture was always on the expensive side. Gimson died soon after the end of the First World War; Sidney Barnsley survived him and lived till 1926, after which Peter Waals continued to produce furniture with several of Gimson's craftsmen until his death in 1937. Apart from the simple oak pieces, there were special pieces made of more exotic woods (often walnut) and sometimes inlaid with ivory or mother-of-pearl; the handles were all designed and made in the workshop, and when not made of wood were of forged polished steel.

At about the time of Gimson's death another furniture designer, Gordon Russell, set up a workshop nearby in Broadway where skilled craftsmen executed his ideas. To begin with his work was very close in feeling to Gimson's and the Barnsleys', but in the 1930s Russell turned to machine production, designing fine pieces for a much wider market. The Cotswold tradition also had a profound influence on furniture produced by factory methods, particularly in the case of Heal and Sons. Ambrose Heal joined his father's firm in 1893 and was much influenced by the Arts and Crafts movement. The simple oak furniture produced by the firm right up to the outbreak of the Second World War must have come somewhere near to William Morris's ideal of honest craftsmanship at reasonable prices. It was designed for industrial production, bringing furniture-making into the modern world and ending those much-laboured Victorian arguments against the machine. In 1915 Ambrose Heal was one of the founder members of the Design and Industries Association.

In America there was also fine hand-crafted furniture along with architect-designed pieces and a commercial range of simple, well-crafted pieces known as Mission furniture. The most successful and best-known of the furniture manufacturers was Gustav Stickley, who made his first Arts and Crafts furniture in 1898 and continued designing and producing until bankruptcy forced him out of business in 1916. Stickley admitted, 'I had no idea of attempting to create a new style, but merely tried to make furniture which would be simple, durable, comfortable, and fitted for the place it was to occupy. It seemed to me that the only way to do this was to cut loose from all tradition and to do away with all ornamentation, returning to the plain principles of construction.' The furniture was made mostly of oak joints dowelled into place, and the style has been described as 'boldly functional', and 'so solidly made as to be almost indestructible'. For Stickley decorative effects achieved through applied ornamentation were ugly and dishonest.

Stickley began working in the British Arts and Crafts tradition, but as his style developed it became simpler, and in the later period he achieved a simplification and standardization of construction that was suited to mass production. Another of the manufacturers of Arts and Crafts furniture in America was Roycroft Enterprises founded by Elbert Hubbard, whose admiration for William Morris's socialist ideals led him to establish an American Guild known as the Roycrofters. The Roycroft workshop was a great success, producing a variety of Arts and Crafts items, including books, metalwork, decorative objects and a line of furniture. In architecture the Arts and Crafts philosophy was most successfully applied by Charles and Henry Greene, 'two brothers whose work epitomizes Arts and Crafts at their highest level'. The brothers were architects and interior designers, and in their interiors the structure of the house, its joints and motifs, were repeated in appropriate scale in each piece of furniture, rug, light fixture and accessory for the house. Craftsmen were hired to work in various media under the close scrutiny of the Greenes, each contributing to the project their special skills and reflecting the Greenes' uncompromising philosophy. The Greene brothers were based in California, and used local craftsmen to execute their designs; in particular they had a close association with master craftsmen Peter and John Hall.

The Greenes' furniture combined functionalism with aestheticism, and was far removed from the simple linearity of Gustav Stickley. The decoration, however, was never gratuitous, but a love of construction led these architect-designers to highlight structure, turning joinery into decoration. To avoid separation joinery, they devised a scheme of ebony splints (in contrast to the paler woods used for the furniture) with inset screws cupped with ebony pegs, and this is the most recognizable 'decorative feature' of their furniture. Their style has been described as the result of 'exposure to the interiors of William Morris, adaptations of the Swiss mountain chalet, and the motifs and structure of Japanese architecture'.

But throughout the first half of the twentieth century the greatest exponent of Arts and Crafts ideals was Frank Lloyd Wright. He has already been referred to as one of the 'modernists' of the 1890s, and without belonging to any sort of avant-garde he remained in the forefront of American modernism throughout his life. His furniture has been criticized for being uncomfortable, but comfort was an incidental rather than a primary consideration for him. He admired William Morris for 'preaching the gospel of simplicity', and his own furniture designs emphasized this aspect as well as the importance of design creating a sense of unity and harmony. Although his style evolved and changed during the course of a very long life, his furniture always remained in essence 'architectural rather than merely utilitarian objects, a part of a larger sculptural whole'.

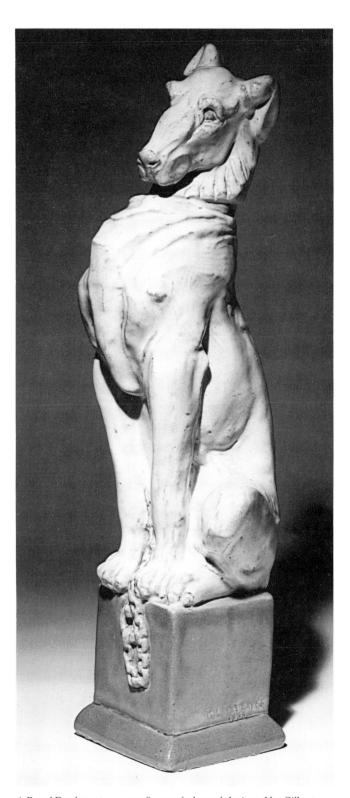

A Royal Doulton stoneware figure of a hound designed by Gilbert Bayes, the dog seated on a stepped rectangular base and glazed in blue, green, white and pale brown slip; 50 cm. high, impressed signature, dated 1935.

A Roberts and Belk silver and parcel gilt cup and cover on octagonal
marble stand, designed by W.P. Belk, the cup with repoussé
decoration, a band of putti above the foot and the finial cast as a
seated maiden; stamped maker's mark, Sheffield hallmarks for 1919.
Printed label on base "R.A. Exhibition of British Art in Industry
1935". 43 ozs.

A massive Doulton and Co. faience baluster vase decorated by
Florence Lewis, circa 1893; 193 cm. high, painted marks Doulton &
Co. London, F.L. monogram.

A selection of Tonwerke Kandern pottery by Professor Max Laüger, all with applied relief decoration, circa 1910; right-hand vase 31.5 cm high, impressed monogram MLK.

While Arts and Crafts furniture seems to have been designed or inspired primarily by architects in the first half of the twentieth century, pottery and glass were made by designers within the appropriate industries, and it became a tradition for potteries and glassworks to open studio departments where art glass and art pottery were made principally for the sake of prestige. In England the way was led by Doulton, who had already established this tradition in the late nineteenth century, and who developed it on a much wider scale in the twentieth. Their stoneware pottery was created by a team of distinguished artists including Frank Butler, Mark V. Marshall, Edith Lupton and Eliza Simmance. The range of their wares was remarkable and showed a real eagerness for experiment, which can be seen in their ranges of Sung and Chang, Titanian or Flambé. There were also the ever-popular figurines, still avidly collected today, Toby jugs and commemorative wares.

Doulton and most of the other potteries cared little for fashion. It was much more a matter of a continuing tradition within the industry. In the case of Doulton, the studio department was merely an adjunct, albeit an important one, to the mainstream of manufacture wares. The same is true of other larger firms like Minton, Worcester and Wedgwood, though the scale of their studio enterprise could not compare with Doulton's.

There were smaller firms whose output was limited to studio pottery, notably the Staffordshire pottery of William Moorcroft, who began as a designer for James Macintyre and Co. at Burslem, designing their 'Florian' and 'Aurelian' wares. Moorcroft established his own pottery in 1913. Throughout its history the Moorcroft style is immediately recognizable, with stylized plant and flower forms in richly coloured glazes. There were other such potteries, including Ruskin, Foley, Bernard Moore and Pilkingtons, mainly in the area of Stoke-on-Trent, creating their own styles which were neither old-fashioned nor modern; their importance in the history of design lies in the fact that they trod the middle ground, catering for a much wider and longer-lasting market, and their work is as valid in the history of design as the more fashionable extremes of taste.

Elsewhere in Europe popular taste in ceramics was catered for in much the same way, with studio departments forming a part of the larger potteries, and the occasional smaller firms devoted exclusively to art pottery. In Germany there were a great many of the smaller firms and a far greater variety of design than in England. Peculiar to Germany was the tradition of stoneware tankards and jugs which were up-dated, particularly at the firms of Reinhold Merkelbach and Westerwald. One of the most prolific German designers was Professor

Max Läuger, most of whose designs were executed by Tonwerke Kandern in the Black Forest region. At the firm of Karlsruhe there was a strong bias towards sculpture, and ceramic sculpture was generally popular in Germany as well as Austria (where many of the Wiener Werkstätte potters went in for it). In general German studio pottery leant more towards art with greater recognition for the individual. At the larger companies like Meissen, Nymphenburg and Rosenthal there was perhaps more concern with unique pieces or limited editions, and the quality of porcelain produced by these manufacturers was outstanding.

In France the serious studio potters like Ernest Chapelet, Emile Decoeur, Auguste Delaherche and Seraphin Soudbinine were really the first of the artist potters in the sense that they set out to produce works of art rather than artefacts. There was also a stronger tradition of artist-decorated pottery, some of it pure Art Deco, but some, like the pottery of Raoul Dufy and Jean Mayodon, belonging to a different category. In Scandinavia most of the art pottery was produced by the few major companies, Royal Copenhagen and Bing and Grøndahl in Denmark and Rørstrand in Sweden.

In America the strong Arts and Crafts tradition in furniture was paralleled among potters. The lead was taken by the Rookwood Pottery in Cincinnati, founded in 1880, which grew into the foremost art pottery in America, a position it held for nearly 40 years. In spirit the Rookwood Pottery always remained deeply rooted in a Victorian craft tradition, and later attempts to update this resulted in failure. The range of Rookwood was nevertheless remarkable, from unique pieces to a mail order catalogue for their standard wares.

With the success of Rookwood, many others followed suit. The Grueby pottery made its mark around the turn of the century by introducing matt glazes, often in a shade of green. Grueby pottery was often used in conjunction with Stickley furniture and belongs to the same tradition, 'a happy merger of mercantile principles and the high ideals of art'. Van Briggle carried the experiments with matt glazes further. There were of course numerous other pottery firms, a few of the most important being Weller, Roseville Pottery Co., Adelaide Alsopp Robineau, Fulper Pottery Co., the Marblehead Pottery Co., and of course the sophisticated pottery creations of the Tiffany studios, where craftsmen remained anonymous.

The situation with glass was essentially the same as with pottery, and there was a quantity of glass produced during the first part of the century which one would categorize as neither Art Nouveau nor Art Deco. For instance the discovery and development of pâte de verre by Daum and Argy Rousseau was more of a glass discovery than a fashion discovery. Lalique's glass is synonymous with Art Deco, and yet the most complex of his pieces, unique pieces made by the lost-wax process, belong more to a craft tradition. In Italy Paolo Venini was responsible for reviving the glass industry, which had suffered a reversal of fortune lasting almost a century. The bright new palette of colours he introduced

'The Plains', a Steuben crystal-footed bowl and cover designed by Lloyd Atkins, the engraving design by Bruce More, deep wheel-engraved with a bison leading a herd; 33 cm. high, base engraved Steuben.

on to the glass scene during the 1930s was very refreshing. There were few developments in America, although Frederic Carder, the founder of Steuben glass, worked there successfully for over half a century, introducing technical and artistic changes into the glass industry.

But it was at Orrefors in Sweden that studio glass developed away from mainstream fashion in the most interesting way. There the team of Simon Gate and Edward Hald ran a studio glass department, inventing the new 'Graal' technique and also furthering the art of engraving with a whole range of new technical ideas. In the Graal technique the main decoration lay between two layers of glass, and the glass underwent a process of reheating so that any image was 'artistically' distorted at this stage. The chief innovation in engraving was a method of deep copper-wheel engraving which resulted in a dramatic three-dimensional effect. Edward Hald and Simon Gate were both very much contemporary designers, not untouched by the craze for Art Deco, but their work once again fits more comfortably into an Arts and Crafts tradition. Another such example was the wide range of enamelled glass made in Austria,

An Ernest Gimson walnut bureau executed by Sidney Barnsley, the
panelled fall front enclosing a fitted interior, the drawers with carved
rosewood handles; 128.5 cm. high, 83.5 cm. wide.

A Gordon Russell oak dining table and six chairs, the seats with
brown leather covers; table 177.7cm. wide, applied with metal label
inscribed 'Russell and Sons, Broadway, Worcs.'

Bohemia and Germany. The art of glass enamelling was
well-established in these countries, and an essential
part of a glass artist's training. Perhaps for this reason
the approach remained essentially an academic one,
with its chief exponents, the most distinguished of
whom was Karl Massanetz, coming from a 'Fachschule'
(or 'polytechnic') background. The areas of Stein-
schönau and Haida (now part of Czechoslovakia) were
the main sources for this type of glass, which was particularly popular during the first quarter of the century.

Metalwork and jewellery also continued to flourish
in the hands of both Art Deco and Arts and Crafts designers. In France, where the Art Deco tradition was
so strong, it tended to force virtually all design into a
single decorative style, but elsewhere, particularly in
Germany, Britain, Scandinavia and the United States,
metalworkers evolved along with the other types of
artist craftsmen. There is certainly a wide choice for
twentieth-century jewellery or silver collectors apart
from the jazzy geometry of the Art Deco designers, just
as there is in all categories of twentieth-century decorative arts. But perhaps the most outstanding metal-
worker in this later Arts and Crafts tradition was the

Danish silversmith Georg Jensen, whose workshops
were established in Copenhagen in 1904. Jensen himself
was an inspired designer, but a number of other designers and craftsmen have always been associated with
the firm, their work being produced under their own
names but executed by Jensen. However, the name
Georg Jensen is associated with a particular style in silver which is greatly influenced by the original owner's
taste. Perhaps the most independent of the Jensen designers in pre-war years was Johann Rohde, although
even his work is very much in the 'Jensen style'.

Georg Jensen had studied sculpture and tried his
hand at various aspects of decorative art before becoming an independent silversmith at the age of 40. Following in the tradition of so many Art Nouveau designers
he found inspiration in the world of flowers and insects,
turning it into a highly personal language that once
again defies description. Weaving in and out of the
boundaries of Art Nouveau, Art Deco and Arts and
Crafts, he is a representative of the many strong individualists who would never wholly adopt one style or
the other, preferring to borrow as widely as possible
and ending up with a personal contemporary idiom.

1

2

3

4

5

6

7

American Arts & Crafts is almost entirely indebted for its inspiration to the English design movement of that name which had had its heyday two decades before in the 1880s. The American equivalent did not get underway until after the turn of the century and was at the height of its popularity between 1910 and 1920, although the style continued for about two years after that. It was honesty of craftsmanship that the Americans found so appealing in British Arts & Crafts.

1.   A copper table lamp by Roycroft, the shade fitted with four screened celeophane panels; 37 cm. high, impressed with firm's mark (replacement finial).

2.   A slatted oak settle by Courtland Cabinet Co.; 154 cm. wide, applied with firm's paper label. There were several designers working in the Arts and Crafts style of Gustav Stickley in the early years of the 20th century.

3.   An oak straddle chair by Roycroft, circa 1906; 87 cm. high; branded with Roycroft insignia.

4. An oak spindle child's bed by Gustav Stickley circa 1907. 150 cm. long, 108.5 cm. high. Stickley could turn his hand to design in every category of furniture.

5. A copper jardiniere by Gustav Stickley circa 1905, 48 cm. high; stamped firm's mark and 'The Craftsman Workshops, Gustav Stickley Als Ik Kan.'

6. An oak and iron sideboard by Gustav Stickley circa 1903. 174.6 cm. wide, 122.5 cm. high.

7. An inlaid oak and glass cabinet by The Cincinnati Shop of the Crafters; 146 cm. high; applied paper label.

8. A leaded glass, gilt metal and wood chandelier, designed by George Grant Elmslie, Chicago 1924, made for the Old Second National Bank of Aurora, Illinois. 55 cm. high.

9. An oak and leather Morris chair by L. and J.G. Stickley, circa 1912, with adjustable back 88.2 cm. wide. The name and the style of this chair show the influence of the English Arts and Crafts Movement in the United States.

10. An oak cellarette by the Shop of the Crafters at Cincinnati, with two small doors with pewter hinges, circa 1905; 159 cm. high.

11. A Honduras mahogany armchair with square ebony pegs, the vertical splat inlaid with silver vine, abalone, copper, pewter and exotic wood florets and with leather seat, designed by Charles and Henry Greene, executed in the workshop of Peter Hall, for the Robert R. Blacker House, Pasadena. California. 1907–09; 107 cm. high; 63 cm. wide, stamped 11.

12. An oak sideboard designed by Harvey Ellis, executed by Gustav Stickley, circa 1904; 137 cm. wide, 108 cm. high; stamped maker's marks, model no. 800.

13. A hammered copper and wrought iron table by Dirk van Erp, San Francisco, circa 1910; 45.5 cm. diam, 63 cm. high. Stamped with the windmill logo and marker's name.

8

9

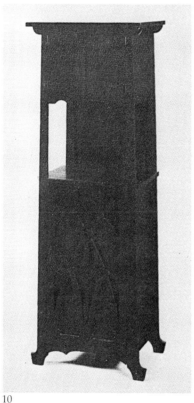

10

11

12

13

1

The most luxurious Arts & Crafts in America was produced on the West Coast by Charles and Henry Greene. Their designs combined simplicity with luxury which their wealthy clientele could well afford. The simplicity was born of a deep concern for functionalism, they also greatly admired the aesthetics of Japanese architecture and this is evident in the interior as well as the exterior of the buildings they designed. Despite these influences they created a style which was completely American.

1. A fine and important inlaid Honduras mahogany desk with fall front designed by Greene and Greene, executed in the workshop of Peter Hall for the living room of the Charles M. Pratt House, Ojai, California, circa 1909; 118.8 cm. wide, 122.6 cm. high, 56.5 cm. deep. Branded three times – Sumner Greene His True Mark.

2

2.   An oak and redwood dry bar, the top inlaid with a silvered copper liner, designed by Charles and Henry Greene, executed by the workshops of Peter Hall for the billiards room of the Robert R. Blacker House, Pasadena, California, circa 1907; 190.5cm. wide, 116.8cm. high, unsigned.

3.   An inlaid Honduras mahogany and ebony side chair with leather seat and a similar serving table designed by Charles and Henry Greene for the dining room of the Robert R. Blacker house, Pasadena, California, 1907–9, executed in the workshop of Peter Hall; chair – 110.5cm. high; table 91.5cm. wide, 75.5cm. high.

4.   A walnut and ebony dining table designed by Greene and Greene, executed in the workshops of Peter Hall for the Charles M. Pratt house, California circa 1909, the shoe-footed legs joined by leather covered stretchers; 151.7cm. long 69.5cm. high, branded in two places – His True Mark Sumner Greene.

3

1

2

3

American Studio Pottery enjoyed a period of creativity and popularity during the first two decades of the twentieth century, and a great many small studios opened up during this time. American taste was principally for matt glazes, particularly in the more popular ranges of studio ceramics. One of the reasons for this was that matt glazes fitted in better with the somewhat stark look of American Arts and Crafts furniture, which had a natural finish allowing the grain of the wood to show through. Furniture of this period tended to be in the heavier looking woods, of which oak was the favourite.

1. A spherical earthenware vase with two loop handles by Fulper, covered in a black and olive glaze; 27 cm. high, impressed Fulper.

2. An earthenware vase by Grueby sculpted with broad overlapping petals; 23 cm. high, impressed Grueby Pottery Boston U.S.A.

3. 'Lorelei', an earthenware vase by the Van Briggle Pottery, the body moulded with a female figure in flowing robes; 26 cm. high, incised AA mark, Van Briggle Colo. Spgs, design introduced circa 1900.

4

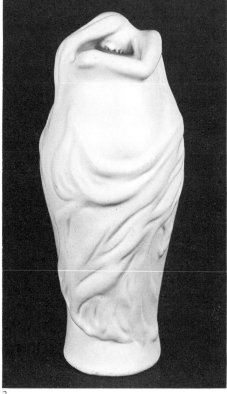

5

4. An avocado coloured earthenware vase moulded on the neck with a band of arrowroot leaves by Van Briggle, 1905; 27 cm. high, inscribed with firm's marks.

5. Two loop-handled earthenware vases by George E. Ohr; 21 cm. and 17 cm. high; impressed G.E. Ohr, Biloxi, Miss. The handles on these vases show a French influence with their looping curves.

6. An earthenware seven-handled vase moulded with leaves, designed by George Kendrick for Grueby; 18.5 cm. high-impressed with firm's marks and artists's monogram. Inspiration from plant forms is in evidence again here.

7. A large earthenware vase by Jacques Sicard for Weller Pottery, decorated with iridescent dandelions; 57 cm. high; painted Sicardo Weller.

8. An earthenware lamp with copper shade inset with mica (a type of cellophane), the shade by Dirk van Erp, the base (drilled) by Grueby; shade 45 cm. diam., vase 32.5 cm. high, impressed Grueby.

9. A square earthenware tile painted with a turtle by Grueby of Boston; 15.5 cm. square.

10. An earthenware 'Effigy' bowl by Fulper, three 'grotesque' seated figures supporting the shallow bowl, covered in a matt, speckled blue glaze; 19 cm. high, printed Fulper.

6

7

8

10

1

Apart from the restrained semi-abstract decoration of American studio pottery, there was a fashion for naturalistic landscapes in soft colours, and also for realistic portraits of Indians in their full regalia. Rookwood produced a range of wares in a shiny dark brown glaze decorated in this manner; the painting on them is of outstanding quality and they are highly prized by collectors. There was also a vogue for silver overlay work on some of the more expensive ware, in naturalistic styles influenced by Art Nouveau. Fulper went in for a range of ceramic lamps enlivened by small panels of stained glass.

2

3

4

5

1. A silver overlaid pottery vase by Weller; 26 cm. high; impressed Lowelsa Weller 502 7.

A silver overlaid pottery ewer by Rookwood and Gorham 1894, decorated by Edward Abel; 19 cm. high; impressed artists's monogram and firm's marks.

A silver overlaid pottery wine flask by Rookwood and Gorham decorated by Olga G. Reed, 1892; 28 cm. high; impressed artist's monogram and firm's marks.

2. An earthenware vase by Grueby, executed by Ruth Erickson; 42.5 cm. high, impressed Grueby Pottery Boston, U.S.A., inscribed R.E.

3. A fine silver overlay earthenware vase by Rookwood and Gorham, 1900, painted with an Indian brave by Matthew Daly; 25.5 cm. high, inscribed 'Jumping Thunder' by M.A. Daly, vase and silver overlay impressed with firm's marks.

4. An earthenware vase by George E. Ohr, with applied serpentine handles; 26 cm. high, impressed Glo. E. Ohr, Biloxi, Miss.

5. A leaded glass and earthenware table lamp by Fulper circa 1910; 58.5 cm. high, diameter of shade 39.5 cm. Base with ink stamp monogram Fulper.

6. A fine earthenware plaque by Rookwood, 1886, decorated by William P. McDonald with a standing Indian chief; 28.5 × 59 cm, impressed with firm's marks and WPMcD.

7. A fine pottery vase by Rookwood decorated by Frederick Rotherbusch, 'Vellum' glazed; 28 cm. high, impressed with artist's monogram and firm's marks, dated 1924.

6

7

1

2

3

4

5

6

7

Some of the best crafted artefacts produced anywhere in the world at this period were American, but they have only recently been noticed outside America. There are several reasons for this, one of them being that the Americans were somewhat diffident about new design in their own country, and had a conscience about the extent of their borrowing from Europe. There was also a tentativeness about using purely American subjects (like Indians) for decorative purposes among young people, the majority of whom still felt their roots to be in Europe, and were shy of their new surroudings.

1.   An earthenware vase by Rookwood, 1924, decorated by Carl Schmidt with sailing vessels; 24.5 cm. high; impressed with firm's marks and artist's monogram.

2.   A pottery vase by Rookwood, 1900, painted with the head of an Indian Warrior; 26 cm. high; firm's impressed marks and inscribed with a tomahawk and the words 'Kills Alone Sioux'.

3.   A Rookwood slender oviform earthenware vase painted by Sara Sax, 1903; 19 cm. high, 'Iris' glazed and with firm's impressed mark, 901D and artist's incised initial.

4.   A large pottery plaque by Rookwood decorated by Edward T. Hurley with birch trees in a landscape; 36 × 32 cm., impressed with firm's marks and artist's monogram, 1947.

5.   A Rookwood earthenware mug painted with an Indian brave by Sadie Markland, inscribed 'Shoshone Comanche Buffalo Hump'; 13 cm. high; impressed with firm's mark and artist's monogram, 1898.

6.   An early Rookwood pottery bowl painted by Albert Valentien, 1886; 25.5 cm. high; impressed Rookwood 276 and incised artist's initials.

7.   A large earthenware vase by Rookwood 1883, painted with flying swallows beneath pendant wisteria blossoms; 61 cm. high, impressed marks.

1

2

American interior decoration in the first part of the century was a curious mixture of Victorian and modern. Linearity, as practised by Frank Lloyd Wright and popularized by Gustav Stickley, belongs definitely to the design aesthetic of the twentieth century. But leather upholstery and heavy grained woods hark back to earlier styles. Interiors were dimly lit by Tiffany style lamps, their thick coloured stained glass shades giving an almost medieval glow to American interiors of this period. The heaviness is particularly noticeable in contrast with much racier styles of the 1920s and 1930s. Colour schemes were mainly dark with a few pastel shades thrown in for light relief.

3

4

1.   An oak spindle porch swing by Gustav Stickley circa 1906, the seat supported by steel and leather straps and with waterproof canvas upholstered seat and cushions; 181.5cm. wide, with original paper label, inscribed model no. 223.

2.   A pair of bronze fire dogs by Tiffany Studios, with tongs, shovel and fork, all cast with Celtic inspired decoration, the finials of each piece inset with Favrile glass orbs. Height of dogs 59.5cm.

3.   Two oak armchairs upholstered in leather, designed by Purcell, Feick and Elmslie for the Merchants Bank of Winona, Minnesota, circa 1911–12; 92cm. high, 61.5cm. wide.

4.   An oak director's table with splayed legs on 'shoe' feet by Gustav Stickley, circa 1912; 183cm. wide, branded signature.
    A set of six oak and rush seated high back spindle chairs by Gustav Stickley circa 1905; 116.5cm. high, 3 stamped Model no. 384.

1

2

There were many technical inventions in the glass world during the early part of the century. In France the art of the reconstituting pâte de verre from crushed glass was rediscovered and developed mainly by Daum, Walter and Argy-Rousseau. In Scandinavia, and particularly at Orrefors, there were new copper-wheel engraving techniques where areas were hollowed out to given them prominence, and one of the most original innovations was the 'Graal' technique where glass was reheated after an initial design had been applied, resulting in decorative distortion of the design.

1.   Examples of overlay glass vases and a bowl by Orrefors and Kosta; left-hand vase 32.3cm. high, signed Orrefors in the overlay; bowl 29.3cm. wide, engraved Kosta Wennerberg AEB 391 on the base.

2.   A pâte-de-verre flared glass vase and a box and cover by G. Argy-Rousseau, 7.5cm. high and 13.2cm. wide, moulded marks G. Argy Rousseau.
     A pâte-de-verre rounded triangular dish and a figure of a seated woman by Almeric Walter, 20.8cm. wide and 20.5cm. high, moulded A. Walter Nancy, H. Bergé Sc. and A. Walter, Nancy.

3.   An Orrefors 'Graal' glass vase designed by Simon Gate and executed by Knut Bergkvist and Heinrich Wollman, the clear glass decorated with blue flowerheads; 25.5cm. high, engraved Graal 1920 KB HW no. 937 on the base.

4.   'Vindrosen', a fine engraved glass plate designed by Edward Hald and engraved by A. Diessner with nude figures, ships, an aeroplane, waves and stars; 38.5cm. diam., engraved Orrefors Hald 477 1929 AD.

5.   An Argy-Rousseau pâte-de-verre vase and a poudrier and cover, 15cm. high and 15cm. diam.
     A Walter pâte-de-verre shaped rectangular marine plaque and a Walter dish modelled by Henri Bergé; 28cm. and 17.5cm. wide, moulded marks. The method of reheating ground glass gave pâte-de-verre pieces their subtle colour variations and thickly textured matt appearance.

3

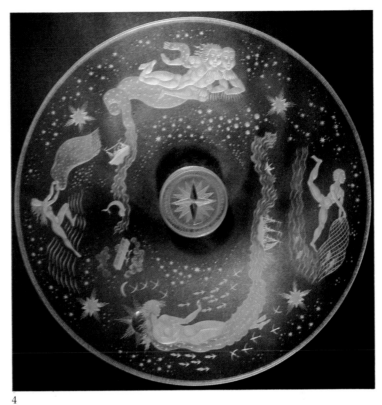

4

5

1

2

3

There is great variety in studio glass from the first part of the twentieth century and a demand both for coloured glass and clear glass. In Scandinavia and at Steuben in the United States there was a preference for clear glass which showed off engraving to its best advantage. In Bohemia there was a vogue for glass painted with enamel colours, and in France glass was either opalescent or brilliantly coloured. There was virtually no clear studio glass produced in France at this time. Iridescent glass also continued to be popular, especially in America.

1. An Orrefors glass presentation vase by Simon Gate and E. Wejdljch presented to the Lord Mayor and Lady Mayoress of London to commemorate their visit to the Stockholm Exhibition in 1930; 28.5cm. high; inscribed Orrefors 1928, S. Gate E. Wejdljch No. 333.

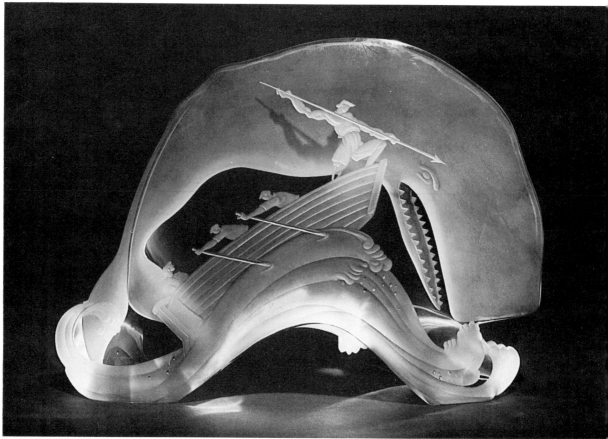

4

2. A François Decorchemont pâte-de-cristal glass dish of midnight blue colour, 1930s; 18 cm. wide; impressed mark Decorchemont, engraved no. C401.

3. A glass vase and cover attributed to Fachschule Haida, circa 1910, the amber and satin finished glass painted with polychrome enamels; 32 cm. high.

4. 'Moby Dick', a Steuben cut and engraved crystal glass sculpture, the glass designed by Donald Pollard, and the engraving by Sidney Waugh, on wood and perspex illuminated base; 28 cm. wide, engraved Steuben signature.

5. An Orrefors clear glass vase engraved by Simon Gate with a nude female figure; 26 cm. high, etched S. Gate Orrefors Sweden and dated 18–4–1949, numbered B6.

6. A cire perdue glass vase by René Lalique, finely modelled with pendant vines and clusters of berried foliage; 16 cm. high, inscribed 194–20. R. Lalique. In this "lost wax" process, the mould was broken in order to extricate the finished vase, so each piece was unique, as the mould could never be used again.

7. A bronze mounted Favrile glass vase; 31.5 cm. high.
A gold Favrile glass 'millefiore' vase; 23 cm. high.
A gold Favrile glass bud vase; 30.5 cm. high. All by Tiffany Studios, inscribed with initials or L.C. Tiffany Favrile.

8. Two engraved and applied glass vases, the left one designed by Vicke Lindstrand and engraved by Karl Rössler, the right one designed by Simon Gate and engraved by Vicke Lindstrand, both raised on circular black feet; 18.8 cm. and 15.5 cm. high, engraved maker's marks on the base.

9. An Amaryllis applied Favrile glass vase by Tiffany Studios; 10 cm. high, inscribed L.C.T. T1844.

5

6

7

8

9

1

2

The Arts & Crafts tradition continued well into the twentieth century in England and is still alive today. Morris & Co., started by William Morris, continued to produce his most popular designs like the Sussex chair and some new designs in the Arts & Crafts manner long after his death. In a completely different but related style the Cotswold Furniture designers (Gimson, the Barnsleys, Gordon Russell and Peter Waals) stood for quality craftsmanship, and their ideas were shared by Ambrose Heal in his store on Tottenham Court Road.

3

1.   A Heal's oak chest with gallery top, three drawers and two panelled cupboards, circa 1910; 98.6cm. high, 120.7cm. wide.

2.   One of a pair of Robert Thompson 'Mouseman' oak armchairs, the toprail carved with feline heads and with square leather strap seats; dated 1928. The carved mouse 'signature' which was Thompson's hallmark can be seen running up the support beneath the armrest on the left.

3.   A Morris & Company mahogany breakfront dresser with pierced and carved scrolling acanthus pediment, the drawers mounted with silvered metal drop handles; 213.5cm. high, 216cm. wide, 54cm. deep, circa 1895.

4.   A wool carpet designed by Frank Brangwyn for Templetons circa 1930; 291 × 69cm., woven initials F.B.

5.   A suite of oak furniture framed by chequered inlaid lines executed by Peter Waals, assisted by P. Burchett, 1928; bedside cabinet at left 91.6cm. high, table 93.7cm wide.

4

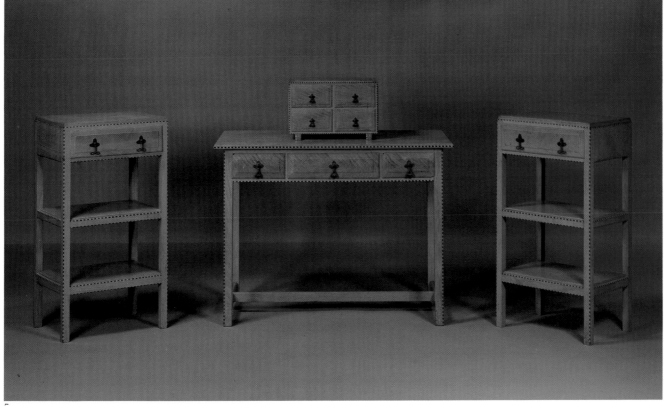

5

1

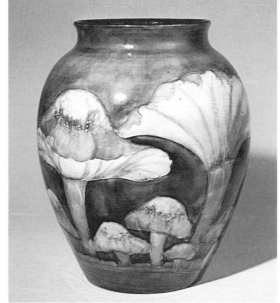

2

3

4

5

6

British Studio Pottery was still dominated by the department devoted to that area at Royal Doulton. Other Staffordshire potteries followed suit, but there were also many smaller studios, often run by a single potter. Of the medium-sized concerns Moorcroft, Ruskin and Foley are among the best known. There were also several sculptors in ceramic at this period, and two of the leading ones, Charles Vyse and Phoebe Stabler, are seen here. During the 1920s artists like Bernard Leach and William Staite-Murray were to introduce the idea of the potter as artist rather than craftsman.

1. One of a pair of Moorcroft Macintyre pottery vases painted with cornflowers and foliage; 30 cm. high, printed Macintyre mark, signed in green W. Moorcroft. Moorcroft designed for the Macintyre factory before setting up his own pottery.

2. A large Moorcroft vase painted in the 'Claremont' toadstool pattern; 33.9 cm. high; impressed Moorcroft, Burslem England 189. Indistinct green painted signature and hand-signed printed paper label.

3. A Moorcroft Macintyre Florian Ware bonbonniere and cover with rich gilt detailing; 21.5 cm. hgh, printed Macintyre mark M2412.

4. A large Ruskin low-fired crystalline glaze vase on the left; 41.5 cm. high; impressed Ruskin England 1926.

On the right, a large Ruskin high-fired transmutation glaze vase with matching stand; 36 cm. high including stand; impressed Ruskin England, circa 1930.

5. 'The Gypsies', a Charles Vyse earthenware group, painted in bright colours; 27 cm. high, painted artist's monogram and Chelsea 1925.

6. A Harold and Phoebe Stabler stoneware group of two putti seated on a caparisoned bull, glazed in natural colours; 33 cm. wide, impressed marks and Poole mark. The Stablers worked for other potteries as well as for Poole.

7. A Bernard Moore tall bottle-shaped vase decorated with herons in sang-de-boeuf lustre on a shaded red and brown ground; 51.8 cm. high, signed Bernard Moore, circa 1920.

8. A Royal Doulton Chang bowl decorated by Charles Noke and Harry Nixon, and a Chang vase by the same artists. This pottery was given the name Chang because of its imitation of early Chinese glazes. Bowl 23.6 cm. diam., vase 25.4 cm. high, both with printed Royal Doulton marks, painted Chang and artists' monograms.

9. A Della Robbia vase and cover incised and painted by C.A. Walker; 30.5 cm. high, incised Della Robbia galleon mark, & C.A.W., dated 1898, numbered 31.

10. A Foley-Shelley 'Intarsio' pottery umbrella and cane stand painted with foliage and a fish-scale pattern on a brown and green ground; 70 cm. high, printed marks.

11. A Bernard Leach large earthenware dish; 41.8 cm diam. BL script monogram circa 1923. Bernard Leach had spent eleven years in Japan (1909–1920) studying potting and decorating techniques there before setting up his own pottery at St. Ives in Cornwall.

7

8

9

10

11

1

The ceramics industry was very interested in attracting famous artists and sculptors to do designs for them, and some examples of this marriage of art and industry are seen here. Gilbert Bayes was one of the leading sculptors of his day and designed a number of such garden statues as that illustrated here for Royal Doulton. Frank Brangwyn designed furniture and carpets as well as ceramics, and the bright colouring seen here on a Wilkinson wall plaque borrowed from a House of Lords commission looks particularly rich. Josef Wackerle executed a number of designs for Nymphenburg.

2

1.   A Wilkinson Royal
Staffordshire pottery wall
plaque, painted by Clarice Cliff,
illustrating a scene from one of
the panels designed for the
Royal Gallery of the House of
Lords by Frank Brangwyn in
1925 and first exhibited at
Olympia in 1933; 44 cm. diam.
with printed facsimile Clarice
Cliff signature.

2.   The 'Lily-Maid', a Royal
Doulton polychrome glazed
stoneware fountain figure
designed by Gilbert Bayes, the
fountain spout concealed in a
bouquet of flowers held up in
her right hand; 61.5 cm. high,
inscribed Gilbert Bayes.

3.   A pair of Nymphenburg
porcelain figures designed by
Prof. Josef Wackerle as stylized
Eighteenth Century fops, on
circular bases; 55 cm. and 56 cm.
high, impressed and printed
Nymphenburg marks, circa
1925.

4.   Six items of lustre ware
from the Pilkington Royal
Lancastrian Pottery, designed
and decorated by artists
including Walter Crane, William
S. Mycock and Richard Joyce,
dating between 1906–1927. Vase
at left 21.8 cm. high, impressed
firm's and painted artist's
marks.

3

4

1

2

1.   A stoneware tureen and cover attributed to Reinhold Merkelbach and the design to Richard Riemerschmid, decorated with a design in relief of stylised leaves and flowers; 33.5 cm. high.

2.   'The Wave and The Rock', a Royal Copenhagen porcelain group designed by Teodor Lundberg in 1897; 46 cm. high, impressed artist's monogram dated 1897, printed marks, numbered 168, 1132, made circa 1930.

3.   A Fraureuth porcelain box and domed cover, blue and white with black and gilt stylized foliate hand-painted decoration; 21 cm. high; printed mark Fraureuth Kunstabteilung, circa 1920.

4.   An earthenware vase of flattened spherical form by Edouard Cazaux, circa 1930; 33.5 cm. high, painted Cazaux Evolution, Made in France.

5.   A Rosenthal figural porcelain group by A. Caasmann (after a group in a painting by Franz von Stuck) of three Bacchanalian figures on a shaped base; 20.1 cm. high, printed factory marks and impressed artist's signature, circa 1920.

3   4   5

6. A white-glazed porcelain figure of a nude female with a snake, detailed with gilt by Gebrüder Heubach, Thüringen, circa 1915; 35 cm. high, marked Heubach Kunst Porzellan, Modell Freireuth. The female and the serpent usually represented evil in the Symbolist art of the late 19th and early 20th century.

7. A Meissen porcelain group by W. Zügel modelled as a polar bear with her cub; 22 cm. wide, marked W. Zügel 1906 and the Meissen crossed swords mark.

8. A Royal Copenhagen stoneware figure of David and Goliath modelled by Arno Malinowski, covered in a celadon crackle glaze; 68 cm. high, impressed artist's monogram and manufacturer's printed mark, 1932.

9. A selection of Tonwerke Kandern pottery designed by Max Lauger, applied with foliage and linear decoration in heavy slip; jug on left 26 cm. high, impressed monogram of Tonwerke Kandern combined with artist's monogram, circa 1900.

10. A lustre pottery plate by Clement Massier, decorated with a Mediterranean landscape, 49.5 cm. diam; signed Clement Massier Golf Juan 1909 and with blindstamp.

6

7

8

9

10

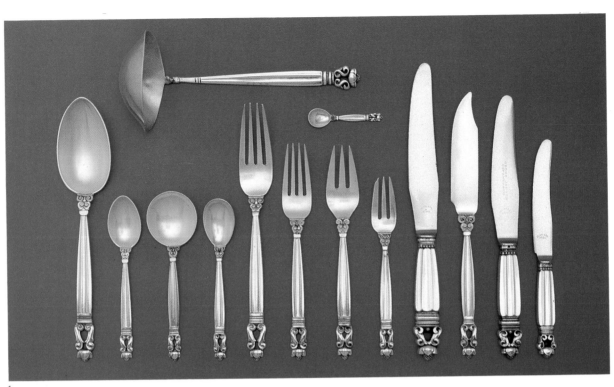

1

2

Georg Jensen undoubtedly counts as one of the greatest twentieth-century silversmiths. He is remarkable mainly for his virtuosity as a silversmith, some of which he managed to pass on to the craftsmen he trained and employed. His own designs were traditional but no less attractive for that. He was a designer with as much taste as skill, and produced what can only be called twentieth-century classics. There is a timeless feeling about his designs. He also encouraged other designers whose work was produced at Georg Jensen, and one of the most successful of these was Johan Rhode.

1.   Part of a Georg Jensen 180 piece 'Acorn' pattern table service first designed in 1915 by Johan Rohde; stamped firm's marks, weight 181 ozs. not including knives.

2.   A pair of fine silver candelabra designed by Georg Jensen, 1920, executed by Georg Jensen Silversmithy, entirely handcrafted; 26.5 cm. high, each impressed Denmark, Georg Jensen Sterling 383A. 194 troy ozs. net. weight.

3.   A fine silver compote designed by Georg Jensen, 1918, executed by Georg Jensen Silversmithy; 30.5 cm. high, impressed 925. S Denmark GJ Sterling 264B. 53 troy ozs.

3

In the first half of the twentieth century the continuing tradition of silversmithing was strongest in Britain, Scandinavia, and the German-speaking countries. In Scandinavia silversmithing was dominated by the figure of Georg Jensen, but other firms like A. Michelsen and Evald Nielsen also produced distinguished wares. In Britain there was no such dominant figure, but many distinguished individuals (Omar Ramsden, John Paul Cooper, Edward Spencer) and a high degree of originality. In Germany and Austria too there was great skill and great variety in the field of metalwork, especially among the Wiener Werkstätte designers.

1. A brass candlestick of inverted trumpet shape by Robert R. Jarvie, Chicago, Illinois; 15.5 cm. high, incised Jarvie.

2. An Omar Ramsden nine carat beaten gold cigarette case with cut steel relief decoration on the obverse and reverse in the Gothic style; 11.3 × 8.8 cm. with O.R. maker's monogram and gold mark for 1922, also engraved Omar Ramsden me fecit MCMXXII.

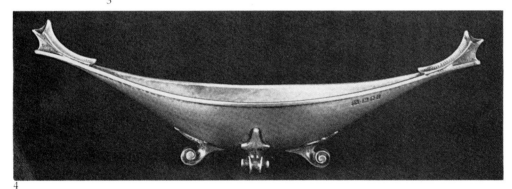

3. An Omar Ramsden silver and burr walnut mazer, on raised circular silver foot; 31 cm. diam. London hallmarks for 1938, makers monogram O.R and engraved Omar Ramsden me fecit (wood cracked).

4. A boat-shaped hammered silver bowl with four scroll feet by Omar Ramsden; 25 cm. wide; inscribed Omar Ramsden Me Fecit; impressed hallmarks for 1931, 5 troy ozs. weight.

5. A silver caddy spoon by Bernard Instone with cloisonné enamelled handle; 7 cm. long, stamped hallmarks for Birmingham 1928.

6. A Danish oval two-handled salmon dish and cover designed by Johan Rohde for Georg Jensen, the finial composed of grapes, shells and fish; 76.5 cm long, 6.650 kg.

7. A silver vase and cover, pierced and repoussé with a grapevine design, by Eduard Friedman, Vienna circa 1920; 27.5 cm. high, impressed hallmarks and Austrian punchmarks, 24.5 troy ozs.

8. An Art Nouveau seven light candelabra by Krausnicku Company; 59 cm. high, stamped marks Krausnicku Co. Gross weight 63 ozs.

9. A Georg Jensen silver four-piece tea and coffee service in the 'Blossom' design, with handles of turned ivory; height of coffee pot, 21.2 cm., all stamped with maker's marks, 1905. 62 ozs, 5 dwts. gross weight.

10. Part of a Charles Boyton 78-piece silver table service, armorial crests on the handles. London hallmarks for 1947, maker's mark CB and facsimile signatures, Charles Boyton.

11. Two pieces of jewellery by Georg Jensen, a silver and moonstone brooch designed as a flower basket and a silver and labradorite necklace 47 cm. long; firm's impressed marks.

7

8

9

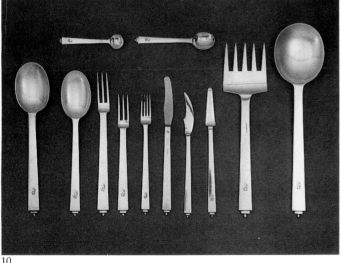

10

11

(*Above*)   A pair of large porcelain vases and covers by Sèvres,
designed by René Crevel, circa 1925; 72.5 cm. high, painted marks.

(*Opposite*)   'Message of Love', a bronze figure cast from a model by
Pierre Le Faguays, poised on a black onyx pedestal; 45.8 cm. high,
signed Le Faguays, stamped Bronze, France.

CHAPTER 4

Art Deco

Art Deco was undoubtedly one of the liveliest and most comprehensive of twentieth century decorative trends, embracing a complete lifestyle. Decorative arts, fine arts and fashion were all involved, and no aspect of living escaped the designer's clutches during the years between the wars. Cars, handbags, bathroom fittings, silver, glass, haircuts, jewellery and lighting were if possible all meant to fit into a single scheme. The complete flapper recognized no other style, and allowed room only for what captured the spirit of the age (which had to be brand-new). There was little sentiment for what had gone before. Although the teachings of Ruskin and Morris preached unity of style, they could never have foreseen anything as radical or total as Art Deco. No earlier style had ever been as demanding, for it was not really possible to achieve the desired effect without adopting the challenge of Art Deco wholeheartedly, drastically short hair for the girls, Oxford bags for the men and geometric design absolutely everywhere.

Even though the contrast with Art Nouveau could not have been more striking, the new geometry of Art Deco was also a logical reaction against this earlier style and had already been hinted at by the clear symmetry of artists like Charles Rennie Mackintosh, Josef Hoffmann, and the Wiener Werkstätte designers. It was as much a consequence of Art Nouveau as a reaction against it. There was no sudden change of gear; it took almost twenty years for Art Deco to come together and form a complete picture as seen at the 1925 Paris Exhibition. The first hints of a radical change came with Paul Poiret and his emancipated view of women's fashion. He literally released their bodies from imprisonment by deciding that it was time for the corset to be abandoned. One type of imprisonment was, however, quickly replaced by another, with hobble skirts which forced the wearer to take mincing steps. Poiret also decided that it was time to put an end to Victorian prudishness, and much to the (simulated) horror of middle-class Paris, his dresses allowed women to show off their ankles for the first time ever in fashion history. As if this was not enough change, the clothes had an air of exoticism about them, with aigrettes and pantaloons reminiscent of harem costume. This is said to have been as a result of the first appearance of Diaghilev's Ballets Russes in Paris in 1909, with costumes by Leon Bakst in a bright palette of colours which Poiret says liberated him from eighteenth-century refinement. 'Now I have let some wolves into the sheepfold, those lively reds, greens, purples and blues make all the rest sit up.' Poiret, as well as creating new fashions, decided that his clothes needed a totally new environment to set them off, and this he created with dramatic effect at the legendary parties he gave, each of them with a theme, be it 1001 nights or some other Middle Eastern fantasy. The fountains flowing with champagne bankrupted him but he none the less managed to dominate Paris fashion for nearly a decade both as interior decorator and dress designer.

The syntax of Art Deco was largely created by interior decorators, for in the new society that emerged after the First World War they had considerable influence. The new rich wanted to show off their wealth in a way that would make them socially acceptable, and to do this they needed help. The easiest way was of course to create a totally new look which did not run the risk of comparison, and with so much that was new in a 'Brave New World' where 'the great life of the machine had shaken society, snapped all chains, opened all doors, and cast its eyes in every direction', this was not difficult. Designers and decorators made a conscious effort to break with the past, relying on a new aesthetic which had a number of sources ranging from Cubism to the clean lines of the machine age. However it is accounted for, basic geometry was an essential feature of all decorative design. Flowers and all the other symbols of Art Deco became formalized and geometric, while some of the symbols like the sunburst and the lightning ziggurat were chosen just because of their geometry.

But French Art Deco could never break completely with the past; just as with Art Nouveau, there was often Rococo somewhere in the background. However geometric the flowers, the overall effect remained florid, as for instance in the wrought ironwork of Edgar Brandt and the woodcarving on a piece of furniture by Paul Follot. The best of French Art Deco was always expensive, making use of exotic woods and luxury materials like shagreen, ivory or mother-of-pearl. Art Deco designers borrowed freely from Egyptian culture (the discovery of Tutankhamun's tomb in 1923 started an Egyptian craze), from Fauvism, Cubism, Futurism and Negro art, subjecting every style to a fashionable brand of formal geometry. Apart from this superimposed geometry the Art Deco designers were not particularly original; Art Deco was a decorative mania without any great intellectual background. The world of fashion and of interior design were closely related in Paris at this time, and worked together to create a suitable new environment for the flapper, 'the free and easy boy girl with shingled hair, a cigarette, a driving licence'. It was something of an innovation too that women were involved professionally in this world, with important figures like Jean Lanvin and Coco Chanel.

The new lifestyle of the 1920s was largely one without domestic help, and much simpler than in Victorian or Edwardian times. Kitchens were no longer relegated 'below stairs', and together with bathrooms became more integrated into everyday life, their decoration being treated with the same attention to style as other living quarters. The dressing table became a shrine to fashion and the cocktail cabinet a shrine to 'the cocktail hour', both reflections of social change, and both concerned with surface decoration rather than inner structure, unlike the more academic forms of modernism.

All the industries involved with the decorative arts set out accordingly to make things as attractive and as instantly appealing as possible. There were basically two different kinds of French Art Deco, both of which were equally important, one concerned with the mass market, the other with unashamed luxury. The luxurious variety was seen at its most splendid at the 1925 Paris Exhibition, the pride of which was Jacques-Emile Ruhlmann's 'Hôtel du Collectionneur' with furniture and decoration only affordable by the very richest clients. It was also seen in the prestigious furnishings of ocean liners like the *Normandie*, intended as a showcase for French luxury. But at the same time the quality of design using ordinary materials improved beyond recognition. Various large stores, realizing the business potential of interior decoration, employed famous designers to open departments for them. Louis Sue and

André Mare started the Compagnie des Arts, which provided well-designed furniture at reasonable prices; Paul Follot worked for Bon Marché, Maurice Dufrène for Galeries Lafayette, and at Printemps there was L'Atelier Primavera. René Lalique, one of the most successful industrialists of the period between the wars, supplied them all with glass.

By 1918 Lalique had completely abandoned his career as a jeweller and had set up a glass factory outside Paris. His aim was to combine good design with quality in products that would reach as wide a market as possible. He was involved in several major design commissions, including the decorative glass fittings for the *Ile de France* and the *Normandie* as well as important commissions outside France. But above all, he was known for glass manufactured by his company for the retail trade. The range was enormous, with scent bottles, vases, boxes, jewellery, all kinds of light fittings from lamps to chandeliers, car mascots, figures and clocks. These were made in moulds, sometimes in a combination of clear and frosted glass, sometimes in opalescent glass, and sometimes in strong colours, notably in brilliant blue, amber and deep reds, emerald greens, and occasionally black. In a wide range of decoration including plants, insects, flowers, and human and mythical figures he made use of the contemporary fashion for stylized geometry, so that any of his pieces could be easily incorporated into an Art Deco interior. His style was much copied, almost to the point of plagiarism in the case of Sabino, whose glassworks produced vases and decorative objects in a similar blue-white opalescent glass.

Another influential glass artist at this time was Maurice Marinot, who worked in a very different way. He started as a painter exhibiting at the Salon d'Automne with the Fauve artists, but was captivated by the magic of glass and decided to use that as his medium for artistic expression. He was the first twentieth-century glass artist to work in this way, a forerunner of the much later major developments in the international Studio Glass Movement which swept America in the 1960s. After the earlier enamelled pieces which he designed and gave to a small glassworks belonging to the Brothers Viard to be manufactured, he worked on the glass himself, using deep acid-etched abstract geometric designs. His work influenced others like Henri Navarre and André Thuret, and the Daum factory used this style to revive its fortunes with a series of commercially produced heavy glass vessels with bold geometric designs. Daum, together with Alméric Walter, François Emile Décorchemont and Gabriel Argy-Rousseau, also helped to develop and make popular pâte de verre, with a variety of decorative objects including lamps, pendants and small pieces with sculptural decorations. With the exception of Maurice Marinot (who in some ways might fit more easily into a chapter about Arts and Crafts), the French 'art glass' industry catered for the luxury end of popular taste. As in other areas of the decorative arts industries, the widely extended new middle classes were keen on decorating their homes, providing a larger middle market than there had ever been before. The

A Hagenauer wall sculpture in fruitwood with copper wire hair, 1920s; 28 cm. high, impressed monogram WHW.

French glassmakers, perhaps by sheer superiority of numbers, and led and inspired by a giant in the industry in the figure of René Lalique, seem to have attracted the most attention.

One of the reasons why Art Deco is so collectable today is that goods for this so-called middle market were extremely well designed and well made; the overall quality of mass-produced articles had improved beyond recognition. Excellent new cheaper materials like plastic helped the lower end of the market, even though plastic was occasionally considered exotic enough to be used in conjunction with precious metals and gemstones, as in some pieces of Cartier jewellery. Plastic was widely and decoratively used, sometimes in imitation of more expensive materials like ivory and amber, but essentially because it lent itself to moulding processes and could be made in virtually any shape or colour. It was popular for jewellery and small objects, radios and lamps. Art Deco lighting in general used electricity with far greater abandon than earlier decorative styles. The earliest electric light fittings imitated oil lamps or chandeliers, and Art Nouveau light fixtures tended to be devised in such a way that the electric parts were either hidden or worked into the decoration, in the guise of flowerheads or insect's eyes. But by the 1920s electrically illuminated glass was used in a thousand different ways from such classic designs as Lalique's Firebird Lamp to the heavy acid-etched Daum chandeliers or the dimly lit pâte de verre lamps by Argy-Rousseau. Theatrical lighting effects were very much part of Art Deco.

Some of the most popular decorative items of this period were the bronze and ivory figures, mostly of exotic female dancers, with cheaper versions in spelter and ivoreen. Bronze and ivory figures rather like Lalique glass were a brand of 'pop art', undemanding, fun and easy to display. They were produced in large quantities by a variety of designers, the most famous being Démètre Chiparus and Ferdinand Preiss. Sculpture of all sort featured in Art Deco interiors from these 'kitsch' pieces to the highly sophisticated work of Gustave Miklos or Lambert-Rucki.

As novelty was so important, any new idea that caught on was much in demand. Cigarette holders and powder compacts are two such ideas. They came in an endless variety of shapes and sizes. Motoring and speed were all the rage, and anything to do with these subjects was treated to streamlining effects. The cocktail hour had become an essential part of life, and the cocktail bar was crowded with witty novelties like cocktail shakers in the shape of dumb-bells or aeroplanes, and cigarette lighters modelled as Negro barmen. Kitsch was an important part of Art Deco and one of the most imaginative aspects of it. It was certainly a contrast to the overindulgent luxury of the most respected designers and worlds apart from the rarified atmosphere they created for their splendid environments. Only rarely (as in the case of Lalique) were products from the mass market acceptable at the top end of the scale, but both extremes hold equal fascination for the art historian.

The master furniture makers, among whom were Jacques-Emile Ruhlmann, Jules Leleu, Clément Rousseau and Armand-Albert Rateau, all tended towards the highly decorative (as opposed to the stark modernist) style of Art Deco. Probably it also suited their luxury-loving clientele better. All of them referred to earlier styles in their work; Rateau, who worked almost exclusively in bronze, harked back to antiquity in pieces reminiscent of Pompeii. Ruhlmann was continuing the great French traditions of furniture established by a long line of distinguished furniture makers from the Louis XIV period onwards. Although there is an element of pastiche in his work, it was done in the spirit of homage to the past, an aspect that would no doubt have reassured his modern clientele, easing them into twentieth-century taste.

Ruhlmann personifies the French Art Deco style, and his style dominated the period. He was of course much more than a furniture designer, creating total environments (curtains, carpets, light-fittings and door furniture), completely designed by himself and made to his own prestigious standards of craftsmanship. He was above all a showman, and used exotic materials (silver, ivory, bronze, sharkskin and rare woods) to the greatest exotic effect. His greatest moment of glory was the invitation to decorate an entire pavilion at the 1925 Paris Exhibition. He took the opportunity in this Hôtel du Collectionneur to work in conjunction with the other designers he admired the most. The pavilion was designed by the architect Pierre Patout, the exterior decorated with a bas-relief frieze by Joseph Bernard. Inside there was ironwork by Edgar Brandt, lacquer by Jean Dunand and furniture by Jallot and Rapin. There was a 'clique' of these top designers whose work appeared together in the various Paris salons. Their styles were either similar or complementary, intended to create an atmosphere of out-and-out luxury.

Edgar Brandt made ironwork that was hand-forged

A fine macassar ebony, marquetry, giltwood and marble commode
by Süe et Mare incorporating doors decorated to a design by
Mathurin Méheut, circa 1925; 84.5 cm. high, 173 cm. wide, 66 cm.
deep.

and delicate beyond belief (suggesting wirework rather
than iron), or else worked in solid cast bronze as with
his famous 'Serpent' lamp. Henri Rapin, as well as
designing furniture, was artistic director at the Sèvres
porcelain factory, which produced a series of outstanding pieces including monumental fountains and
chandeliers, many of them designed by himself. Jean
Dunand worked in enamelled metal and also designed
bookbindings, but is known above all for his lacquer
work which incorporated designs in crushed eggshell.
The art of lacquer enjoyed a revival during this period,
the laborious techniques involved making it rare and
costly and therefore highly suitable for a luxury market.
Dunand used lacquer in furniture, either directly on the
surface or in separate panels that were incorporated.
Eileen Gray, the British designer who lived and worked
in Paris, was also a lacquer artist, though her designs
fitted more into the modernist scheme of things. The

silver of Jean Puiforcat, often set with semi-preciou
materials such as rock crystal or lapis lazuli, also fitte
into the category of sheer luxury, along with the silve
and enamel vases by Camille Fauré, the thick enam
applied in bold brightly coloured geometric patterns.
It was also a great period of French jewellery an
objects of vertu such as the mystery clocks made by Ca
tier, many of them intricate mechanical tours de force i
which all the working parts were set with preciou
stones. Jewellery, too, was either abstract in design o
decorated with stylized Art Deco motifs. Apart from th
major jewellers, Cartier, Boucheron, Van Cleef an
Arpels, there was a handful of smaller firms like Lacloch
Frères, and individual designers (Templier, Desprè
Georges Fouquet and Jean Dunand), who designe
jewellery as well. The new method of invisible settin
devised by Van Cleef was very popular and much usec
There were also a few new ideas like the fashion fo
dress clips which could either be worn separately o
together as a large brooch. Necklaces were longer tha
before, probably owing to the flat-chested look whic
was so much *en vogue*. The smart modern accessory wa

a 'minaudière' or evening vanity bag made of gold or silver and often set with precious stones. Inside were fitted compartments for lipstick, rouge and whatever else the flapper required. Cigarette holders were of course *de rigueur*, and the longer the better.

The rest of Europe looked longingly at Paris fashion and Art Deco, without ever entering into the spirit of it in the same way. In England there were isolated examples, but it did not overwhelm the look of things. Only one department store had a really 'modern' department, and that was Waring and Gillow where a Russian-born Frenchman, Serge Chermayeff, was in charge of the Art Deco image. There were a few 'modernist' furniture designers, but on the whole the French style of Art Deco did not lend itself to English middle-class, let alone upper-class lifestyles. The nearest a purely English designer got to Art Deco was Clarice Cliff with her jazzy hand-painted ceramics, particularly the range of 'Bizarre' patterns with bold geometric shapes in bright colours. There was a British pavilion at the 1925 Paris Exhibition, but it was rather tame by comparison with French design, with more or less traditional items by Wedgwood and Worcester; a few items more in keeping with the times included some attractive Poole pottery and Wedgwood ceramics decorated by Alfred and Louise Powell.

The French Art Deco influence was more evident in some of the British sculptors like Eric Gill and Richard Garbe. There was also very fine English metalwork such as that designed by R.Y. Gleadowe and H.G. Murphy, but perhaps even this owed more to Arts and Crafts than to Art Deco. An anglicized version of Art Deco was, however, to be seen in some of the smart new London hotels (which were not on the whole catering for Londoners). The Savoy, Claridges, and the Park Lane Hotel (with its magnificent Art Deco ballroom) are the closest the British ever came to a total Art Deco look.

The main difference between France and the other European countries in the period between the wars was that it was only in France that interior decorators were allowed to run wild and exert the powerful influence they did. Nevertheless every European country had its own version of Art Deco, and there were some outstanding European designers other than the French ones. In Italy Gio Ponti was the best-known of the furniture designers, but there were others like Sigmund Pollitzer and Guglielmo Ulrich. Ponti also designed some very attractive pieces for Richard Ginori, some in an updated baroque style with elaborate gilding and putti, others in a more modern idiom, notably a series of vases decorated with sporting subjects. During the 1930s the Torino-based Lenci Pottery produced a series of colourful caricature-like figures in a distinctive style combining wit and sophistication.

The Belgians did not make the same sort of contribution to Art Deco as they had to Art Nouveau; in fact apart from the lively pottery of Boch Frères, there was little Belgian Art Deco. Boch was a branch of the German firm of Villeroy and Boch, and known both by this name and as Keramis, a pottery established by them at La Louvière. In Austria the Wiener Werkstätte continued until 1932, and during this later period produced some beautiful work, particularly under the artistic direction of Dagobert Peche from 1917 to 1923. Peche himself was a versatile designer, at his best perhaps in metalwork. Unlike the more restrained modernist Wiener Werkstätte artists, Peche sought his inspiration in the rich tradition of Austrian Baroque. There were also a number of good ceramic designers at the Wiener Werkstätte during this period, many of whom looked to folk art for their inspiration. Much of the work was figurative and sculptural and very mannered. Gudrun Baudisch and Vally Wieselthier were two of the most successful of the Wiener Werkstätte potters in this 'folk' style. Other ceramic artists like Michael Powolny produced work that was more baroque in feeling, while Ernest Wahliss, who designed for Serapis Fayence, came closest to French Art Deco. The best-known Austrian decorative objects outside the Wiener Werkstätte were the metal and wood sculptures of Karl Hagenauer.

The Scandinavian countries were affected least of all by Art Deco, where its influence was seen primarily in the work of large established firms like Royal Copenhagen and Georg Jensen in Denmark and to a certain extent in the Swedish glass industry. Of the smaller firms Gustavsberg had an 'Art Deco' range of vases and other pieces in pale green porcelain inlaid with silver, designed by Wilhelm Kage.

In America the influence of French Art Deco was felt most strongly in architectural design, particularly in New York. Several of the skyscrapers built in the late 1920s and 1930s are pure Art Deco. The best-known are the Chrysler Building, the Chanin Building, the Rockefeller Plaza and Radio City Music Hall. Many of the American architects had studied in France and adapted what they had learnt there to their own environment. In skyscraper architecture everything was on a larger scale, and this is particularly noticeable in the sculptural decoration, like the Paul Manship sculpture of Prometheus on the Rockefeller Plaza. The most famous and beloved Art Deco interior in New York is that of Radio City Music Hall, designed by the Rockefeller Centre architects in conjunction with Donald Deskey. The Art Deco style as it is used here is described as 'innocent but never corny'. Radio City Hall was for moviegoers, and, like the Hollywood movies shown there, intended to bring into their lives all the grandeur the 1930s could summon up. In the period between the wars 'Movie Madness' pervaded America. A number of Art Deco picture palaces were built across the country, and all eyes were on 'Hollywood' for the next new style as seen in the movies. It is difficult to include films in any history of decorative art, but if there was such a thing as American Art Deco, it was in the work of such Hollywood directors as Busby Berkeley, both in the set and costume designs of his musical routines. No history of Art Deco can really be considered complete without taking into account the Hollywood Musical.

1

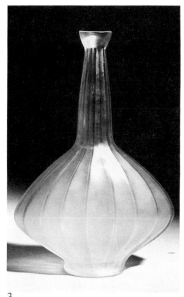

2

3

4

5

Quite apart from his skill as a glassmaker, Lalique's work was remarkable for its sheer inventiveness. His use of glass in lighting was highly original, and lighting appliances designed by him were often more sculptural than functional. Unlike most other lamps of the period, Lalique lamps are today highly prized collectors' items, as are his range of perfume flasks, clocks and car mascots. Lalique's imaginative use of glass extended its possibilities far beyond what had hitherto been considered a commercially viable proposition in glass.

1. 'Douze Figurines avec Bouchon' by René Lalique, a bottle and stopper in satin-finished glass moulded with pairs of nude figures, heightened with traces of brown staining, the stopper moulded with a kneeling nude; 28.5cm. high, etched R. Lalique, numbered 6.

2. A clear and frosted glass carafe and stopper by René Lalique; 38.8cm. high, engraved R. Lalique.

3. A Lalique ribbed flask in clear and satin finished glass, circa 1930; 24.5cm. high, moulded Lalique signature.

4. 'L'Oiseau De Feu', a Lalique glass and bronze table lamp; 43.5cm. wide, engraved R. Lalique.

5. 'Tête D'Aigle,' 'Tête de Coq', and 'Longchamps', by René Lalique, three car radiator mascots in clear and satin finished glass; the Tête de Coq 17.9cm. high; moulded R. Lalique, France.

6. A clear and frosted glass clock by René Lalique, the circular face set in a thick arched frame, enclosed in a garland of flowers and flanked by maidens moulded in intaglio, raised on an electrified nickel-plated base; 36cm. high, etched R. Lalique France.

7. 'Naiades', a frosted and clear glass clock by René Lalique, moulded in intaglio with mermaids; 11.5cm. square, moulded R. Lalique, etched script mark R. Lalique France.

8. 'Deux Paons', a clear and frosted glass luminaire by René

Lalique, raised on an electrified black bakelite base; 45 cm. high, inscribed Lalique.

9. 'Yeso', a Lalique frosted glass luminaire, the semi-circular panel intaglio moulded with goldfish, with electrified metal base; 52 cm. long, etched R. Lalique France.

10. 'Victoire', a car radiator mascot in clear and satin finished glass by René Lalique; 24.7 cm. wide, moulded R. Lalique France.

11. 'Grenouille', a Lalique car mascot in clear and satin finished glass, moulded as a seated frog; 6.3 cm. high, engraved R. Lalique France, moulded Lalique France.

6

7

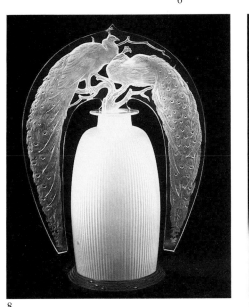
8

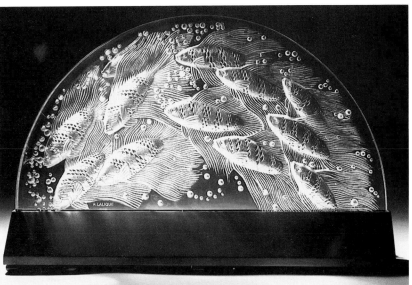
9

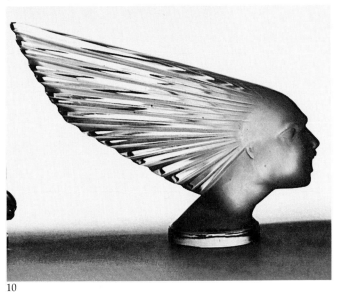
10

11

1

Lalique was best known for vases, the designs for most of which can be found in the Catalogue des verreries de René Lalique, *published in 1932. Models were made in clear and satin-finished glass, sometimes with additional green, blue or brown staining. The same models are often to be found in opalescent glass, a milky blue substance reminiscent of the semi-precious stone from which it derives its name. Some models were also manufactured in a range of brilliant gem-like colours, of which a bright emerald green, rich ruby red, and singing blue are perhaps the most spectacular.*

2

1. A rare black glass and silvered bronze box and cover by René Lalique, the two silvered bronze hinges and clasp cast as scarabs, the black glass moulded with brambles and detailed in white; 19 cm. wide, 8.5 cm. high, inscribed R. Lalique.

2. A selection of Lalique coloured, moulded glass vases, mistletoe vase, bottom right 19 cm. high, moulded and etched marks circa 1930.

3. 'Serpent', a frosted ruby coloured glass vase by René Lalique, moulded as a coiled serpent; 26 cm. high, moulded R. Lalique on the base.

4. A selection of moulded, coloured glass vases by René Lalique; bramble vase lower left 23.5 cm. high, all etched or moulded R. Lalique.

3

4

1

2

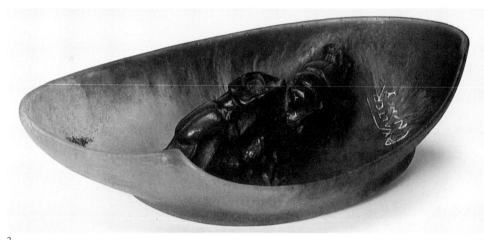

3

There were many original ideas in glass during the Art Deco period, most of them from France. Pâte-de-verre was successfully revived by Almeric Walter and Gabriel Argy-Rousseau, both of whom made small objects with sculptural decorations well suited to this technique. There was also a fashion for heavy-walled glass, sometimes internally decorated with tiny air bubbles, and sometimes with a deep acid-cut geometric design as in the Daum pieces seen here. In Sweden there were new techniques for wheel engraving and the remarkable internally decorated pieces in the new Graal technique invented at Orrefors.

1. A thick-walled glass vase by Henri Navarre, the clear glass heavily mottled with amethyst and green; 17.5cm. high, inscribed H. Navarre 700.

2. A Graal glass vase designed by Edward Hald and executed by Knut Bergkvist, the bell-shaped green glass decorated with birds and flowers; 14.5cm. high, engraved Graal 1928KB-EH no. 3112.

3. A pâte-de-verre dish by Almeric Walter, modelled by Bergé with two beetles at the centre; 28cm. wide, moulded A. Walter Nancy, Bergé Sc. Like Gallé at the turn of the century, artists at Nancy were still using botanical subjects as a source of inspiration.

4

5

4. An elliptical engraved bowl and underplate by Orrefors, circa 1925, the bowl engraved with nude female figures by Simon Gate; 12 cm. high, inscribed SG 109 29 P.

5. An etched and frosted glass table lamp by Daum, circa 1930, 48.5 cm. high, etched Daum, Nancy, France.

6. A Daum deeply etched goblet-shaped glass vase; 37.5 cm. high, etched Daum, Nancy, France.

7. A large etched and engraved glass vase by Aristide-Michel Colotte, carved with elephants and African women, on deep hexagonal base; 30 cm. high, engraved Colotte Nancy, pièce unique.

8. A pâte-de-verre cylindrical box and cover by Gabriel Argy-Rousseau, the cover modelled with a grotesque mask within an ivy leaf border; 15 cm. diam., moulded G. Argy-Rousseau, France.

9. An Argy-Rousseau pâte-de-verre and wrought iron night light, circa 1925; 23 cm. high, moulded G. Argy-Rousseau.

10. A large etched glass vase by Daum, the thick transparent emerald ground etched with slender columns; 39.5 cm. high, inscribed Daum Nancy France. circa 1930.

6

7

9

10

8

Maurice Marinot came to glass via fine art, having started life as a painter. His attitude to glass always remained that of the artist working his material in the privacy of his own studio, away from the glass industry, and in this respect he was the forerunner of the International Studio Glass Movement of the 1960s. It was not customary during the 1920s for glass artists to handle the material themselves. They designed pieces for a team of craftsmen to make.

1.   A fine two-handled etched glass vase by Daum, of thick transparent sapphire coloured glass, circa 1930; 37 cm. high, inscribed Daum, Nancy France.

2.   A bottle and stopper and a vase in glass by Maurice Marinot, both etched, polished and internally decorated; 13.2 cm. and 13.5 cm. high, both incised Marinot.

3.   An engraved glass bottle and stopper by Maurice Marinot, decorated with internal inclusions; 19.7 cm. high, engraved Marinot on base.

4.   A glass flask and stopper by Maurice Marinot, the thick clear glass encasing an oxidized red and green layer profusely scattered with bubbles; 16.6 cm. high, engraved Marinot.

1

2

3

4

1

2

3

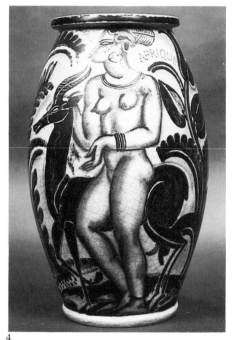

4

5

6

During the period between the wars ceramics were on the whole brightly coloured, and there were some fashionable new colours like orange; silver streaks could always be relied upon for a jazzy accent. Naturalistic subjects were transformed almost beyond recognition by geometric stylization so that they would merge into the general decorative scheme. There was a vogue for figurines, either young maidens or dancing couples, and once again the human form became elongated or cylindrical to suit the dictates of fashion.

1.   An earthenware vase by René Buthaud circa 1928; 33 cm. high, painted with artist's monogram.

2.   A rare pottery wall plaque by Clarice Cliff, possibly inspired by the Ballets Russes; 44.3 cm. diam. Painted 'Bizarre' by Clarice Cliff. A.J. Wilkinson, Burslem, England. Pre-1930.

3.   An earthenware vase painted with centaurs by René Buthaud circa 1925; 35 cm. high, painted with artist's monogram.

4.   An 'Africaine' crackled earthenware vase by René Buthaud circa 1931; 43 cm. high, inscribed 'Afrique' and painted artist's initials R.B. Artists at this time were influenced by African cultures as a result of the French colonization of Africa and the West Indies.

5.   A Longwy crackled creamware vase wtih stylized

foliate relief decoration; 23.5 cm. high, marked Longwy France, circa 1920.

6. Four Boch Frères, Belgium earthenware vases and a bowl painted in bright colours, centre vase 29 cm. high, circa 1915–1925, all with firm's marks.

7. A Continental polychrome porcelain group after a design by Claire Vokhart, 1913; 33 cm. high. This group is probably based on the impersonation of characters from the popular contemporary 'Ballets Russes'.

8. An earthenware sculpture by the Wiener Werkstätte, designed by Gudrun Baudisch as a woman's head, in green, blue and orange on a white ground; 24 cm. high, inscribed WW Made in Austria 345 GB5.

9. A Meissen white-glazed porcelain figure of a courtesan by Paul Scheurich; 46.7 cm. high, inscribed Scheurich, blue Meissen crossed swords mark.

10. A Goldscheider pottery bat girl, her short dress forming a winged cape; 47.5 cm. high; printed Goldscheider factory mark and inscribed Lorenzl.

11. A Clarice Cliff 'Fantasque Bizarre' tea for two set, painted with stylized trees in bright colours, printed marks and facsimile signature. Ceramics in increasingly vivid colours and stylised designs were a reflection of the bright new 'Jazz' age.

12. 'Butterfly', a Royal Doulton porcelain figure designed by L. Harradine, HN720, circa 1925; 16 cm. high. Girls in theatrical costumes and fancy dress were popular themes for potters.

7

8

9

10

11

12

1

2

Three of the most popular subjects in Art Deco design are seen here; the Ginori porcelain box and cover is surmounted by a dancing couple. The success and influence of Diaghilev's Ballets Russes was such that dancing figures featured heavily in all aspects of design. Jazz was very much an invention of the times and a popular subject with designers, particularly groups of Negro jazz musicians. Closely related was the craze for African Art, which had so influenced Cubist painters earlier in the century. It was only to be expected that it would find its way into the decorative arts.

1.   'Omaggio Agli Snob' – a Richard Ginori porcelain box and cover designed by Gio Ponti, the cover with elaborate sculptural relief of a male and female dancer before a stylized tree; 28.2 cm. high, printed and painted marks including Gio Ponti, Richard Ginori and 1925.

2.   'Age of Jazz', a Clarice Cliff two-sided painted pottery plaque on rectangular base; 14 cm. high, printed marks.

3.   A fine large earthenware vase with scalloped handles by René Buthaud, circa 1931, both sides embossed with a nude African woman amidst palm fronds, on a crazed ground; 37 cm. high, painted initials R.B.

3

1

Tea and coffee sets were much in demand, and by tradition silver was popular for ceremonial occasions. During this time it was often combined with ivory; lucite combined with silver as in the set by Ravinet D'Enteret is more uncommon, though plastics were beginning to be used in combination with precious metals and gems even by Cartier. The shiny characteristics of silver and silver plate fitted well into the bright and brittle look of Art Deco, and bronze accessories, either in the form of objects in themselves or as decorative features on furniture, added the much sought after touch of luxury.

1. An enamel and scarab bangle by E. Philippe in the Egyptian style, the amethyst and cornelian scarabs of the Middle Kingdom and Late Period; inscribed E. Philippe à Paris deposé, French poinçon marks. After the discovery of Tutankhamun's tomb by Lord Caernarvon and Howard Carter in 1922 there was a vogue for jewellery and other applied arts in the Egyptianesque style.

2. An Austrian white metal and enamel cigarette case, the enamel by F. Zwichl depicting an open Samson car in black, red and cream enamels and with engine-turned borders; stamped Made in Austria.

2

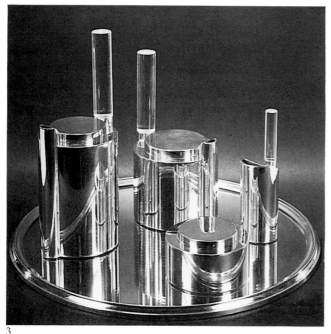

3

4

3.   A five-piece silver-plated coffee service with clear lucite handles by Ravinet d'Enteret; tray 40 cm. diam, impressed firm's marks. Design has become extremely angular, in this instance almost taking over from the functional.

4.   A silver and ivory coffee and tea service designed by Dagobert Peche for the Wiener Werkstätte circa 1920, each piece with hammered scalloped body and beaded rim and with handle and finial of ivory; tray 43.5 cm. wide, impressed firm's marks, designer's mark and Austrian hall-mark. 89 troy ozs. gross weight.

5.   A silvered bronze mirror by Emile-Jacques Ruhlmann, raised on ribbed, tapering splayed feet; 46 cm. high.

6.   A pair of Artificers Guild Ltd. silver and narwhal tazzas, designed by Edward Spencer, the domed feet set with cone-shaped aventurine cabochons; bowls 19.4 cm. wide; stamped – Designed by Edward Spencer, maker's mark and London hallmark for 1926.

7.   A silvered bronze urn by Edgar Brandt cast with a frieze of nude figures; 123 cm. high, the stepped plinth impressed E. Brandt France.

8.   A Georg Jensen three-peice coffee set designed by Johan Rohde, the scroll handles set with discs, circa 1920; coffee pot 21.7 cm. high, stamped Dessin J.R. Georg Jensen 312. 34oz. 12 dwts. gross weight.

5

6

7

8

There were a number of master jewellers and master metal-workers in France at this time, whose clientele were the rich and the new rich of upper-middle-class society. The clothes they wore were designed by leading Paris couturiers, and a fashion for modernity meant that new jewellery was in demand. Luxurious objects were also sought by decorators using the furniture of the top French designers like Ruhlmann and Leleu.

1.   A gilt bronze clock by Süe et Mare, circa 1924, the upper section cast with stylized flowers, the circular body raised on two scrolled feet, on black onyx base; 33.5 cm. high.

2.   A silvered bronze and black onyx mantel clock by Albert Cheuret circa 1930, of an Egyptian inspired design; 42.5 cm. wide, inscribed Albert Cheuret.

3.   A monumental inlaid metal vase and pedestal by Claudius Linossier for the 1925 Paris Exhibition, the urn inlaid with silver and patinated in colours, on fruit-wood pedestal; vase 80 cm. high, the pedestal 90 cm. high. Inscribed Cl. Linossier.

4.   A jade, diamond and enamelled platinum pendant by Georges Fouquet, 1924, suspended on a jade and onyx chain; pendant 12.5 cm. long, impressed G. Fouquet 19720 and with French poinçons.

1

2

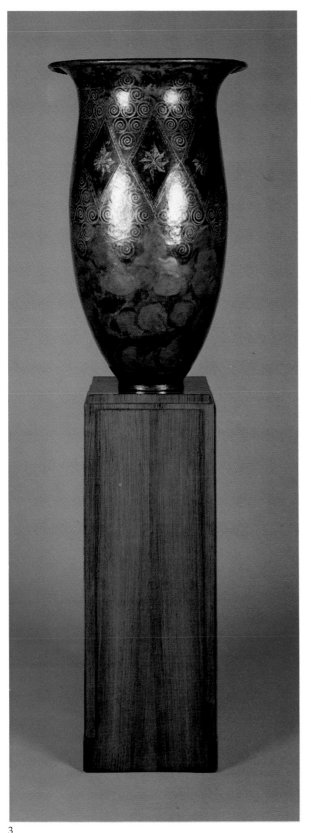

3

4

1

2

4

3

5

Bronze and ivory figures were a vital accessory either as sculpture or as a vehicle for lighting. The bronze was finished in a variety of patinas from dull gold to bright green, and often heightened with cold-painted colouring. Ivory was used for the face and hands and occasionally coloured with flesh tones. The most popular subjects for these figures were dancers in exotic Middle Eastern costume (obviously influenced by the Ballets Russes) and young flappers suitably attired in trouser suits and wearing high heels or in fashionable flat-chested dresses with dropped waists and with aigrettes in their hair.

1. 'Faun et Nymph', a dark brown patinated bronze group cast from a model by Pierre Le Faguays, on green marble base; 69.5 cm. wide, 52.3 cm. high, inscribed Le Faguays and impressed with the Gold-scheider 'Le Stele' foundry seal.

2. A bronze and ivory figure of a harem dancer cast and carved from a model by Pierre de Faguays, mounted between two flambeaux light fittings; 48.7 cm. wide, signed Le Faguays.

3. 'The Black Leather Suit', a bronze and ivory figure cast and carved from a model by Bruno Zach; 72 cm. high, inscribed Bruno Zach and stamped with founder's monogram. Zach was appreciated for his female sculptures in rather erotic costumes or poses.

4. 'The Aristocrats', a cold-painted bronze and ivory group of a medieval woman with two borzois, cast and carved from a model by Professor Otto Poertzel, on elaborate stepped onyx base; 48.9 cm. high, inscribed Prof. Poertzel and impressed with the Preiss-Kassler foundry seal.

5. 'Ankara Dancer', a parcel gilt bronze and ivory figure of a snake dancer, cast and carved from a model by Claire Jeanne Roberte Colinet, on waisted marble plinth; 63.8 cm. high, stamped 11 and inscribed Cl. J.R. Colinet.

6. 'Profil de femme', an ivory plaque by Bela Vöros, mounted in an ebonized wood plaque on rectangular base; 11.2 × 14.4cm. inscribed monogram in the ivory.

7. 'Hoop Girl' and 'Sonny Boy', cold-painted bronze and ivory figures cast from models by F. Preiss, on green onyx bases; 20.6cm. and 21cm. high, both inscribed F. Preiss.

8. 'Torch Dancer', a cold-painted bronze and ivory figure cast and carved from a model by Ferdinand Preiss, on onyx plinth; 40cm. high, inscribed in the bronze F. Preiss.

9. 'The Sisters', a fine cold-painted, gilt bronze and ivory group of two exotic dancers, cast and carved from a model by Demêtre Chiparus; 46.8cm. high including variegated onyx base, signed Chiparus. This group is thought to represent 'The Dolly Sisters', a popular singing and dancing duo in the 20's.

10. 'Towards The Unknown', a bronze and ivory group cast from a model by Claire Jeanne Roberte Colinet; 41cm. wide, signed. Female figures in action were a popular theme for sculptors at this period.

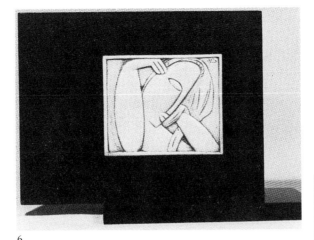

6

7

8

9

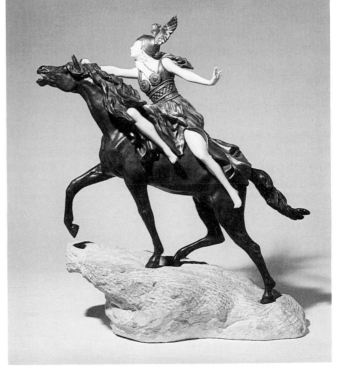

10

1

All the figures illustrated here are by Demêtre Chiparus, and all of them in exotic costume sometimes of Middle Eastern and sometimes of medieval inspiration. 'Les Amis de Toujours' was one of his most popular works, although for modern tastes its heavy sentimentality borders on sickliness. Its heaviness did, however, fit with the elaborate woods and exotic mountings used by French furniture makers, which are sometimes considered to be no more than a kind of updated Victorianism, or neo-romanticism.

1. 'Russian Dancers', a cold-painted silvered and gilt bronze and ivory group of cymbal dancers, cast and carved from a model by Demêtre Chiparus, on elaborate red and black marble base; 60.3 cm. high, signed D.H. Chiparus and inscribed Etling –

Paris. The two dancers might represent Vaslav Nijinsky and Ida Rubenstein dancing in the Ballets Russes production of 'Scheherazade' first performed in Paris in 1910.

2. 'Les Amis de Toujours', a gilt and silver cold-painted bronze and ivory group cast and carved from a model by Demêtre Chiparus; 62.5 cm. high, signed Chiparus, the bronze stamped LNJL Paris.

3. 'Civa', a polychromed bronze and ivory figure of a temple goddess cast and carved from a model by Demêtre Chiparus, the faceted marble plinth enclosing a light fitting; 55 cm. high, including plinth, central plaque inscribed 'Civa' par D.H. Chiparus. These bronze or bronze and ivory figures became increasingly popular in the late 20's and 30's, many showing eastern influence.

2

1

2

3

4

5

6

There is a great variety in popular Art Deco sculpture, some of which was heavily romantic and some very saucy. Much of it is pure kitsch and should not be taken too seriously. It can be either mildly erotic as in the work of Bruno Zach, heavily romantic as in Chiparus, or light and airy as in Preiss. Chiparus and Preiss were certainly the most prolific popular sculptors, but in France particularly there were many commercial artists working in a similar idiom, all of them more concerned with interior design than with fine art.

1.   'Couple Dansant', a French bronze group of two dancers with a high, rich brownish black patina, cast from a model by Joseph Bernard; 58.2cm high, inscribed J. Bernard No. 4 ©, impressed with the Valsuani foundry seal and with French customs seal.

2.   A dark brown and silvered bronze figure of a nude dancer within a circle of stylized petals cast from a model by Alexander Kéléty, on grey marble base; 40.2cm. high, inscribed A. Kelety.

3.   Nude Girl with Shawl, a silvered bronze figure cast from a model by Lorenzl, decoration by Crejo, with a cold-painted floral design on the shawl, on an oval onyx base; 37.5cm, inscribed Lorenzl, enamelled Crejo.

4.   'The Clown's Dream', a bronze and marble figure cast and carved from a model by Demêtre Chiparus, gilt and greenish brown cold-painted patina; 74.2cm. high, inscribed by the founders Gazan (one hand damaged).

5.   A cold-painted bronze and ivory figure of Pierrette cast and carved from a model by Paul Philippe, on stepped bronze and verde antico base; 37.8cm. high, inscribed P. Philippe and circular founder's mark.

6.   'March Winds', cast from a model by Richard Garbe, bronze on a stepped marble base; 48.6cm. high, signed in the bronze Richard Garbe and dated 1922.

7. An onyx and marble mantel clock mounted with a nude ivory figure cast and carved from a model by Ferdinand Preiss; 26cm high, signed F. Preiss.

8. A bronze, marble and glass figural lamp cast from a model by M. Le Verrier, circa 1925; 86.2cm. high, signed M. Le Verrier.

9. 'Leaving For The Crusade', a rare silvered, gilt and cold-painted bronze and ivory group of an equestrian knight and a maiden, cast and carved from a model by Pierre de Faguays on a shaped onyx base; 58.2cm. high, signed P. Le Faguays, stamped Bronze and impress LN and JL foundry seal.

10. 'The Riding Crop', a cold-painted bronze figure cast from a model by Bruno Zach, on veined black marble base; 30.5cm. high, inscribed Zach, Austria.

11. An onyx and silvered bronze mantel clock cast from a model by Georges Lavroff; 38.2in. high, 56.8cm. wide, sleeping nymph inscribed G. Lavroff.

12. A bronze and ivory figure of an exotic dancer cast and carved from a model by Gerdago, cold-painted in polychrome, on stepped onyx base; 33.4cm. high, inscribed Gerdago and founder's stamp.

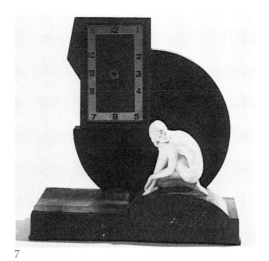

7

8

9

10

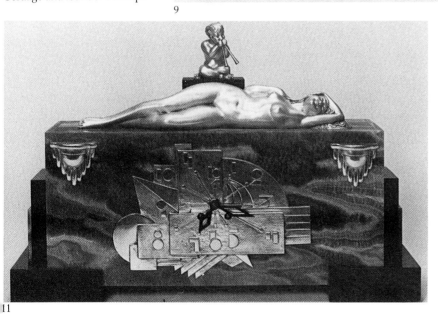

11

12

Lacquer was rediscovered in Europe during this period, and even though Eileen Gray, one of the master craftsmen working in this idiom, was an English-woman, Paris was the only place in Europe where lacquer artists worked. Jean Dunand and Eileen Gray are considered the two greatest Art Deco design-ners in lacquer, and Eileen Gray mastered the art of executing lacquer work herself, a time-consuming and laborious pro-cess, as well as being a health hazard owing to the cold damp conditions it requires.

1. A fine lacquered wood panel by Jean Dunand circa 1929 for Mme Jacoubovitch, Paris; 246 × 241.5 cm. Signed.

2. A fine lacquer and ivory commode bombé by Jean Dunand, outlined in ivory and with ivory sabots, the door lacquered with stylized foliage; 89.5 cm. wide, 89 cm. high, painted Jean Dunand.

3. A fine lacquer and shagreen (sharkskin) 'bateau' bed of gondola shape in caramel lacquer on a shagreen covered plinth; 152.5 cm. wide, 240.5 cm. long, unsigned. This bed was illustrated in the French magazine 'Mobilier et Decoration' in January 1937.

2

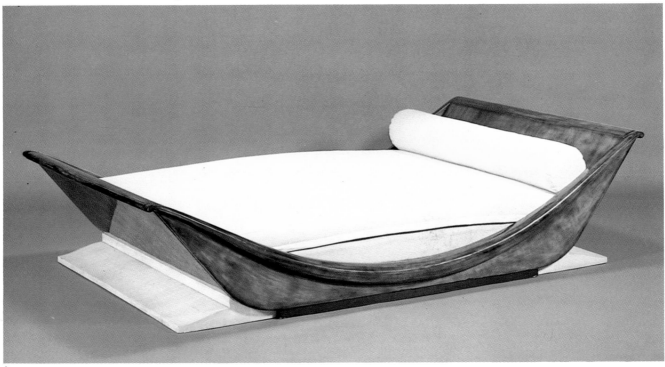

3

1

2

Lacquer was used by Dunand on metal as well as wood, and examples of both processes are seen here. On metal the most popular colour combination was black and red. Lacquer was used in conjunction with crushed eggshell, carefully arranged in geometric patterns and laid into a surface. Used in varying degrees of density, eggshell can give a surprising three-dimensional effect.

1.   A reproduction of a photograph from the magazine 'L'illustration', 1932, showing the Dunand bed in situ.

2.   A black lacquer, gilt and mother-of-pearl king-size bed by Jean Dunand, 1930, for Mme Berthelot, 191 cm. wide, 221 cm. long, 152 cm. high, signed.

3.   A coquille d'oeuf (eggshell) and red lacquered metal box and cover, 17 cm. diam, lacquered Jean Dunand. Unusual and exotic materials were widely used to provide unique finishes on objects and furniture.

4.   A lacquered metal and coquille d'oeuf box, by Jean Dunand circa 1925, probably from a design by Jean Lambert-Rucki; 10 cm. diam.; lacquered in red – Jean Dunand.

5.   A lacquered and coquille d'oeuf silver cigarette box circa 1925; 13.5 cm. wide, impressed with French poinçons.

3

4

5

Sofas and armchairs were usually heavy in design in traditional
Art Deco interiors. The gondola
shape was reasonably popular
(as seen here in a Betty Joel
chaise longue); otherwise sofas
often had loose inset cushions
(either a single one with long
cylindrical cushions as armrests
or three cushions in an upholstered frame). Armchairs were
sometimes very angular in design, but the 'bergère' type with
rounded back and sides was also
popular, particularly in France.
The angular style was the more
modern of the two, while the
'bergère' fitted better into the
more exotic style of Art Deco.

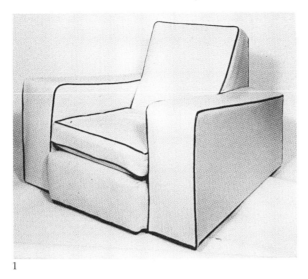

1

2

1.   A pair of cream leather
armchairs with brown edging by
Gordon Russell circa 1937;
94 cm. wide, 68.5 cm. high.

2.   One of a pair of mahogany
bergères inlaid with ivory
stringing, by Jules Leleu; 81.3 cm
wide, 74.9 cm. high, stamped
Leleu.

3.   A beechwood chaise longue
by Betty Joel, of gondola form
upholstered in cream silk with
fringed trim, circa 1930; 194 cm.
long.

4.   An ivory inlaid burl walnut
canapé by Emile-Jacques
Ruhlmann, on brass bun feet,
upholstered in velvet; 178 cm.
long, 88 cm. wide.

5.   One of a pair of French
macassar ebony and leather
armchairs, circa 1930,
unsigned.

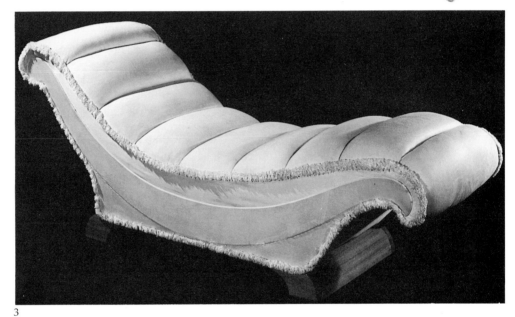

3

4

5

Piano design enjoyed a new lease of life, with all sorts of exotic models appearing. The most popular (probably largely due to its convenient size) was the baby grand; its stubby rounded end fitted well into a modern or 'moderne' interior. The Ruhlmann piano illustrated here is at once classical and modern. The angular shape is untypical of Ruhlmann, while the lyre-shaped pedal frame is of neo-classical inspiration and more what one would expect of this designer. Light sycamore veneer was a popular finish for Art Deco pianos, sometimes with a simple geometric design in a darker wood; lacquer was also popular, and there is even a famous all-glass piano designed by Pierre Legrain.

1. A white lacquered wood baby grand piano and stool by Collard and Collard; 97.5 cm. high, 142 cm. wide, 157 cm. deep.

2. A macassar ebony, amboyna and bronze boudoir grand piano, the case by Emile-Jacques Ruhlmann, the instrument by Gaveau, Paris. Piano No. 89795, circa 1930–31. 150 cm. long. 141 cm. wide, 100 cm. high, signed Ruhlmann in bronze, Gaveau, paris gilt stamped. Of the six known pianos built by Ruhlmann all were unique in design.

1

1

A cross-section of work by some of the top French furniture designers is seen here, making for variety within a given set of rules. All the pieces have originality while confirming to the dictates of Art Deco fashion. The Lalique table is perhaps somewhat impractical, but when one considers the frequent use of lacquer and highly polished surfaces in exotic woods, this does not seem to have been a prime consideration. Wrought iron and parchment were also popular. Nos. 3 and 4 show how a similar idea could look completely different with the use of differring material.

2

3

4

5

1.   A bronze and marble table by Armand Rateau, Paris, circa 1924, the base cast as four birds surmounting spheres, the black marble top inlaid with white marble stringing; 32.5cm. high, stamped A.J. Rateau Paris.
  This table was originally created on commission for Jean Lanvin, the couturier.

2.   A French bureau de dame, decorated in a matt crackled polish and painted in low relief with stylized fruit and flowers; 120cm. high.

3.   A glass and metal illuminated table by Lalique and Sabino, circa 1937 for a Jean Lanvin commission; 139.5cm. diam., 73.5cm. high, inscribed Lalique and Sabino.

4.   A macassar ebony circular table with chrome rimmed base, by Jules Leleu, circa 1930; 119.5cm. diam, 73.5cm. high. This model was produced to accept leaves for extension and seems to have been created for one of the dining rooms on the 'Normandie', see 'L'Illustration', June 1935.

5.   A French wrought iron wall mirror, circa 1925; 93cm. wide, unsigned.

6.   A palisander wood, silvered-bronze and ivory dressing table mirror, by Emile-Jacques Ruhlmann, circa 1921; 35cm. high, branded Ruhlmann 1921.

7.   A moulded and carved mahogany console with marble top by Dominique; 149.8cm. wide, 109.2cm. high, 53.3cm. deep.

8.   A wrought iron console by Edgar Brandt, the top and base of macassar ebony; 149.5cm. wide, 96.5cm. high, stamped E. Brandt.

9.   A mahogany cabinet by Jacques Adnet, the two doors covered with squares of shagreen; 159cm. high, 84cm. wide, unsigned, circa 1930.

10.   A rosewood and walnut secretaire à abbatant designed by Dominique, inlaid with gilt metal stringing; 157cm. high, 83cm. wide, 42.5cm. deep.

6

7

8

9

10

1

The Art Deco period was nothing if not luxury-loving, and apart from jewellery which by its very definition involves expensive materials, this is best seen in the use of exotic woods and semi-precious fittings in furniture. Rosewood, macassar ebony, amboyna and zebra wood are just a few examples of woods used by the makers of luxury furniture. Added to this were fittings in bronze, and decoration of ivory, mother-of-pearl, shagreen, eggshell and elaborate marquetry, all of which involved either expense or labour and made furniture such as that illustrated here available to few; even so it was much in demand.

1. A macassar ebony and rosewood commode attributed to Maurice Dufrêne, with inset 'verde antico' marble top above carved ivory panels; 128 cm. wide.

2

2. A silver-leafed wood petite commode incised with outlandish contemporary scenes, and with onyx keyholes, by Atelier Martine, decorated by Leo Fontan; 85.7 cm. wide, 74.9 cm. high, incised Leo Fontan, 1923.

3. A burr walnut and marquetry jewellery cabinet on stand by Gustavo Pulitzer, commissed for a Trieste family in the 1920's; 178 cm. high, 154.7 cm. wide.

1

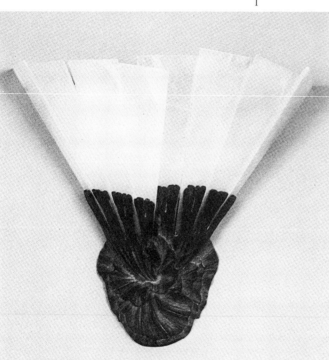

2

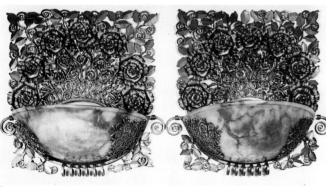

3

4

Until the 1920s lighting was looked upon as mainly functional. Edwardian lamps are hardly notable for their beauty, and designers were on the whole content to copy the principles of gas and oil lighting. But as lighting became an important part of modern decorative schemes, designers in all areas of the decorative arts became interested in the artistic possibilities of lighting. Shades were made of alabaster, glass and sometimes ceramic, and bases were very often of wrought iron, bronze and ceramics. Wall lights, often in metal and glass, became increasingly popular, providing a softer form of illumination than overhead lighting.

1. A lacquered metal and coquille d'oeuf table lamp by Auguste-Claude Heiligenstein, the circular foot inlaid with crushed eggshell, raised on a lacquered wood base; 28 cm. high, inscribed Aug. Heiligenstein 1926.

2. A bronze and alabaster wall light by Albert Cheuret; 35 cm. high, signed.

3. A pair of Edgar Brandt wrought iron and alabaster wall light appliques; 55 cm. high, signed Brandt.

4. A Rosenthal white porcelain standing lamp designed by Gerhard Schliepstein, the six separate parts fitted together and held in place by a metal rod, printed Rosenthal, Selb Bavaria, circa 1927.

5. One of a pair of bronze wall lights cast from models by F. Carbasius; 58.9 cm. high, one inscribed F. Carbasius, both stamped Brons Gieteru Deplastier A. Binder Harlem.

6. A bronze table lamp by Philippe, the two stylized nude figures standing on a stepped onyx base; height including vellum shade 80 cm., signed.

7.   One of four massive
Odeonesque gilt metal and
frosted glass wall lights; 158cm.
high.

8.   A wrought iron standard
lamp by Edgar Brandt; 155.5cm.
high, unsigned.

9.   A wrought iron table lamp
by Edgar Brandt, with two bell-
shaped mottled glass pendant
shades; 49.5cm. high; base
impressed Brandt.

10.   A pair of alabaster and
bronze table lamps by Armand-
Albert Rateau, the alabaster
shades raised on the backs of
four stylized bronze deer; 46cm.
high, impressed. A.A. Rateau,
Paris (restoration to one lamp
rim).

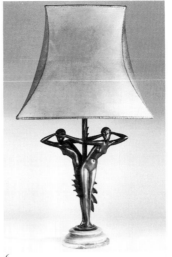

6

5

9

7

8

10

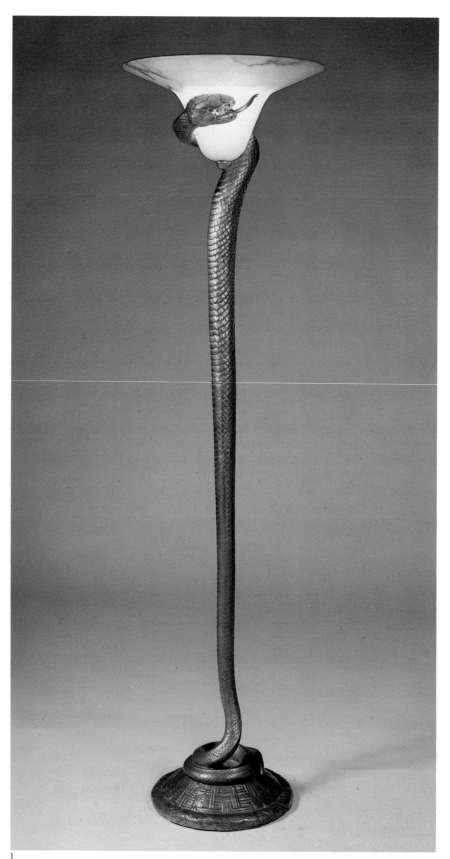

Edgar Brandt was without doubt the greatest craftsman in wrought iron during the 1920s. The intricate delicacy of some of his work seems in direct defiance of the intransigent material in which he was working. Often designs rely on a bolder and more sculptural approach, and one of his best-known works was the serpent lamp, which was made both as a table lamp and as a floor lamp. Brandt lamps are invariably found in conjunction with Daum shades, sometimes in opaque glass with a heavily pitted surface, sometimes in mottled glass, and sometimes in glass with an acid-cut design.

1.   'La Tentation', a gilt bronze and alabaster floor lamp by Edgar Brandt, the cobra column supported by a domed foot cast as a woven basket; 170 cm. high, impressed E. Brandt.

2.   A Daum Frères and Edgar Brandt chandelier in wrought iron and etched amber glass, exhibited at the Paris Exhibition, 'Arts Decoratifs et Industriels Modernes', in 1925; 155 cm. high, 91 cm. diam., glass engraved Daum, Nancy France, iron stamped E. Brandt.

1

All the symbols of Art Deco rely on streamlining through geometry, with rough edges removed by a linear approach. In contrast to the undulating lines of Art Nouveau, Art Deco sought to simplify nature rather than to elaborate upon it. This rule applied to every area of the decorative arts including fashion. In many instances the same symbols appear in Art Nouveau and Art Deco (flowers and birds are common to both) but in different guises. There were some new symbols as well, like the sunburst, the leaping gazelle, Negro jazz musicians, the fountain and the lightning ziggurat.

1. A monumental porcelain and bronze luminaire by Sèvres, decorated by Jean Beaumont and potted by Charles Fritz; 51 cm. high, incised and printed marks.

2. 'Source de la Fontaine', a frosted glass sculpture by René Lalique, the female figure with clam shell headdress and water cascading over her body; 56 cm. high, including ebonized wood base, inscribed R. Lalique France. These figures originally formed part of a 17-cascade fountain shown at the International Exhibition of 1929. This was the first example of a new conception in decorative statuary.

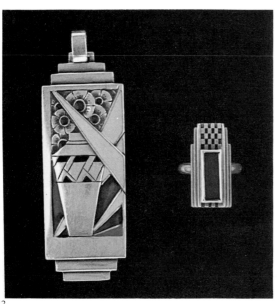

3. Left: An enamelled silver pendant with a stylized floral design by E. David; 7.5 cm. long, stamped E.D.
Right: A silver and carnelian ring by R. Portall.

4. A terracotta sculpture of an accordion player by Jan & Joel Martel; 31 cm. high; inscribed J. Martel.

5. A gilt wood mantel clock by Leon Jallot; 28 cm. high, impressed with artist's monogram.

6. 'Suzanne', a Lalique amber glass nude female figure holding drapery; 23 cm. high, moulded R. Lalique.

7. 'Jazz', an earthenware bowl executed for Viktor Schreckengost for Cowan, circa 1931, with a highly stylized sgraffito decoration; 33.5 cm. high, painted and impressed marks.

8. Geometrically shaped earthenware vases by T. Robert Lallemant, circa 1930; 35.4 cm. high and 25.5 cm. high, painted T.R. Lallemant, France.

9. A coquille d'oeuf (eggshell), red and black lacquered silver cigarette case by Jean Dunand; 9 cm. high, lacquered J.D.

10. An early 'locust' vase in emerald green glass by René Lalique; 27 cm. high, inscribed R. Lalique.

11. A wrought-iron firescreen by Wilhelm Hunt Diederich, depicting a pack of greyhounds in chase; 132 cm. wide, 112 cm. high, unsigned.

12. A ceramic wall mask attributed to Elena König Scavina for Lenci; 36 cm. high, painted Lenci Torino Italy M.

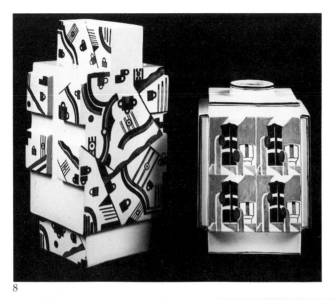

8

9

10

11

12

Easy chair designed in 1924 by Gerrit Rietveld, of ebonized wooden
billets and carved plywood, with wooden arms, the back and seats
edged in white. This chair is one of only five and was originally
designed for the Schröderhuis.

A chrome and wood table lamp by Donald Deskey; 40.5 cm. high,
unsigned.

CHAPTER 5

Bauhaus and its Influence

The Bauhaus was founded in Weimar in 1919 by the German architect Walter Gropius, and its influence has been one of the main factors in shaping modern design. The great difference between Art Deco and the Bauhaus style is that whereas Art Deco was a modern interpretation of decorative ideas which mainly affected the surface of things, the Bauhaus designers dug deep into the foundations of design history and tackled the problems of design in the modern world at source. Although the philosophies and ideas of the Bauhaus evolved during the 1920s in time to affect some of the more radical Art Deco designers, its influence did not affect the mass market until the 1930s both in Europe and in America. This influence became even stronger during the 1940s in America, with many refugees who had been Bauhaus students emigrating there to continue their careers; its effect is still discernible today in the Western world seventy years after its foundation. Now that the ideas of the Bauhaus thinkers have been absorbed into design history, it is difficult to realize how far in advance of their time they were. The Bauhaus was accused of art Bolshevism, particularly by a German bourgeoisie steeped in a historical art tradition, and even the art academies in Germany had difficulty in accepting their own highly important avant-garde.

Of course the Bauhaus style did not develop in a vacuum: styles in art and architecture never do. There had been a process of intellectual reappraisal in the design world ever since the radical theories of the English art critics and architect-designers of the late nineteenth century; Christopher Dresser and E. W. Godwin had already been preoccupied with simplicity and clearness of construction in the late 1870s, and in its way the famous Godwin ebonized sideboard, an example of which is in the Victoria and Albert Museum, was just as

far in advance of its time as any Bauhaus design, anticipating many important twentieth-century ideas. One of the most important early twentieth-century books on design was *Das Englische Haus* by Hermann Muthesius, written after a seven-year spell in England as a supplementary trade attaché at the German Embassy. In 1907, under Muthesius leadership, some of the more enterprising German manufacturers, together with architects and designers, formed the Deutscher Werkbund to improve standards of quality in industrial design, which included mass-produced low-cost furniture (at this period mainly in bentwood). In Vienna the Austrian architects were also waging war on decoration, and in an essay entitled *Ornament and Crime* Adolf Loos wrote, 'I have evolved the following maxim, and pronounce it to the world: the evolution of culture marches with the elimination of ornament from useful objects.' But one factor remained a constant source of inspiration for every single one of the architects, designers and critics mentioned so far, and that was the aesthetics of Japanese art. The ideas of the Western avant-garde owe more to Japan than one sometimes realizes.

The most obvious precursor of Bauhaus ideology was 'De Stijl' in Holland. This was in fact the name of a magazine edited by the Dutch painter, designer and writer Theo van Doesburg from 1917 to 1931; De Stijl is Dutch for Style. The artists associated with De Stijl were mainly architects and painters, headed by Gerrit Rietveld and Piet Mondrian. The most compact visual statement of this style is made by Rietveld's Red-blue Armchair, a sculptural object whose structure is as clear as a skeleton or scaffolding. Rietveld said about this chair, 'the construction is attuned to the parts to insure that no part dominates or is subordinate to others. In this way, the whole stands freely and clearly in space,

(*Right*)   A thick, black speckled, deeply etched glass vase by Daum, circa 1930; 29 cm. high, etched Daum, Nancy France.

(*Far Right*)   An etched, heavily walled glass vase by Daum; 44.5 cm. high, etched signature.

and the form stands out from the material.' Once again there is a strong Japanese quality to Rietveld's early furniture, and it also takes into account Cubism. Among the De Stijl group there was also a thrill at modern inventions like speed and machinery. Van Doesburg wrote, 'the machine is, par excellence, a phenomenon of spiritual discipline. Materialism as a way of life and art took handicraft as its direct psychological expression. The new spiritual artistic sensibility of the twentieth century has not only felt the beauty of the machine, but has also taken cognizance of its unlimited expressive possibilities for the arts.'

Combined with these influences there were other important factors, such as the rectilinearity of the Dutch landscape that lent itself so well to geometry, the Amsterdam school of architecture led by J. J. P. Oude, H. P. Berlage and P. J. Klaarhammer, and equally significant was the fact of Holland's neutrality during the First World War, which allowed artistic and philosophical ideas to develop with minimum interruption. During the second decade of the twentieth-century, it fell to Holland to develop the new ideas in architecture and design that had come out of Europe and America during the first decade. De Stijl ideology struggled for a set of principles that could be applied to art and design, and is best expressed by some of Van Doesburg's exhortations in his journal *De Stijl*. 'As soon as the artists in the various branches of plastic art have realized that they must speak a universal language, they will no longer cling to their individuality with such anxiety. They will serve a general principle far beyond the limitations of individuality. By serving the general principle, they will be made to produce, of their own accord, an organic style. ... Let's refresh ourselves with things that are not Art: the bathroom, the W.C., the bathtubs, the telescope, the bicycle, the auto, the subways, the flat-iron. There are many people who know how to make such good unartistic things. But they are hindered, and their movements are dictated, by the priests of Art. Art, whose

functions nobody knows, hinders the function of life. For the sake of progress we must destroy Art.'

Such radical thinking in Holland was matched by the forthright ideas of the Russian avant-garde. As with De Stijl in Holland, the Suprematists and later the Constructivists were mainly concerned with painting and architecture. But one of the first questions to be established after the Revolution was the function of art within the new society, and artists became directly involved in the planning and regeneration of industry and the applied arts. The chief source of inspiration for the new revolutionary designers was folk art combined with the new symbols of socialism (the hammer and sickle, of course, as well as tractors and other farm implements). The new look in the applied arts was seen principally in textile design and in ceramics. The designers came from the ranks of Constructivism, Suprematism and Fauvism, all of which were separate strands of the Russian avant-garde.

The Suprematists, headed by Kazimir Malevich, made the greatest contribution to the applied arts, particularly in the field of ceramic design, and there are many outstanding examples of their work. Malevich designed a teapot and two cups ('half-cups') and Nikolaj Suetin a teapot and inkstand, as well as many other designs. 'Their aim was to create an ideal, abstract form built upon the principles of 'economic geometry' which was free from any other stylistic reference.' Apart from the manufacture of tea-sets and household ware in this style, there was a vogue for a new type of figurine that chronicled revolutionary society. 'The new ceramic sculptures of dockers, activists, partisans and militia girls left no doubt about the fundamental changes which had taken place.' All Russian ceramics of this period are characterized by dazzling colours and virtuoso brushstrokes, which were executed on blanks of white porcelain taken over from the Imperial Porcelain Factory. One French critic wrote that in the chinaware, 'the revolution has found its highest and clearest expression.' The philosophy of the new designers was succinctly expressed in the famous saying of Bachunin, 'the spirit of destruction is at the same time the spirit of creation'.

Such a sentiment, whether it was the result of thinking in revolutionary Russia, neutral Holland or war-weary Germany, was at the core of Western European avant-garde design, and it found its strongest and most practical expression in the ideas of the Bauhaus. German opinion after the First World War was sharply divided between those who believed in the past and tried to cling on to it, and those who wanted to find a new lifestyle to take them into the future. The latter, even outside Germany, were drawn to the Bauhaus as to a magnet. Western tradition in the applied arts, despite the socialist dreams of William Morris and his followers, had been heavily biased towards upper-class tastes, and at the Royal Manufacturies of Europe designers were involved in the manufacture of decorative material destined for the courts and their imitators in the middle classes. New thinking in the applied arts struggled for a more productive co-operation between art and life.

Gropius had been one of the leaders of the Werkbund in Germany after studying with the architect Behrens, but his single-minded devotion to the reconciliation of art and industry drove him to break away from the Werkbund in order to establish something new. Although basically an architect, Gropius extended his interest into the whole field of the arts. The first Proclamation of the Weimar Bauhaus urged, 'Architects, sculptors, painters, we must all turn to the crafts', and do away with class distinctions which set up an arrogant barrier between craftsman and artist. Bauhaus designers were intent on improving the total environment. They approached modern problems of design realistically in a modern atmosphere, and their interest extended to typography, paintings, prints, theatre art, architecture and industrial objects of all kinds. Bauhaus students were expected to be involved primarily with industry and mass-production rather than with individual craftsmanship, and were taught to disregard conventional distinctions between the 'fine' and 'applied' arts. Designers were not to be thought of merely as decorators but as having a vital function in society, aware of all aspects of living, the artistic, the technical, the social, the economic and the spiritual.

There were many famous names among the teachers at the Bauhaus. At the very beginning Gropius appointed Johannes Itten, Lyonel Feininger and Gerhard Marcks, but those who were involved later included Paul Klee, Oskar Schlemmer, Wassily Kandinsky and Laszlo Moholy-Nagy. Many classics of twentieth-century design came from the Bauhaus workshop. In the carpentry workshop Marcel Breuer designed the famous chair with a fabric seat and backrest. In the pottery workshop Otto Lindig and Theo Bogler worked on designs for industry, some of which were produced by the Staatliche Porzellanmanufaktur in Berlin. The best-known of the designers for the metal workshop were Marianne Brandt and Wilhelm Wagenfeld, the first

A polished chromium hat stand made for Bazzi in Milan; 51.6 cm. high, circular base with metal rectangular label 'Bazzi Milano'.

for her metal and wood tea-set, the second for his metal and glass lamp which is still being reproduced today. Gropius also designed for the metal workshops. But perhaps more than such objects the Bauhaus was renowned for its creative education programme, unparalleled in any other European country.

And yet the Bauhaus was forced to close in Weimar because of hostile reaction from the government, whom they accused in a letter of 'having permitted and approved the frustration of culturally important and always non-political efforts through the intrigues of hostile political parties'. Still under Gropius's direction, it moved in 1925 to Dessau at the invitation of the mayor of that town, and reopened in a new building now considered to be perhaps the most important structure of its decade.

It was at this Bauhaus that Marcel Breuer designed his first tubular chair in 1925, and a series of tables with tubular supports. The new designs were epoch-making in a number of ways, including Breuer's own reasoning behind the furniture he created. He said, 'the new interior should not be a self-portrait of the architect, nor should it attempt to fix in advance the personal environment of the occupant. And so we have furnishings, rooms and buildings allowing as much change and as many transpositions and different combinations as

(*Left*) An enamelled glass vase by Daum, decorated with two Amazons hunting deer, heightened with gilding; 28 cm. high, engraved Daum, Nancy France.

(*Opposite*) 'Bat Dancer', a bronze and ivory figure cast from a model by Ferdinand Preiss, cold painted in green and yellow, on a stepped onyx base; 23.6 cm. high, inscribed on base F. Preiss.

possible ... Any object properly and practically designed would "fit" in any room in which it is used as would any object, like a flower or human being.' It was the aim of Bauhaus designers to work in industry with a view to producing on as large a scale as possible. Inevitably this called for simplification and standardization of design. Bauhaus designers were frequent visitors to the factories, and factory technicians frequent visitors to the Bauhaus design workshop. After Gropius left the Bauhaus in 1928 there were two more directors before the school was closed by the national socialist regime in 1933. One of these was the well-known Berlin architect Ludwig Mies van der Rohe.

In Germany the effects of Bauhaus teaching were felt strongly during the late 1920s and the 1930s, partly because some of the teachers moved on to open departments in art colleges elsewhere. The effect of Bauhaus design was also very noticeable in one or two areas of industry, and nowhere more than in the production of

items using tubular steel, in particular the chair. Although the use of iron and steel in furniture has its roots as far back as the 1820s, it was not extensively used until the 1920s, mainly because of its heaviness before that time. Tubular steel was invented for use in the bicycle industry and later to make furniture for aeroplane interiors. From this it was a natural progression to domestic furniture. Early tubular steel furniture has much in common with bentwood designs, and in fact this popular new material took over almost entirely from wood, which had been so popular in the earlier part of the century. Marcel Breuer, for instance, more or less 'translated' his designs from wood to steel. His ideas on construction owed much to Rietveld, and the relationship between the Red-blue Armchair and the Breuer wood and fabric chair is easy to see. The latter is in turn closely related to the famous Wassily Chair. The wood and fabric chair was a cross between Rietveld's chair and a deck-chair, borrowing the idea of a fabric seat and back-rest from the deck-chair. Unquestionably, however, the basic idea worked far better in tubular steel, as has been proved by the continuing life of the Wassily Chair, which has never been out of production since its first appearance in 1925. It was incidentally given its name because it was first designed for use in Wassily Kandinsky's department at the Dessau Bauhaus.

But the designs in tubular steel would never have been possible without the 'adventure' of bentwood particularly as explored by the Thonet Brothers in Vienna. Although Thonet had been in existence since 1844, it was the Secession architect Adolf Loos who saw the possibility of bentwood serving the cause of modern design. The other Viennese bentwood manufacturers J. & J. Kohn had Gustav Siegel, a pupil of Josef Hoffmann, as their chief designer. Both firms, in their experiments to adapt bentwood techniques to the needs of modern architectural interiors, invented a technology that went far beyond fashion. In 1900 a bentwood chair by Gustav Siegel won the gold medal at the Paris Exhibition. Many of the 'classics' of Vienna Secession design were fashioned in bentwood, after designs by Wagner, Hoffman and Moser. It is doubtful, however, whether these Viennese architects could have had any idea of the far-reaching effects of their simple designs. Their simplicity suited both the modern 'functional' aesthetic of these designers and were of vital importance for mass-production techniques. The success of Thonet and Kohn

furniture made their simple, almost 'anonymous' style popular for practically any kind of interior, whether it was domestic, industrial, or a public building like a restaurant or a hospital. Such universality fitted in well with Bauhaus ideals, and it was not surprising that Bauhaus designers were fascinated by tubular steel as the natural successor to bentwood.

Marcel Breuer was the first of the Bauhaus designers to experiment with tubular steel and to see the beauty of a material that was (unlike straight-sided wood) flexible enough to bend continuously this way and that without the constructional problems of joinery. No thought was required any longer to switch from a horizontal to a vertical plane of design. One continous line could now be used to design an entire chair frame. As a material, tubular steel was also far lighter and more durable than wood. Mies van der Rohe immediately saw the advantages of this new material and designed his first tubular steel chair in 1927. The problem of 'finish' was easily resolved by the use of chromium plating, both the ideal technical solution and providing a twentieth-century look, that suited the machine age and severed all connections with earlier traditions of furniture design. Although the Wassily Chair was probably one of the first tubular steel chairs, the great breakthrough in design construction was the cantilever chair as thought out by Mies van der Rohe and Mart Stamm, which made its first appearance in 1927. During the next five years

'A Savage drinking from the Stream', a bronze figure cast after a model by J. De Roncourt, on a green and brown marble base; 81.6 cm wide, inscribed J. De Roncourt.

there followed endless improvements and adaptations of this idea, with arms, without arms, with a multitude of different approaches to supporting the seat and to the basic cantilever approach. News of the German experiments travelled fast and soon designers all over Europe and America were making use both of the material and of the new constructional ideas that accompanied it. It was used by J. J. Adnet, Jean Prouve and Pierre Chareau in France, by Alvar Aalto in Finland, and was a great favourite with the Swiss architect Le Corbusier, particularly in his collaboration with Charlotte Perriand. Together they designed their famous adjustable chaise longue in 1928, which, after the prototype had been made in their own workshop, was produced by Thonet, who had the foresight to move with the times and switch from bentwood to tubular steel production.

The new approach to architecture as seen in the work of the major European architects was the chief factor in what became known as the 'International Style', a term coined by Henry-Russell Hitchcock and Philip Johnson in 1932 in their book *The International Style: Architecture since 1922*. They wrote: 'There is now a single body of discipline, fixed enough to integrate contemporary style as a reality and yet elastic enough to permit individual interpretation and to encourage general growth.' The style evolved as a result of De Stijl and the Bauhaus, and the chief exponents were Rietveld, Gropius, Breuer, Mies van der Rohe and Le Corbusier, all of them architects. Their architecture had a profound effect on interior design, and their designs for furniture distinguished by grace, elegance of line and clarity of form were as important for the history of furniture as their buildings were for architecture. Both their architecture

and their plans for interior design, with its strong orientation to the requirements of modern production, found wide acceptance in the New World. It was, however, not until after the Second World War that many of their designs (for instance Mies van der Rohe's Barcelona Chair and Le Corbusier's chaise longue) went into mass-production, at a time when low production costs were foremost in people's minds. Even so their presence was felt strongly throughout the late 1920s and the 1930s. Alongside the show-stopping Hôtel du Collectionneur at the 1925 Paris Exhibition was Le Corbusier's Pavillon de L'Esprit Nouveau, with rectilinear built-in furniture and comfortable chairs sparsely dotted about.

While the Ruhlmann style marked the end of an era, the Pavillon de L'Esprit Nouveau marked new beginnings, and there is no doubt which of the two had a greater effect on modern design. The French brand of modernism was in its way as stylishly elegant as conventional Art Deco. Evidence of a new approach was to be seen principally in a new choice of materials. Chrome, steel or aluminium replaced expensive woods, largely as a result of the successful Bauhaus designs as executed by Thonet. But in France these were still used as 'luxury' materials rather than with a view to mass production. The futurist designs of Pierre Chareau were hardly suitable for the mass market, and were sculptural rather than practical in approach. Both Chareau and the other modernist designers (and of course architects) found that glass was both from an aesthetic and practical point of view one of the easiest materials to use in conjunction with metal, and one of Chareau's most famous designs was his 'Maison de Verre' in Paris. Chareau, together with other French designers including René Herbst and Jean Prouve started the Union des Artistes Modernes in 1930. There was never a real feeling for out-and-out modernisn in Paris, where elegance

A pair of Barcelona chairs designed in the 1930s by Mies van der Rohe and still being produced today, the leather seat and back cushions on chromium plated steel X-shaped frames. These chairs circa 1960.

and luxury were slow to die. There was a great appetite for modernism, but so long as it did not smack too much of socialist thinking! Paradoxically, in the hands of master craftsmen such as Eileen Gray, Georges Fouquet and Jean Dunand it resulted in a style that owed everything and yet nothing to the Bauhaus aesthetic.

Eileen Gray and Jean Dunand both did much to revive the art of lacquer, Dunand more in a traditional French Art Deco manner, Eileen Gray in a highly original modernist style. In his foreword to the catalogue of the Eileen Gray exhibition at the Victoria and Albert Museum in 1979 Roy Strong writes, 'there was no simple united march of the avant-garde towards a brighter future, and within the Modern Movement itself there were disparities of approach ranging from the haute couture of Moderne to the engaged functionalism of International Modern.' Eileen Gray was one of the most distinguished designers at work in Paris during these inter-war years. Her transition from exquisite hand-made lacquer objets de luxe to purposefully functional architecture and furniture employing industrial materials reflects indeed a creative evolution exemplary of the most advanced taste of her age. Though she spent most of her life in Paris, Eileen Gray was born in Ireland and brought up in London; she first began to be interested in lacquer during her studies at the Slade School. Lacquer is a demanding process requiring much patience and diligence, each of the twenty or so layers needing three days in a humid room to harden before a further layer can be applied. Eileen Gray made tables, screens and a variety of exquisite small pieces of furniture in lacquer, but later became involved in the design

and execution of whole interiors including furniture, carpets, lighting fixtures, and entire new walls of lacquer. She began designing in a decorative style but progressed to a more modernist and architectural approach, one of the best examples of the later style being the 'Transat' chair designed in 1927 which had a padded leather seat slung within a lacquer frame and chromed steel 'joints'. She was also one of the rare instances of a designer who turned architect, designing a house for herself to live in at Roque Brune in the south of France.

Germany was the country perhaps least influenced by Bauhaus design. Apart from the involvement of those closely associated with its teachings, reaction was largely unfavourable, leading to its dissolution and the departure of most of its teachers to other parts of Europe or to America. Marcel Breuer, for instance, spent some time in England designing for Isokon, who took over production of his laminated wood chaise longue designed in 1935. There were a number of modernist British designers and architects, of whom the most commercially successful was Ambrose Heal, whose stylish steel and leather armchair was compared in the *Architectural Review* to the work of Marcel Breuer, though not very favourably. Herbert Read wrote, 'the beautiful curves of the Breuer chair, its simplicity and functional efficiency are replaced by senselessly scalloped arms and bowed legs, sharp points, chest traps and more than a suggestion of antiquarianism and the price has gone up to 10 guineas.' Whether it is fair to compare Heal's work with Breuer's is questionable, but Herbert Read quite rightly implied that Bauhaus thinking had not been properly understood. It was in fact many decades before the daring simplicity and economy of Bauhaus design was fully appreciated and used to its best advantage. Until then it remained a gospel of truth more than anything.

1

Some designers during the Art Deco period preferred the abstraction of pure geometry to figural symbols. Total abstraction is always more demanding, and it was therefore used sparingly by designers working with a sophisticated clientele in mind. Pure geometry lent itself to carpet design as that was an area in which naturalistic representation could be awkward.

1. An Edward KcKnight Kauffer modernist hand-knotted wool carpet, woven with a geometric linear design, circa 1935; 209.5 × 139.8cm., woven with artist's monogram.

2. A wool rug by Myrbor, circa 1937, with an abstract motif possibly designed by Miro; 143 × 203cm. Woven Myrbor and bearing a lead seal from the 1937 Paris Exposition Internationale.

3. A wool rug by Ivan da Silva Bruhns woven with a geometric design. 386 × 289.5cm., woven signature, circa 1928.

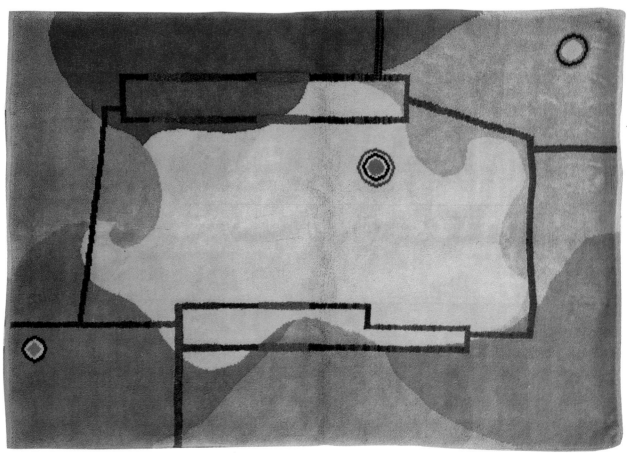

2

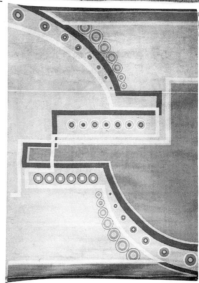

One of the main influences in this period was Cubism, which was more easily applicable in two-dimensional design, and for that reason most often discernible in carpet or textile design. Geometric carpets of this period are often in strong colours and difficult to incorporate in anything but a totally modernist interior. Their geometry can also be demanding as it needs room and cannot be cluttered with furniture; the strong shapes cannot stand interference from furniture contours projecting on to their field, and are best left without anything on them except perhaps a simple glass-topped table.

1.   A wool rug designed by Fernand Leger, possibly executed by Myrbor, woven with a Cubist design; 139.5 × 256.5cm., Leger woven on the reverse.

2.   A hand tufted wool rug by Jules Leleu; 114.5cm. × 73cm. J.L. monogram worked in one corner.

3.   A wool carpet attributed to Marion Dorn, woven in colours with a geometric design; 367 × 216cm. unsigned.

4.   A modernist wool pile rug designed by Terence Prentis; 246 × 191cm. one corner with TP monogram.

5.   'Concrete Mixer', a woven wool carpet after a design by Man Ray. No. 2/6; 144 × 104cm. Woven signature.

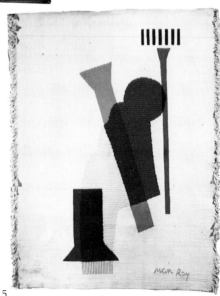

Lighters, wrist-watches and plastic were among the novelties of the period; plastic had been in existence for well over half a century, but early plastic was mottled, and the bright colours used during the 1920s were an innovation. Plastic also imitated rarer materials such as ivory and amber. Lighters tended to be machine-like, and the most famous brand was Dunhill, the design of which took positive pride in the mechanism being an important part of the design. Cartier wrist-watches (most of them with Jaeger Le Coultre movements) were sleek and of a simple elegance that made them a popular accessory.

1.   A Jaeger-Le-Coultre Duoplan 18 carat gold back winder wrist watch with leather strap, circa 1935.

2.   A selection of English and Continental cigarette lighters dating from 1920 to 1962, lighter at bottom right with BP monogram, 4.2cm. high.

3.   A pair of diamond and sapphire ear pendants, the hexagonal frames emphasising their severe geometric styling.

4.   A Cartier gold wrist watch with articulated strap, the hexagonal winder set with a sapphire.

5.   An ebony and ivory expanding bracelet, the tooth shaped segments threaded on elastic, by Georges Bastard, Paris; 4.5cm. wide, circa 1920.

1

2

3

4

5

1. A silver-plated and oynx clock by Jean Puiforcat, the twelve circular silver discs set with onyx studs mounted with stylized silver-plated Arabic numerals; 26 cm. high, impressed Puiforcat.

Jean Puiforcat was outstanding among French silversmiths, producing a modernist range of wares that remained unsurpassed in France during the period between the wars. Designs were boldly geometric, and often silver was used in conjunction with semi-precious materials such as lapis lazuli and rock-crystal. Simple machine-turned engraving was the most frequent design to be found on the metal itself. In England there were a number of fine silversmiths, many of whom designed for the Goldsmiths and Silversmiths Company, while a few, like H.G. Murphy and Omar Ramsden, had their own workshops.

2. A Wakeley & Wheeler silver cup and cover with mother-of-pearl finial designed by R.Y. Gleadowe, carved and engraved by G.T. Friend and retailed by the Goldsmiths and Silversmiths Company; 37 cm. high. Birmingham silver marks for 1938. R. Gleadowe's printed signature and retailer's marks (30 ozs. 10 dwt.)

3. A fine silver and lapis-lazuli tureen and cover by Jean Puiforcat, circa 1927, with twin four-pronged lapis-lazuli handles, the cover with a four-sectioned lapis-lazuli finial; 26.5 cm. high, signed and impressed with French poinçons; 153 troy ozs. net weight.

2

3

1

Bauhaus design philosophy attempted to deal with bare essentials, or at least discover what they were. It is perhaps for this reason that chair design features so strongly, as the complexity of designing a chair involves so many of the basic principles of design. Ludwig Mies van der Rohe and Marcel Breuer were directly involved in the Bauhaus, and some of their designs, particularly chair designs, were of seminal importance to the Bauhaus aesthetic. Both Breuer and Mies van der Rohe were fascinated by the possibilities of tubular steel, Breuer as a logical outcome of his experiments in wood and laminated wood. Glass and ceramics were among the other experimental workshops run by the Bauhaus.

1. A Cassina chromium-plated and pony skin chaise longue originally designed in 1928 by Le Corbusier; 160 cm. wide. (Cassina have produced this design since 1965).

2. A chromium-plated tubular steel and cane 'MR' armchair, side chair and stool, designed by Mies van der Rohe, 1926, executed by Berliner Metallgewerbe, Joseph Muller, Berlin, circa 1930; armchair 82.5 cm. high (some damage to wickerwork).

2

3

4

5

3. A laminated beechwood open armchair designed by Alvar Aalto and manufactured by Finmar Ltd., London.

4. A laminated plywood chaise longue designed by Marcel Breuer and manufactured by the Isokon Furniture Company; 130 cm. long.

5. A pair of chromed steel and upholstered 'Brno' arm chairs by Mies van der Rohe, designed in 1930; 58 cm. wide, 81.5 cm. high. (This chair was one of a series designed for the Tugendhat house in Brno, Czechoslovakia).

6. A pair of tubular steel 'Brno' armchairs designed by Ludwig Mies van der Rohe, 1929–30, executed by Berliner Metallgewerbe, Joseph Muller, Berlin, or Bamberg Metallwerkstaten, 1934. 80 cm. high, 56 cm. wide. Unsigned.

7. Part of a Schott & Gen. Jenaer Glas heat-resistant tea-set designed by Wilhelm Wagenfeld; teapot 14 cm. high. Printed Jenaer Glas mark.

8. Four earthenware cups and saucers, grey glazed, by Otto Lindig for Staatliches Bauhaus, Weimar, circa 1923. Cups 11 cm. diam., marked with OL monograms.

6

7

8

1

Bauhaus design was deeply influenced by De Stijl, with its far-reaching principles of Neo-Plasticism which sought to go beyond Cubism into the realms of 'Pure Reality'. De Stijl aimed to banish sentimentality and ornament from design, creating harmony by discovering equilibrium in a perfect balance between horizontal and vertical planes. The clearest visual statement of these principles as propounded by Theo van Doesburg and Piet Mondrian is Rietveld's Red/Blue Chair. Seen next to Breuer's oak armchair, Rietveld's influence on the Bauhaus is abundantly clear, and in turn Bauhaus design made a sweeping impression on the rest of Europe.

1. The '1918 Red/Blue Chair' in beech and plywood by Gerrit Rietveld, members stained black with yellow painted ends; 87.5 × 66 × 82 cm. Bears label under seat G.A.v.d. Groenekan, Utrechtseweg 315, DE BILT.

2. An upholstered sycamore folding arm chair with chromed fittings by Eileen Gray, designed in 1926; 89 cm. long, 51 cm. wide, 74.5 cm. high.

3. A rare oak armchair by Marcel Breuer, 1922, the handwoven fabric produced by the Bauhaus weaving workshop; 94.5 cm. high, 56.5 cm. wide. Unsigned.

2

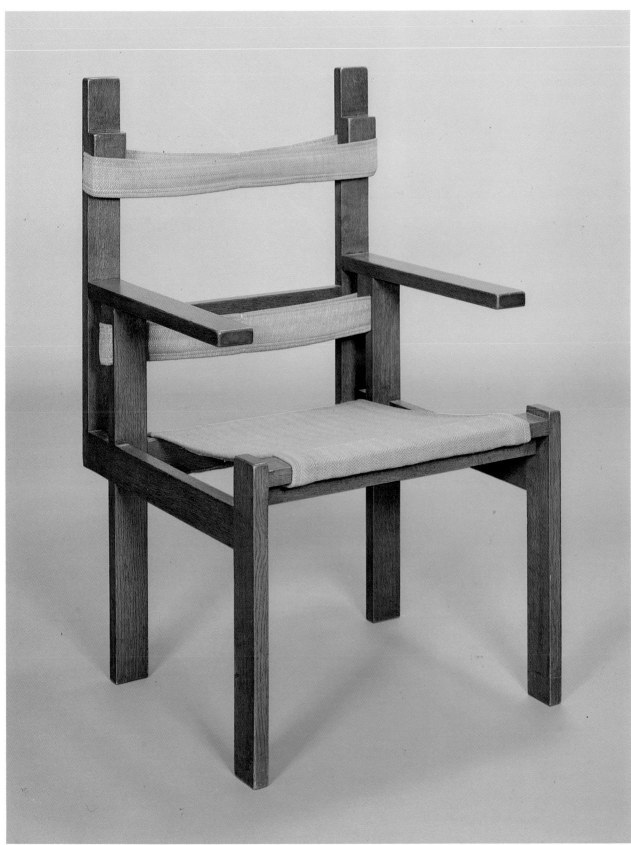

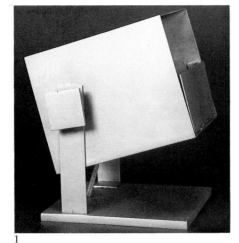

1

2

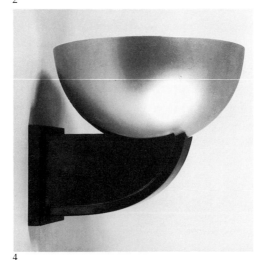

4

Lighting took into account all aspects of modern design technology, availing itself both of improved glass production techniques and the suppler varieties of metal (particularly chromed metal) now available. Aluminium was popular because of its lightness. Angle-poise and counter-balance designs had only recently been discovered (first made popular by Tiffany in table-lamp design), and many variations on this practical idea are to be found in the 1920s and 1930s. Tiers of plate glass also make frequent appearances, popular because of their interesting effects when lit. Glass and chrome are obviously complimentary materials, and designers made the most of this novel combination.

1. A chromed bronze wall lamp by Desny, the square box containing the light fitting, mounted on an articulated wall plinth; 14 cm. high; stamped Desny, Paris, Made in France Deposé.

2. A chromed metal and wood table lamp designed by Donald Deskey with pivoting hemispherical shade; 38.5 cm. high. unsigned.

3. A chromed metal desk lamp, French, circa 1935, the swivel shade on angled arm; 45 cm. high, unsigned.

4. One of a pair of chromed metal wall lights by Jean Perzel; 27.5 cm. high, unsigned.

3

4

5

6

5.   A chromed metal and glass table lamp attributed to Jacques Adnet, circa 1930, the swivel hemispherical shade enclosed in a clear glass disc; 33 cm. high, unsigned.

6.   A bakelite and metal table lamp by Jumo, circa 1930, the bakelite shade supported on an articulated copper and chrome-plated column; 43 cm. high, fully extended, moulded Jumo Brevete, Made in France.

7.   A glass and chromed metal floor lamp by Kuykens, circa 1930, with six glass slabs electrically illuminated from within; 176 cm. high, unsigned.

8.   One of a pair of silvered metal floor lamps. Uplighting was an innovative interior lighting effect in the thirties.

9.   A pivoting metal architect's lamp by Edouard-Wilfred Buquet, raised on a circular wood base; 52 cm. high, impressed Buquet, Paris, circa 1932.

10.   An aluminium, nickel plate and bakelite luminaire of intersecting circles and circle segments in the constructivist style by J. Le Chevalier; 28 cm. high; stamped 'Made in France'.

11.   A chromium-plated metal table lamp by Edouard-Wilfred Buquet, circa 1930; 40.5 cm. high, unsigned.

12.   Two Modernist chrome and glass table lamps; 51.5 and 37 cm. high.

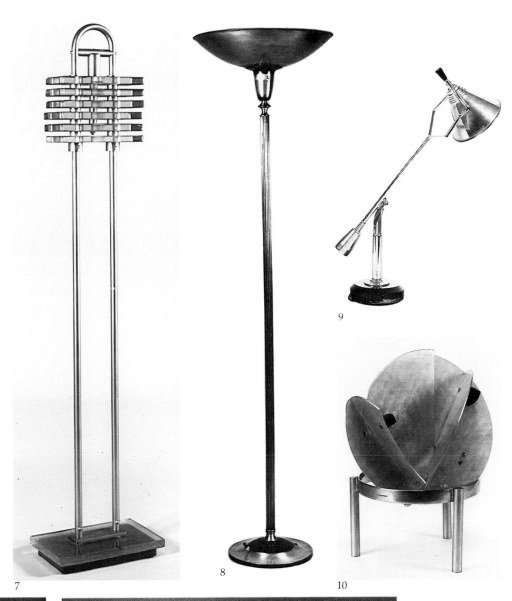

7

8

9

10

11

12

Lamps were often sculpturally conceived, and the contrast of lightness (provided by illuminated glass) and bulk (by materials such as bronze) was an inviting challenge to designers. The two lamps illustrated here can hardly be considered primarily as lighting sources. Both Albert Cheuret and Jean Goulden were masters in the field of metalwork, and both their solutions of combining translucence with solid mass are ingenious. In the Goulden lamp small pools of light act as focal pin-points; in the Cheuret lamp the light adds texture to the three-dimensional effect of the design on the tall column.

1. An enamelled silver and glass table lamp by Jean Goulden of Cubist-inspired form, intersected with opalescent glass panels; 32 cm. high, inscribed Jean Goulden L111 and with French poinçons. 54 troy ozs. gross weight.

2. A silvered bronze floor lamp by Albert Cheuret, circa 1925, the shade composed of spreading planes of alabaster; 174 cm. high, inscribed Albert Cheuret, stamped Made in France.

1

2

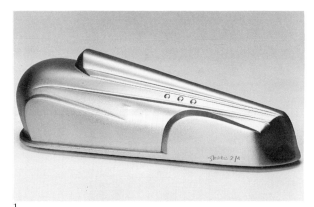

1

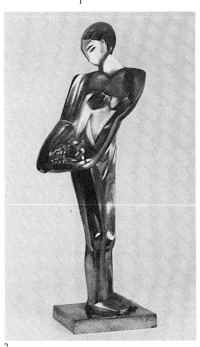

2

3

Sculptors found freedom in the new geometric language of design and made use of it in varying degrees, some exploiting its clear forms to add a sort of formality to conventional design, others letting it take over completely to become an art form of itself. The most extreme examples of this latter concept of design are seen here in the work of Gustav Miklos and Leon-Arthur Tutundjian; while the Bela Vöros pigeons merely emphasize spherical and linear forms already present in nature. In other sculpture seen here the approach is more one of organized symmetry interfering to a lesser degree with natural forms.

1.   'Locomotive In Motion', a chromium-plated bronze sculpture by Gustav Miklos; 26.5cm. long; Impressed G. Miklos 2/4.

2.   'Woman with Fruit Basket', a polished bronze figure cast from a model by Marg Moll; 70.5cm. high. Inscribed Marg Moll, stamped H. Noack Berlin-Friedenau.

3.   'Geometric Head', a bronze cast from a model by Arnold Auerbach; 42.5cm. high, inscribed A. Auerbach, numbered 2/3.

4

5

4. 'The Archer', a bronze figure cast from a model by Lucien Gilbert; 69 cm. high. Inscribed L. Gilbert.

5. One of a pair of American greenish brown patinated bronze figural candlesticks, cast from models by E.P. Seidel; 48.3 cm. high, inscribed artist's signature and stamped XXXII.

6. 'Le Signal', an aluminium sculpture by Leon-Arthur Tutundjian, 1928, mounted on a brushed steel base; 107.5 cm. high. Inscribed 'Le Signal' 4/8 LA Tutundjian 1928 Ginet Fondeur. This is an exceptionally early example of cast aluminium in sculpture.

7. A silvered bronze group of a couple dancing the tango, cast from a model by Jean Jacques Adnet; 34 cm. high; inscribed Adnet.

8. A carved alabaster figure of Venus arising from the sea, by Richard Garbe, mounted on a shaped bronze base; 64.5 cm. high, signed Richard Garbe ARA. 1933.

9. 'Couple de Pigeons', a bronze group by Bela Vörös, cast in 1969 from a model of 1927; 46 cm. wide. Artist's monogram and numbered 1/6.

10. A stoneware group of two nude dancers, of Cubist influence, from a model by E.J. Bachelet for Grès Mougin; 39.2 cm. high. Stamped and impressed Grès Mougin Nancy, E.J. Bachelet Sculpt. 1925.

7

6

8

9

10

Geometry was used as much in two-dimensional as in three-dimensional art forms in the wake of Cubism, and added a much-needed new look to twentieth-century design. In three-dimensional art the smooth planes of brightly polished metals highlighted the angularity of geometric design. In two-dimensional art lacquer, with its ultra-smooth surfaces in glistening colours, was once again a natural technique for showing off geometry. Black and red used together were among the most popular schemes because of the clear contrasts they offered, which were often heightened even further by the use of gold and silver.

1. 'Tour Architecturale', 1924, a black patinated bronze cast from a model by Gustave Miklos; 102.1 cm. high; inscribed G. Miklos 24 and numbered 4/4, with foundry mark Georges Rudier, Fondeur, Paris.

2. A three-leaf lacquered screen by Donald Deskey, composed of three graduated canvas panels painted with a red linear design on a black and silver leaf ground; 197 cm. high, 149 cm. wide, signed Deskey-Vollmer.

The most obvious changes of style brought about by modernism are to be seen in furniture design. Seating became either obviously rectilinear, with armchairs shaped like cubes, or purist about its curves. The most brilliant new designs were often the simplest, as in Eileen Gray's black lacquer screen with its interplay of simple rectangular shapes sharpened by an ingenious system of invisible hingeing. Mirror was often found in furniture design, and in some instances an entire piece of furniture was mirrored. Cocktail parties were a social innovation necessitating a new kind of cabinet specially fitted for this popular pastime.

1.   An ebony macassar veneered desk by Renée Kinsbourg. French, circa 1925, with cantilevered ends for book supports; 115cm. wide; 74cm. high.
    Mme Kinsbourg was one of the few women designers working in this clean, modernist style in the 20's and 30's.

2.   A painted metal high stool with oval black leather seat by Eileen Gray, circa 1932–34, 63cm. high; initialled EG on a plaque on the base.

3.   An American upholstered glass chair, a sheet of tinted green glass wrapped around a velvet upholstered chair seat; 73.6cm. high, unsigned., circa 1920.

4.   A black lacquered wood screen by Eileen Gray, circa 1923, composed of invisibly hinged rectangular panels; 195.5 × 212cm, unsigned.

5.   An English burr-maple and rosewood cocktail cabinet with mirrored and illuminated interior; 123cm. high, 97cm. wide.

6.   A burr-maple veneered cocktail cabinet, the interior fitted with shaped mirrored shelves; 141.1cm. high, 107.2cm. wide, circa 1932, English.

7.   A bird's-eye maple, ebonized and mirror-glazed cocktail cabinet; 163cm. wide, 109.5cm. high, English, 1930's.

5

6

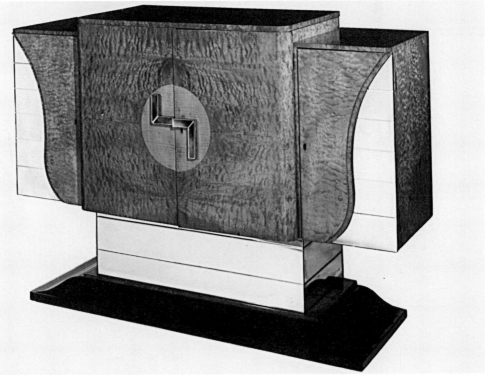

7

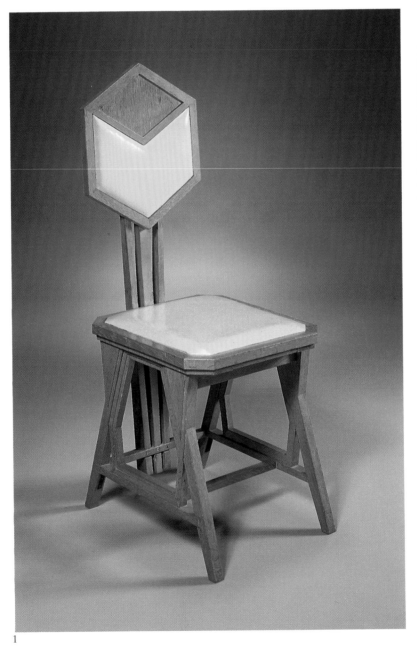

The modernist approach could be seen both in luxury and in mass-produced furniture. All the pieces seen here are of the luxurious variety, and even the Frank Lloyd Wright chair, whose severe appearance suggests a somewhat spartan approach, required detailed joinery and special colour schemes. Many of Ruhlmann's designs harked back to earlier styles, but the desk seen here is among the most successful of his modernist pieces, relying on clean lines and a surprising lack of decoration for this designer, some of whose more elaborate designs depend heavily upon floral geometry, and come close to being overdecorated.

1. An oak side chair designed by Frank Lloyd Wright for the Imperial Hotel, Tokyo, circa 1916–22, with yellow oil cloth seat and back; 96 cm. high.

2. Two painted wood chairs by Josef Urban, circa 1930, the barrel-shaped outer parts with appliqués of mother-of-pearl within yin and yang lozenges, 108 cm. high. A painted wood and mother-of-pearl table en suite, unsigned.

3. A fine macassar ebony and gilt-bronze desk by Emile-Jacques Ruhlmann, made on commission for a New York collector, circa 1929, the demi-lune design with double pedestals on gilt-bronze plinths with joining stretcher; 208 cm. wide, 77 cm. high, stamped Ruhlmann B. Made in France.

1

2

3

1

2

3

4

Both laminated plywood and tubular steel were popular because of their flexibility. The Scandinavians, and particularly Alvar Aalto in Finland, preferred plywood, showing a predilection for natural materials which has remained constant throughout the history of twentieth-century design in Scandinavia. In France the brightness of chrome or tubular steel was offset by leather upholstery or shiny lacquer. There was good as well as bad metal furniture: unfortunately because of the ease of shaping tubular steel, designers often overdid the curves, as with the child's bed seen here, which one feels cannot incorporate enough curves into its design.

1. A tubular black painted steel and wood draughtsman's table/desk, mounted with an articulated lamp, by the English firm PEL, circa 1930; 134.5 cm. wide (including a table chair and desk chair).

2. A chromed steel and glass two tier table by Marcel Breuer, circa 1925; 70 cm. high; top 48 cm. square.

3. One of a pair of beechwood armchairs and a matching table designed by Alvar Aalto for Stylclair, France, 1930. Table 56 cm. high.
   Stylclair, based in Lyons and Paris, was the first to execute this type of chair by Aalto as well as furniture by Marcel Breuer.

4. A walnut veneered, glass and metal desk by Jean-Jacques Adnet; 160 cm. wide, 76 cm. high, unsigned.

5. A chrome table with black glass top designed by Donald Deskey for Deskey – Vollmar Inc. 68.6 cm. high, circa 1930.

6. A pair of upholstered side chairs by Donald Deskey, on cantilevered metal legs; 50 cm. wide.

7. A pair of upholstered bronze chairs by Eugene Printz; 73 cm. high, 47 cm. wide.

8. A chromium-plated steel chaise longue by Jacques Adnet, with adjustable back, upholstered in red; 165 cm. long, circa 1930.

9. 'Mon Beguin', an adaptable chromium-plated tubular child's chair, bed, cradle, swing or table; 56 cm. high (as a table), circa 1930. Ingenious design was applied even to items for infants' use.

5

6

7

8

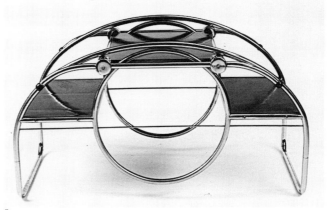

9

1

2

Gold and silver were among the primary colours of Art Deco, and whereas in earlier decorative styles they had been used for enrichment or highlighting, Art Deco designers came to use them quite differently, to achieve coolness and slickness, two strong characteristics of the period. The most frequent use of silver was in the bright finish of chromium-plated metal, but a more discreet colour was to be found in the satin finish of aluminium. Gold was used in large areas in lacquer work, on screens or doors, and sometimes even in contrasting shades for entire walls. Silver leaf was also found used in this way in interior design.

1.   A burled ash and anodized aluminium commode by Marie-Louis Süe, 1933; 141 cm. wide, 89 cm. high, branded MLS.

2.   A lacquered and gold and silver leaf dressing table by Paul Poiret, circa 1929; 173 cm. wide, 132 cm. high. Poiret was a member of New York's Contempora group of designers, which included Paul Lester Weiner, Lucien Bernhard, Vally Wieselthier and Rockwell Kent. His designs were sent from Paris to Contempora for execution in America.

3.   A nickel and glass centre table designed by Eugene Schoen, executed by Valentine Krumm for the Rockefeller Centre, circa 1932. 153 cm. wide, 75 cm. high, signed with stylized initials ES and VK New York.

4.   A lacquered gold and silver leaf double bed by Paul Poiret, circa 1929; 208 cm. long, 239 cm. wide, headboard 92 cm. high.

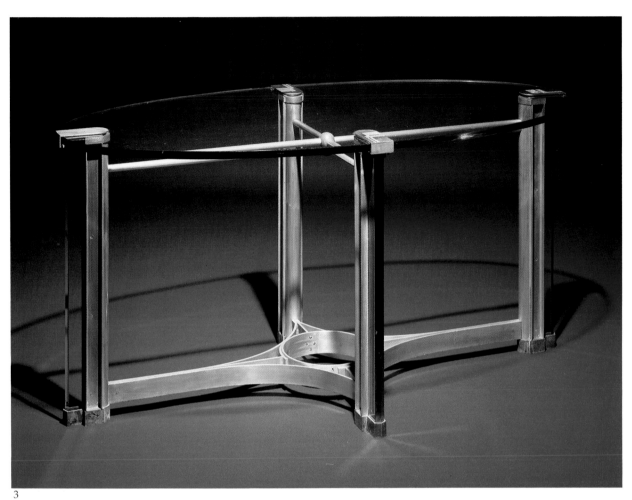

3

4

1

During the Art Nouveau period silver was frequently used in conjunction with enamel, which was often turquoise or green: enamel colours on silver were bolder and more contrasting during the 1920s, particularly as used by Camille Fauré in his vases with thickly applied bright enamelling in geometric patterns. Again in contrast with Art Nouveau when the semiprecious stones used with silver tended to be opaque and rough in texture, the Art Deco metalworkers showed a preference for the transparency and brilliance of rock crystal and rose quartz or the brilliant solid blue of lapis lazuli.

1.   A silver and enamelled cigarette box designed by Harold Stabler for the Goldsmiths & Silversmiths Co. Ltd; 25.3cm. wide; stamped Stabler, HS, London 1935 (64ozs. gross).

2.   A silver and lapis-lazuli urn and cover by Gustave Keller; 34.5cm. high, stamped G. Keller Paris and with French poinçons.

3.   A silver tureen and cover with jade loop handle by Jean E. Puiforcat; 25cm. diam; impressed Made in France. Jean Puiforcat Paris; with French poinçons (57.5 troy ozs. gross weight).

2

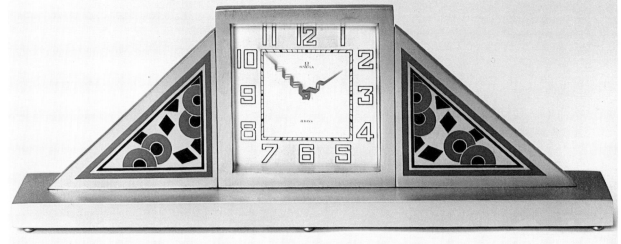

3

4

4.   A blue and black enamelled and chromed metal mantel clock by Omega, in the popular pyramidal style of the period; 40 cm. long.

5.   A silver powder box and cover by J. Tostrup, Norway, circa 1930, guilloche enamelled in green and blue with gilt embellishments; 12 cm. diam; signed J. Tostrup. Oslo N925S.

6.   An English five piece silver and ivory tea service by E. Viner & Co. of octagonal form with angular ivory handles and finials, teapot 29.3 cm. wide, stamped maker's marks London 1935 and Sheffield 1934 (122 ozs. gross weight).

7.   A Limoges vase, brightly coloured enamels on copper, by Camille Fauré, France; 28 cm. high, signed.

8.   Part of a 138 piece silver flatware service by Jean E. Puiforcat, impressed marks (358.5 troy ozs. gross weight).

9.   A Charles Boyton hammered silver teapot with wooden handle and finial; 12.5 cm. high. Charles Boyton facsimile signature. Maker's initials C.B&S and London hallmarks for 1933 (21ozs. 19dwt. gross weight).

5

6

7

9

8

Whereas 1920s bronze and ivory figures were either over-sweet or influenced by the Middle Eastern exoticism of the Ballets Russes, in the 1930s the dancers turned into gymnasts, athletes or sporting figures. We see here a golfer, a javelin thrower and a skater, and even the dancing figures seem athletic rather than balletic. The Olympic sports movement was an important feature of life during the 1930s. This outdoor cult included sun-bathing, a comparative novelty, particularly among the upper classes in Europe, and especially daring for the female sex, which until so recently had not even dared to expose an ankle.

1. 'Sun Worshipper' a cold-painted bronze and ivory figure cast and carved from a model by Ferdinand Preiss, on striped onyx plinth; 18.6 cm. high, signed F. Preiss.

2. Six cold-painted bronze and ivory figures cast and carved from models by Ferdinand Preiss, all on onyx and marble bases; 'The Golfer', lower left, 31.9 cm. high; inscribed F. Preiss or with stamped Preiss and Kassler founder's mark.
    The German admiration and encouragement of physical fitness in the 30's inspired these sculptures.

1

British modernism was on the whole tame and concessionary rather than convinced, particularly in the more popular ranges of mass-produced items. There were a few exceptions, and these are mostly found in the imaginative shapes and decoration of some of the pottery manufacturers' products, such as Shelley, Carlton Ware, some ranges of Royal Doulton and Wedgwood and the ever popular 'Bizarre' and 'Fantasque' patterns of Clarice Cliff. Clarice Cliff also persuaded a number of contemporary British painters to do designs for her, as seen here in the Laura Knight mug: there were also Clarice Cliff designs by Graham Sutherland, Vanessa Bell, Dod Proctor and John Armstrong.

1.   'Boat Race', a pottery goblet designed by Eric Ravilious for Wedgwood, circa 1938; 25.7 cm. high, printed – designed by Eric Ravilious, Wedgwood. Made in England.

2.   A 1930s pottery tea service by Carlton Ware in the 'Modern' design, painted with brightly coloured bands embellished with gilding; teapot 14.2 cm. high, printed marks.

3.   A Clarice Cliff pottery mug designed by Laura Knight; 16 cm. high, printed firm's marks and artist's facsimile signature, circa 1930.

4.   A large Louis Wain pottery vase of Cubist inspiration modelled as a seated cat; 25.4 cm. high, moulded signature.

5.   A selection of Clarice Cliff pottery painted in bright colours with stylized foliage and geometric patterns; plate at left 25.5 cm. diam, printed marks circa 1930.

6.   A Carlton Ware pottery vase, painted in polychrome with stylized trees, birds and foliage detailed with gilt; 26.7 cm. high, marked Carlton Ware, Made in England, circa 1930.

7. 'Spring', a Doulton cream-glazed pottery figure designed by Richard Garbe; 53.5 cm. high. Painted signature, Potted by Doulton & Co. Edition limited to 100. No. 61, 'Spring' by Richard Garbe ARA. Plinth with moulded artist's signature and dated 1932.

8. Part of a Shelley white porcelain coffee set, painted with a foliate motif in orange, black and silver; printed firm's marks. The geometric design emphasized the angular look of the porcelain.

9. Part of a Crown Ducal cream-glazed pottery tea set painted with the 'Orange Tree' pattern in black and orange; printed marks.

6

7

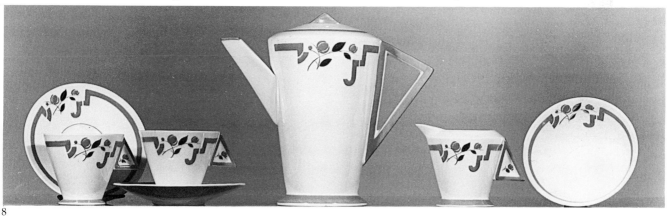

8

9

(*Above*)   An Iittala glass 'cantarelli' vase designed by Tapio Wirkkala, 1946, engraved with fine vertical lines; 19.5 cm. high, engraved signature and Iittala 11/50.

(*Opposite*)   A white-glazed porcelain bottle vase by Lucie Rie with raised spot decoration covered in a matt white glaze, circa 1960; 23.9 cm. high, impressed LR Seal.

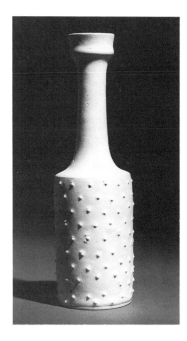

CHAPTER 6

Post-War Design

During the Second World War there was little scope in Europe for the decorative arts; manpower and industry were given over to the urgent needs of producing munitions and defending frontiers, and adornment of any kind was severely rationed. There were no such restrictions in America, and yet 1940s design in America had nothing very new to say. It is perhaps best described as a late flowering of Art Deco, with the sleek linearity of the 1930s becoming fuller and more rounded to provide an altogether bulkier look. One thinks of the chunky radios designed by Russell Wright and solid American kitchen gadgetry which was the envy of war-locked Europe. There were, however, a handful of American architect-designers who, during a period when few houses were being built, turned their talents to furniture, and set a style to be developed in the next decade, with some classics of American design dating from the 1940s, such as the walnut and plate-glass office table designed by the sculptor Isamu Noguchi (1944), Eero Saarinen's Womb Chair of 1948 and some of Charles and Ray Eames's experiments in plywood furniture. Their collection, at first produced by their own 'Evans Products Company', was taken over in 1947 by Herman Miller, who is producing Charles Eames designs to this day. Another American designer, George Nelson, called it at the time 'the most advanced furniture being produced in the whole world today'.

The general effect of material shortages during the Second World War was to make designers revert to a principle of bare essentials. In Britain there was a general moratorium on design and a dulling of colour schemes. Rationing was introduced on foodstuffs, clothing and furniture. War socialism brought the principle of standard design, and a system of 'utility furniture, utility clothes and utility household goods'

was introduced. The utility sign, CC41, became recognized as a guarantee of high-quality material and workmanship and sensible design at a moderate price. In many ways it signified a return to honest craftsmanship, with standard formula high-quality products at a reasonable price. 'The war provided an opportunity for the philosophy of economical, practical, utilitarian standards to be applied to the taste of the nation as a whole.' The Festival of Britain in 1951 was more or less a 'Celebration of Utility', reversing a trend towards fashionable streamlining of earlier decades and pointing the way to a new post-war style. It was Gordon Russell, a furniture maker in the best British tradition of craftsmanship, who as a campaigner in the cause of good design, was the chief instigator of utility.

The predictable post-war reaction to rationing and scarcity was a full swing of the pendulum to the other extreme. Restraint was thrown to the winds with very mixed results. Once again Paris led the fashion world with the New Look invented by Christian Dior, an altogether fuller and more enveloping look than there had been for over thirty years. But Parisian fashion was no longer related to the design world as it had been during the period between the wars, and with very few exceptions French design never quite made it during the 1950s. Modern European design was at its most advanced in Scandinavia and in Italy during this decade and it is above all Italian and Scandinavian designs from the 1950s that are collected today, except in America where there is at present great interest in this period of American design.

During the 1950s Scandinavia, that is Denmark, Norway, Sweden, Iceland and Finland, received a disproportionately large share of world awards for arts and crafts and industrial design. By tradition Scandinavian

design was intimately related to nature, and the natural beauty of the countryside is reflected in an instinctive feeling for proportion and colour, and a particularly effective use of raw materials. Norway, Sweden and Finland, endowed with ample forests, came naturally to learn the best techniques of working wood. Intelligent craftsmanship is perhaps the outstanding feature in Scandinavian design. 'Its essence is the insistence that useful articles should be, not just sturdily constructed, but also beautifully formed.' There was no particular emphasis on modernity in post-war Scandinavian design, more a preoccupation that design should become better and better, and more suited to modern living standards and modern society in general. Alf Hard in his book *Scandinavian Design* expresses succinctly the philosophy behind it. 'When judging the design worthiness of any object, the first consideration must be: How well has the material been used, technically and aesthetically, for the purpose to which it is being put? A bad design violates the nature of its material. And one material should not be made to look like another, even if this is technically possible, because the unique beauty of each will be lost.'

In thinking of Scandinavian design from this period one thinks of teak furniture by a variety of designers, loosely woven curtain fabrics in natural colours that let in just the right amount of light, Danish metalwork (and Henning Koppel's classic designs for Georg Jensen in particular), and the heavy studio glass produced in special departments of the Scandinavian glass industry, but perhaps most successfully at Orrefors and Kosta in Sweden. Some good studio ceramics were produced at Gustavsberg by Stig Lindberg and at Royal Copenhagen by Axel Salto.

Scandinavian furniture, though concerned principally with the Swedish way of life, became internationally popular for its educated discrimination and its ability to blend with other styles. There was a notable absence of gimmicks, and a concern with economy of form that captured the spirit of the times. The long Scandinavian history of woodworking led to sophisticated laminated techniques such as those used by Alvar Aalto in Finland. During the 1950s, teak and walnut were almost synonymous with Scandinavian furniture, particularly Danish. There was a great range of design, with a particular talent for forms which were at once free and restrained, as for instance in the 'Egg', 'Swan' and 'Ant' chairs by Denmark's Arne Jacobsen.

Scandinavian glass reflected a feeling for clean lines and cool colours, and the glass was heavier than elsewhere in Europe. Shapes were functional but free and inventive, and each of the many glass factories adopted an individual style, with the help of a team of resident designers. There were some fascinating technical developments like those of Tapio Wirkkala and Timo Sarpaneva in Finland, who experimented with new kinds of moulds made of tree bark and even of ice. Tapio Wirkkala is now considered one of the great designers of this period, not only for his designs in glass, for he also designed silver, ceramics (some for Rosenthal) and furniture. He is best known for the famous Cantarelli Vase, a masterpiece in clear glass with engraved vertical linear decoration.

Although Wirkkala worked mainly in clear glass during the 1950s, there was a move away from this Scandinavian tradition. Kaj Franck at Nuutajärvi Notsjö and Per Lutken at Holmegaard are recognizable for their precise shapes in a range of restrained colours that never dominate the shape and allow it to be clearly read. The most important glass factories remained Orrefors and Kosta in Sweden. Orrefors was technically the more adventurous of the two, with its range of heavy pieces using the Ariel technique where the design was air-trapped and coloured between layers of glass. Edward Hald continued to be a strong influence on a younger generation of designers, including Ingeborg Lundin,

Erwin Ohrström and Sven Palmqvist, who was responsible for a jewel-like variation on the Ariel technique known as Ravenna glass. But Vicke Lindstrand at Kosta was perhaps the most imaginative of all the Swedish designers in glass at this period, with designs that were completely in tune with current design trends.

In complete contrast, Italian glass design of this period used a glaringly bright palette of colours which only the superb taste of the Murano glassmakers (and above all Venini) prevented from being vulgar. The Italian glass industry had been in the doldrums for most of the twentieth century, but the arrival of Paolo Venini from Milan reversed the downward trend. Although he was not a glassmaker himself, his innate taste, courage and business acumen provided a lead which the other Venetian glass manufacturers followed willingly. Venini knew how to choose his designers, and how to get the best out of them. The two star designers at Venini were Fulvio Bianconi and Carlo Scarpa, whose work changed noticeably after Venini's death in 1959. Bianconi invented the handkerchief vase which has become one of the popular symbols of 1950s design; he was also the inventor of a brightly coloured patchwork technique called 'Pezzato', now considered by collectors to be one of the most prized inventions of this period in glass. Scarpa revived various ancient Roman glassmaking techniques, turning them into lively modern designs: his murrhine wares are a modern-day

version of mosaic glass. In fact most of the so-called modern Venetian techniques at this time had their origins in ancient Venetian traditions which had become stale and had never really been updated for well over a hundred years.

A recurring pattern in the history of twentieth-century glass seems to be that the emergence of a major figure in the glass world heralds a local revival of fortune within the industry. It happened with Gallé at the turn of the century in the glassmaking region in and around Nancy, with Simon Gate and Edward Hald at Orrefors in the heart of the Swedish glass industry during the early part of the century, with Lalique in Paris during the 1920s and with Venini in Venice during his heyday in the 1940s and 1950s. Other Venetian glassmakers took on a new lease of life and there was some imaginative work at Barovier, at Aureliano Toso, where the painter Dino Martens developed his own brand of patchwork glass known as 'Oriente', and at Seguso, where Flavio Poli created solid abstract shapes closer to the Scandinavian style, and a popular kind of special decoration usually in turquoise known as Astrale. The best glass was exhibited at the biennial shows in Venice and the triennial shows in Milan, both of them providing a worldwide panorama of modern decorative and industrial art, and published regularly in *Domus*, an Italian magazine devoted to the decorative arts, which during the 1950s was under the inspired editorship of Gio

(*Far Left*)   A Tapio Wirkkala laminated wood dish, the two-coloured woods emphasizing the shell shape, circa 1950; 28 cm. long, incised artist's monogram TW.

(*Left*)   A four-piece silver and walnut tea service by Tapio Wirkkala; teapot 20 cm. high. inscribed TW, impressed Sterling 925 Made in Finland. 36 troy ounces gross weight.

(*Below*)   A Georg Jensen 18 carat gold necklace designed by Bent Gabriel Petersen gold marks, stamped Georg Jensen. This design was first introduced in 1959.

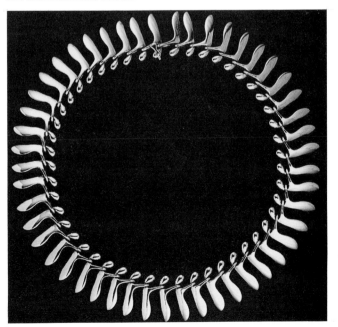

Ponti. It was at these shows and in *Domus* that the many new Italian firms of the 1950s were seen for the first time.

There was a remarkable revival of Italian imaginative power during the 1950s, and experimentation both with new manufacturing processes, and new synthetic materials, Gio Ponti, as well as editing *Domus*, was by now a much revered Italian architect and designer, who had already made his name during the 1930s. It was his enthusiasm and generous co-operation with other designers such as Piero Fornasetti during the 1950s that continued to earn him a place as one of the foremost designers. Once again during this time many of the leading designers were also architects, Franco Albini, Oswaldo Borsani, Carlo de Carli and Marco Zanuso

'Il Grande Pavone' by Paolo De Poli, a massive enamelled copper stylized sculpture on cast iron legs and simulated wood base; 155.7 cm. high, including the base. Signed on the reverse De Poli and dated 1962.

among others, working for Tecno, Casina and Magistretti. Carlo Mollino, a genius and eccentric, stands out from this group. His extraordinary adventures in laminated wood, tables, chairs and sometimes whole interiors, were dreamt up for a handful of rich and discerning clients, and are already considered much prized rarities today, with most pieces in museum collections.

All areas of the decorative arts took on a new vitality, and the art of the potter not least of all. Italian pottery during the 1950s was bright, decorative and asymmetric, with more good potters at work in Italy than during any other decade in the twentieth century. Fausto Melotti, Guido Gambone, Lucio Fontana and Salvatore Meli were among those who created a stir when their work was shown at the Venice and Milan shows. Their work was sometimes very large in scale and often had a tendency towards the sculptural, unlike most other European pottery at the time. Pottery, in contrast to most other areas of Italian decorative arts, which enjoyed a close relationship with industry, was dominated by artist craftsmen working alone in their own studios.

The lone craftsman was much more a figure of the 1960s, for during this decade there was a sudden revival of arts and crafts, and one that has been gathering momentum ever since. It was bound up with the spirit of the 1960s, when hippie culture and pop culture took hold of a younger generation, who had been born during the war. Perhaps in reaction against parents whose youth had been spent at a time when the war imposed severe restrictions, the hippies of Haight Ashbury in San Francisco and pop culture in London with heroes such as John Lennon and David Hockney, were individualists and free-thinkers. In England pop music, serious music, painting and to a certain extent the decorative arts enjoyed a glorious decade. London during the 1960s was the popular cultural centre of the world, with mini-skirts, hipsters and Pop Art providing an artistic syntax that was used worldwide. In the field of decorative arts British pottery in particular was attracting a lot of attention; the pottery scene was dominated (and perhaps still continues to this day to be) by two foreigners, Hans Coper and Lucie Rie, both of them refugees. There were other successful potters too; their names are not altogether fashionable today (Michael Cardew, Michael Casson, Raymond Marshall and Rosemary Wren), but it will soon be time for them to be rediscovered. These were the established potters of the day, the ones whose work merited comment in books such as *Modern Ceramics; Pottery and Porcelain of the World*, published by Spring Books in 1965. A younger generation of potters was also beginning to make an impact at this time; they were unknown in the 1960s, becoming established during the 1970s, and considered establishment today. Such youngsters as Alison Britton, Joanna Constantinides and Jacqui Poncelet, now the teachers of the next generation of British potters, were producing work during the 1960s and 1970s that is beginning to be categorized as belonging to the New Golden Age of British pottery.

'City of Cards', a trompe l'oeil four panel screen printed in colours,
by Piero Fornasetti, circa 1952, the first screen he created, each panel
217 × 50 cm. on castors, unsigned.

In America glassmakers were attracting more attention than potters, and there were developments in studio glass which changed dramatically the whole history of glass. Claims have been made to the effect that more discoveries in glass have been made during the last twenty years than in the entire previous history of glassmaking. The 'International Glass Movement' began with a series of makers, most of whom had begun their artistic life in other fields, turning to glass because it felt like a medium uncluttered by artistic tradition. The three great American names in glass during the 1960s were Dominic Labino, Harvey Littleton and Marvin Lipofsky, all of them still working today. Erwin Eisch in Germany was very tuned into their way of thinking, and no history of post-war glass can be complete without reference to the exciting work that was being done in comparative isolation in Czechoslovakia, where from 1960 to 1985 Stanislav Libensky was Professor of Glass at the School of Applied Arts in Prague.

The greatest innovation was the development in America of a small kiln which enabled the glass artist to create work away from the industry. A new generation of glassmakers worked directly with their material, with some very amorphous results at the beginning of this 'new period', which is characterized by what can only be described as misshapen lumps, such as the early sculptures of Marvin Lipofsky in America, Erwin Eisch in Germany, and Sam Herman in England. Since that time attitudes have changed greatly, techniques and teaching have become much more sophisticated and the technical virtuosity of studio glass today knows no bounds. Highly organized glass exhibitions like 'New Glass, A Worldwide Survey' at Corning in 1979, the Coburg glass prizes of 1977 and 1985, and the numerous glass exhibitions in Japan are a far cry from the early glass symposia in America where a handful of glass enthusiasts exchanged their ideas. Developments in glass artistry over the past 25 years have been unparalleled in any other field of the decorative or fine arts.

There have of course been other developments in the world of design during the 1960s and 1970s. During the late 1960s and the 1970s Art Deco was rediscovered. An exhibition at the Minneapolis Institute of Arts entitled 'The World of Art Deco' caught the public imagination. In London a new store called Biba created by Barbara Hulanicki attempted a complete re-creation of an Art Deco atmosphere; musicals from the 1920s and 1930s were extravagantly revived, and the re-emergence of Art Deco started a trend for nostalgia in the worlds of design and fashion. Vidal Sassoon's new geometric hairstyles were reminiscent of the flappers as seen in Art Deco bronze and ivory figures and were superseded by an updated version of the 1960s 'Victory Roll'. It was during the second half of the 1960s that both Art Nouveau and Art Deco began to be seriously collected, with the first specialist sales in those areas starting up at auction. In a sense, however, these various revivals were light relief or perhaps just adjuncts to the mainstream of new ideas in design.

There can be little doubt that since the mid-1960s Italy

One of a set of three children's chairs in bent plywood by Charles Eames; 37 cm. high.

has been the dominant force in the creation of design. In 1972 the Museum of Modern Art in New York staged a show entitled 'Italy. The New Domestic Landscape'. In his introduction to the catalogue Emilio Ambasz wrote, 'the emergence of Italy during the last decade as the dominant force in consumer-product design has influenced the work of every other European country and is now having its effect in the United States. Italy has become a micromodel in which a wide range of the possibilities, limitations and critical issues of contemporary design are brought into sharp focus.' The same author divides Italian design into three categories: 'the first is conformist, the second is reformist, and the third is rather one of contestation, attempting both enquiry and action.' The conformists were those who continued to refine established forms and functions, using bold colours and an imaginative approach to the new synthetic materials and moulding processes. Those that fall into that category are designers like Joe Colombo, Giancarlo Piretti, Vico Magistretti and Anna Castelli. Their work was mainly concerned with exploring the aesthetic quality of single objects, a chair, a table, a bookcase. The reformists were more concerned with the role of the designer in the new consumer society; they sought to construct a new language of design, reinterpreting earlier styles and ideas, or even ridiculing them with ideas that were pure kitsch. Objects such as the 'Pill Lamp' by Cesare Casati and Emanuele Ponzio, or the Mies Armchair manufactured by Archizoom come to mind. The last group were interested in creating anti-objects in a spirit of contestation which tried to get to the root of the problem. Here, 'the designer's pursuits are either confined to political action and philosophical postulation or else consist of total withdrawal.' In this spirit objects such as 'I Sassi' by Piero Gilardi were created; this is a set of seats modelled as bulky rocks made of polyurethane in different colours and different sizes. Another example was a sofa made of lacquered wood and artificial leopard skin, its contours shaped like the foliage of a tree, by a team of designers, including Andrea Branzi, for Archizoom.

In the late 1960s and early 1970s there were three Italian manufacturers who encouraged avant-garde designers like Branzi, Gilardi, Coretti and Morozzi. They were Archizoom, Gufram and Poltronova. The designs executed by them were challenging in the extreme and therefore strictly limited in their appeal. Even if they managed to find an environment to fit into, they were uncomfortable and highly impractical. Girlardi's rocks were hardly inviting after a hard day's work and demanded considerable athleticism when it came to sitting down on them or getting up from them. But these pieces of furniture, partly because of their rarity, partly because of their intellectual content, and also because they were made of strange synthetic materials which it would be a nightmare to reproduce, will undoubtedly become the most desired of collectors' items in the future, and the fight to own them has already begun.

One of the designers whose work was seen at the New Domestic Landscape Exhibition in 1972 was Ettore Sottsass jun.; he was born in Austria in 1907, came to Italy in the early 1930s and worked in a wide variety of media including painting, architecture, ceramics, jewellery, furniture and tapestries, as well as interior furnishings and industrial design. Sottsass has been the dominant figure in the world of design since the early 1970s. He says of himself, 'It would be difficult to make a catalogue of my work because I have never made monuments for the public drama, only fragile sets for private theatre, for private meditation and solitude.' Sottsass was the first of an important group of architect-designers, most of them younger than himself, to abandon the dictates of commercial design and look for a freer, more sculptural approach; in the mid-1960s Sottsass initiated the movement called 'Anti-Design'. While the established companies and major figures of Italian design went on catering for a more and more sophisticated middle class hungry for luxury and beauty, there was a strong reaction against capitalist values from a younger generation who knew nothing about war and deprivation and were beginning to question the views of the establishment. There was 'a deliberate exploitation of bad taste or kitsch, and eclecticism was seen as a way out of the formal purism of Functionalism'. The products of Anti-Designers were essentially non-commercial. Among other members of the Anti-Design movement were individuals such as Gaetano Pesce and Ugo La Pietra and a number of designers working together in groups, such as Gruppo STRUM and the UFO Group. In Sottsass's work of the late 1960s and 1970s there is a tendency towards mysticism, as in the 'Tantra' and 'Yantra' series of ceramics of 1969 and 1970, which are 'environmental pieces aimed at stimulating meditation and self-awareness'. And there are also references to American and European avant-garde sculpture, as in a series of furniture with bright stripes for Poltronova reminiscent of the imagery of Pop painters such as Lichtenstein and Warhol. During the 1970s Sottsass expressed himself in ceramics, glass, furniture and jewellery as well as creating total environments, sometimes imaginary and sometimes real.

Despite Sottsass and the other radical designers, mainstream Italian design has remained largely the same since the 1960s. The closure of the Triennale exhibitions in 1974 had a marked effect on the dissemination of ideas. But thanks to its avant-garde designers Italy has managed to stay in the forefront of contemporary design. In 1976 the Studio Alchymia was formed, 'as a centre for innovatory design that would be manufactured and sold rather than just imagined'. Its members included the élite of radical design, Alessandro Mendini, Andrea Branzi and of course Sottsass. Mendini, the spokesman for Alchymia, refers to the group as 'Post-radical'. Sottsass describes his own contribution by saying: 'So I have chosen textures like the grit and the mosaics of public conveniences in the underground stations of big cities, like the tight wire netting of suburban fences, or like the spongy paper of government account books, the iconography of non-culture.' Eventually Sottsass broke away from Alchymia, and in 1981 he started his own experimental design company called 'Memphis'. It was successful and has attracted attention worldwide, though even now the appeal in commercial terms is narrow enough to be considered foolhardy. But Sottsass's courage is remarkable and he has managed to carry design a step further. He has found a way forward by harking back first to the geometry of Art Deco and later to the 1950s. But it seems to be a universal truth of the design world that one has to go into reverse in order to proceed.

1

All pieces seen here are Scandinavian, with the exception of the free-form sculpture by the Dutch glass artist A.D. Copier, whose career in glass has already spanned more than sixty years. Scandinavian glass during the 1950s was mostly thick-walled with decoration trapped between layers of glass. Ariel and Graal techniques initiated thirty years earlier at Orrefors were modified by a number of the artists working there at this time, and the new Ravenna technique invented by Sven Palmquist was one of the most brilliant innovations, giving the glass a jewel-like glow by using grains of sand mixed with the coloured glass.

1.   A Leerdam free-form glass sculpture designed by Andries Dirk Copier, circa 1968; 34.5cm. high, engraved Leerdam Unica CK1600 A.D. Copier.

2

2. Graal, Graal & Ariel, and Ariel glass vases by Vicke Lindstrand; 17.4 cm. high, 18 cm. high and 20.2 cm. high, two unsigned, the shell vase signed Lindstrand, Orrefors, Sweden – Ariel on the base.

3. An Orrefors 'Ariel' glass vase, designed by Ingeborg Lundin, circa 1975; 18.5 cm. high, engraved mark Orrefors Ariel Nr. 367E 5 Ingeborg Lundin.

4. Three Orrefors 'Ravenna' glass bowls, designed by Sven Palmquist circa 1955; bowl at left, max. width 20.75 cm., engraved marks.

3

4

1

2

3

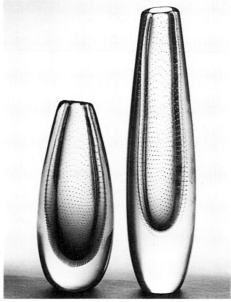

4

5

The Scandinavian method of making studio glass was for a skilled team of technicians to interpret a designer's work partly from drawings and partly in close co-operation with the designer, who was very often a full-time member of staff. Most of the designers involved in the glass industry designed only glass, but Tapio Wirkkala in Finland also did designs for metal, wood, and ceramics. His work in glass showed evidence technically as well as artistically, of a highly original design talent.

1.   An Orrefors 'Ariel' glass vase designed by Ingeborg Lundin, circa 1978, internally coloured olive green and with a design of profiles in Ariel technique; 19 cm. high, engraved mark Orrefors Ariel N197E8 Ingeborg Lundin.

2.   An Orrefors 'Ariel' glass vase designed by Ingeborg Lundin, circa 1970, with a regular design of double striped banding in internal bubbles; 21.5 cm. high, engraved marks.
   An Orrefors 'Ariel' glass bottle vase designed by Edwin Ohrstrom, circa 1965; 22.5 cm. high, engraved marks.
   An Orrefors 'Ariel' glass vase designed by Ingeborg Lundin, circa 1970; 18.5 cm. high, engraved marks.

3.   Four glass vases by Tapio Wirkkala, circa 1960; straight cylindrical vase 26.2 cm. high; all with engraved signatures.

4.   Two Nuutarjarvi Notsjo vases designed by Gunnel Nyman, circa 1945, clear glass over amber with asymmetrical designs of small trapped air bubbles; 23.2 cm. and 33.8 cm. high, signed.

5.   Two Kosta glass vases designed by Vicke Lindstrand, circa 1955, both internally decorated in dark colours; tallest vase 30.5 cm. high, signed in diamond point Kosta.

6.   Three Iittala glass flask vases with tiny spouts, designed by Timo Sarpaneva; circa 1955; tallest vase 39 cm. high, engraved signatures and Iittala 3288.

7.   A Graal glass vase designed by Edward Hald for Orrefors, 1946; 14 cm. high, signed and dated, inscribed Graal no. 2437.

8.   Three Holmegaard globular glass vases with random pierced holes, designed by Michael Bang, circa 1955; largest vase 17.5 cm. high, engraved Holmegaard MB.
   A Holmegaard glass 'flame' vase designed by Per Lutkin, circa 1958; 20 cm. high, engraved Holmegaard PL 1958.

9.   Four Iittala textured, smoked glass vases designed by Timo Sarpaneva, circa 1965; vase on left 19.5 cm. high, engraved signature.

Italian glass was much freer in colour and design than Scandinavian with less emphasis on symmetry and clean lines. The bright (almost garish) colour combinations were much nearer to the lively colour palettes of many Italian and American painters of this period. The Italian glass industry enjoyed a brief creative revival in the postwar decade, which was almost entirely due to the entrepreneurial prowess of Paolo Venini, who began his career before the war, but whose firm produced its most individual work in the last decade of his life. He died in 1959, and with his death the vitality of Italian glass design diminished noticeably.

1

2

1. 'Hibou', an applied glass
vase designed by Pablo Picasso
and made by Aureliano Toso
circa 1955; 37 cm. high.

2. An 'Oriente' glass ewer,
designed by Dino Martens,
executed by Vetreria Aureliano
Toso, circa 1950; 33.5 cm. high,
unsigned.
   A glass sculpture designed by
Dino Martens, executed by
Vetreria Aureliano Toso, circa
1955; 30.5 cm. long, inscribed A.
Toso.
   A glass vase by Luciano Ferro,
executed by A.V.E.M. circa
1950; 37 cm. high, unsigned.

3. An 'Oriente' pezzato glass
vase designed by Dino Martens
for Aureliano Toso, the abstract
face beneath the rim with
features detailed in 'millefiore'
and rod cane insertions; 26 cm.
high.

4. A selection of glass by
Venini, circa 1950.

3

4

1

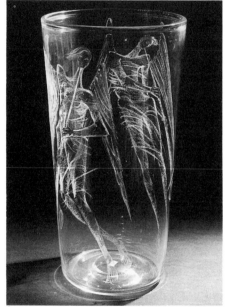

3

2

Patchwork techniques, invented by Fulvio Bianconi at Venini, were very popular during the 1950s, and many of the Italian glassmakers experimented with them. It was a natural progression from the more traditional latticinio *techniques where different coloured threads made a pattern in the glass. Instead of the threads making the pattern, this was now provided by solid blocks of colour. Latticinio, however, was still popular, particularly in combination with another 1950s innovation, the 'fazzoletto' or handkerchief shape also invented by Bianconi. The freedom of shape and unconventional approach to Italian glass of the 1950s led the way to the anarchy of the International Studio Glass movement of later decades.*

1. Two Dale Chihuly glass vases, the coloured glass with abstract motifs; 17.3cm. high and 15.3cm. high; one engraved Chihuly '79 and one Chihuly 1978.

2. A large Sam Herman free-form blown and applied glass vase; 20.5cm. high, engraved Samuel Herman 1973 18.

4

5

3.   A large glass vase designed and engraved by John Hutton, circa 1958/9, stipple engraved with two seraphims; 42.5 cm. high, engraved signature.

4.   A glass 'handkerchief' vase and a chequered design glass vase by Venini, 14 cm. and 21 cm. high, both etched Venini Murano Italia.

5.   A glass 'Sidone' 'vase by Ercole Barovier, executed by Barovier and Tosso, 1958; 21 cm. high.

6.   Two glass decanters and a glass vase by Venini; tallest decanter 42 cm. high, all etched Venini Murano Italia.

7.   A tall glass vase attributed to Ercole Barovier, with turquoise patchwork decoration, circa 1955; 34.6 cm. high.

8.   Three glass 'Fazzoletto' vases designed by Fulvio Bianconi for Venini, circa 1951; largest vase 28 cm. high, all etched Venini, Murano, Italia.

6

7

8

During the 1950s Italian glass became noticeably less concerned with function and more sculptural in shape. Glass was moving closer to fine art, and the Murano glass-makers (unlike those of the previous 100 years) had a keen appetite for artistic invention. Nothing is of course ever entirely new, but traditional techniques were stretched and cajoled to provide some of the most original glass seen in Italy for nearly 300 years. All the techniques seen here, the applied glass in the Barbini vases, the dramatic tartan pattern of the Bianconi vase, and the honeycomb techniques, are examples of this new vitality.

1. Two Pauly applied glass vases, designed by A. Barbini, circa 1955; 25 and 25.3 cm. high, engraved Pauly A. Barbini.

1

2

2. A Venini glass tazza, circa 1960, internally decorated with brightly coloured stripes; 18 cm. high, etched mark Venini Philips.

3. A Venini glass vase, designed by Fulvio Bianconi, 1960; 27.25 cm. high, engraved Bianconi 1960 Fulvio, etched mark Venini, Murano Italia.

4. Left: A Barovier and Toso 'Honeycomb' vase designed by Ercole Barovier, circa 1955; 16.75 cm. high; engraved Barovier & Toso, Murano and with printed paper label.
Right: A Venini glass Honeycomb vase circa 1960; 22.25 cm. high; printed paper label, Venini Murano Venezia N. Made in Italy.

3

4

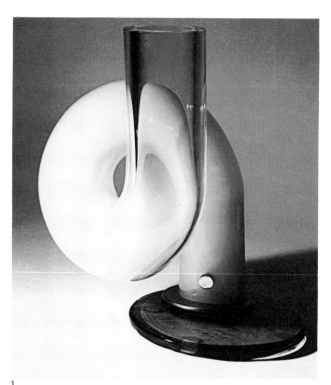

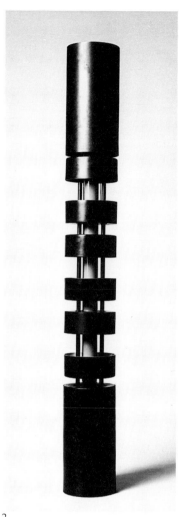

As in the period between the wars, designers paid a great deal of attention to lighting with results ranging from the pure sculpture of the Tecta opaline and clear glass lamp to the pure Kitsch of 'Pillola', the Pop-art object suggesting five gelatin capsules.

1. A glass table lamp by Tecta in opaline and clear class, attached by an aluminium mount to a smoky grey-tinted base, circa 1970; 36.1 cm. high.

2. 'Totem', a painted metal lamp by Serge Mouille, the black painted metal sections enclosing a red fluorescent tube; 103.5 cm. high, unsigned.

3. A Gio Ponti table lamp with white painted metal base and frosted glass spherical shade; 45 cm. high.

4. A 1950s French floor lamp, with black painted stand suspending a white, pleated plastic shade; 162.4 cm. high.

5. A perspex and metal floor lamp designed by Sergio Asti circa 1975, manufactured by Blumendel in a limited edition of 12; 197.2 cm. high.
A Chimera white perspex floor lamp designed by Vico Magistretti, 1969, and manufactured by Artemide; 183 cm. high, and a matching table lamp, 77.9 cm. high.

1

2

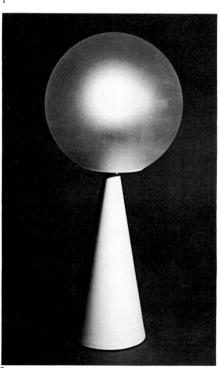

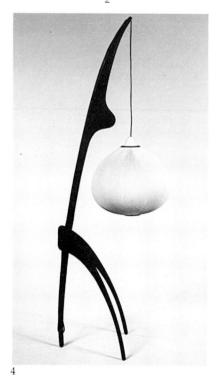

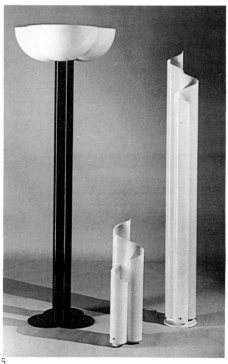

3

4

5

6. An adjustable brass and steel desk lamp designed by Angelo Boccanera, manufactured by Stilnovo, Brevattato, circa 1952. Patent; printed label Milano, Stilnovo. Italy.

7. A 'Girasole' metal and perspex floor lamp designed by Gae Aulenti and manufactured by Kartell, circa 1968; 70.4 cm. high.

8. A brass and glass table lamp by Fontana Arte, circa 1954, the brass shade and stem set with two rhombic sections of thick, green tinted glass; 60 cm. high, unsigned.

9. 'Pillola', a series of five plastic lamps designed by Cesare Casati and Emanuele Ponzio, circa 1968, each of the five gelatin capsules in primary colours, dotted with air vents to dissipate heat, each seated in a clear plastic ring; each capsule 54.5 cm. high, unsigned.

10. 'Taraxacum', a Flos hanging lamp designed by Achille & Piergiacomo Castiglioni, circa 1950, the spun fibre glass shade stretched tightly over a wire frame; 64.5 cm. high.

6

7

8

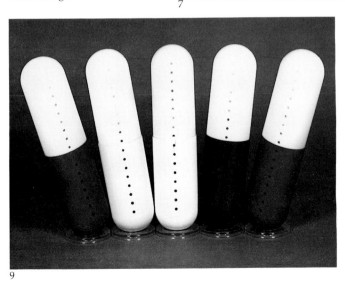

9

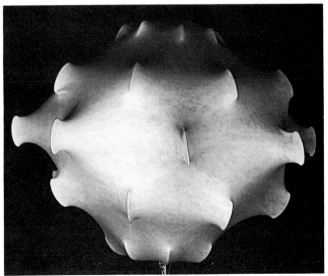

10

Many influences were at work during the 1950s, 1960s, and 1970s. The 1950s were marked by an obsession with asymmetry, probably as a reaction to the sleek lines of Art Deco. There were brash juxtapositions of colour and a liking for spindly shapes. The 1960s were bright and cheerful, and Pop Art had an immediate effect on the decorative arts. The 1970s was dominated by Italian design, with a predilection for moulded plastics in bright primary colours, and a definite empathy with the technology and aesthetics of space-age design. The three illustrations seen here mark clearly the difference in approach from one decade to the next.

1. A white kidney-shaped fibreglass desk and chair by Jean Leleu, the 1969 prototype awarded the Prix de Rome; 221 cm. wide, 75 cm. high, unsigned.

An aluminium floor lamp, four spherical adjustable lights on the disc perimiter, by Lebovici, 1972; 203.5 cm. high, inscribed Lebovici 4/10 1972.

2. 'Boxing Gloves', a pair of chaise longues by De Sede, deeply upholstered in brown and light green hide, circa 1978; 178 cm. long; 112 cm. wide; 85 cm. high.

3. A painted metal wall luminaire-applique by Serge Mouille, 1956–60, with three rod arms supporting five pivoting lamp shades; held to the wall by two brackets; 140 cm. high, 200 cm. wide, one of six, unsigned.

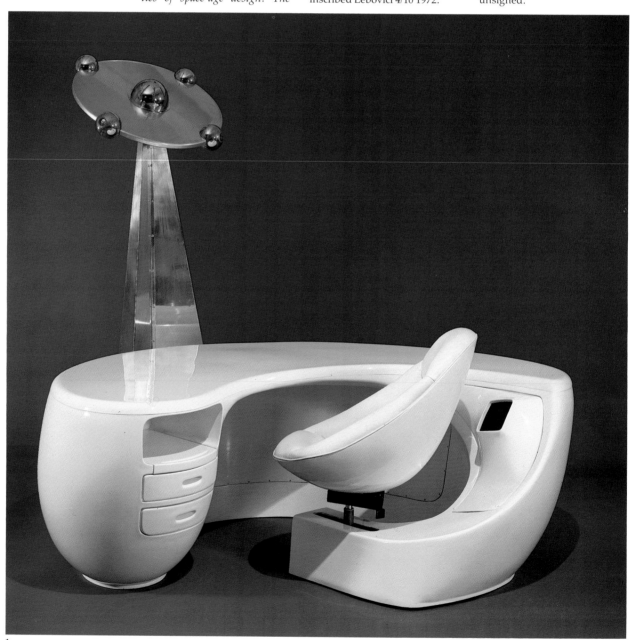

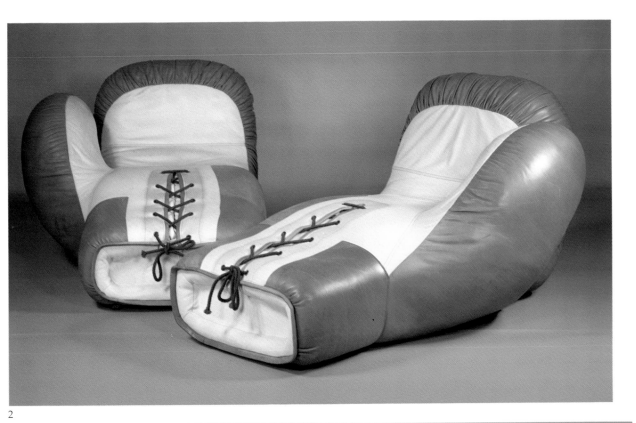

2

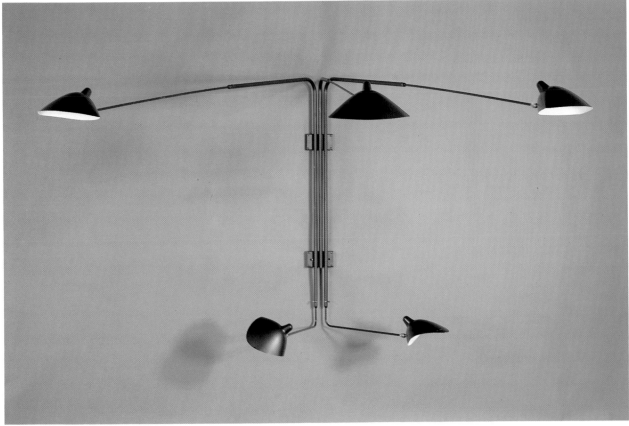

3

1

2

3

4

5

Chair design has always been of seminal importance in -the history of decorative arts. In the preface to an exhibition at the National Gallery of Victoria in 1974 entitled 'One Hundred Modern Chairs', Terance Lane wrote, 'No other article of furniture impinges so closely and intimately on everyday life, or continues to be such a pressing and demanding design problem', and went on to point out how twentieth-century technical inventions have offered 'a means of escape from the tyranny of the four-legged chair, the severely restricting demands of which, sanctioned and reinforced by tradition, have dominated seat furniture for many hundreds of years'.

1.   Two from a set of six high backed aluminium and foam side chairs, designed by Roger Tallon, executed by Jacques Lacloche, Paris 1965; 88 cm. high, unsigned.

2.   A Knoll steel wire armchair and ottoman designed by Harry Bertoia, with dark blue woollen covers.

3.   Three from a set of four nickel-plated steel rod armchairs designed by Warren Platner, 1966, and manufacturerred by Knoll, with hessian upholstered top rails and cushions.

4.   A pair of Ernest Race 'Antelope' chairs designed for the Festival of Britain, 1951, with painted metal rod frames on ball feet, and with plywood seats. Printed labels Race. London England.

5.   Two from a set of six bentwood chairs attributed to George Nelson, circa 1950; 77 cm. high, unsigned.

6.   Two chromium-plated fine tubular steel side chairs upholstered with white vinyl, designed by Charles Eames and manufactured by Herman Miller, 1951.

7.   One of a set of four birch plywood side chairs designed by Charles Eames for Herman Miller, circa 1946; 75 cm. high; applied printed labels, Charles Eames designed Herman Miller – Zeeland – Michigan.

8.   A laminated rosewood lounge chair upholstered in hide, designed by Charles Eames, 1956, and manufactured by Herman Miller, with an Ottoman en suite.

9.   A birch plywood armchair designed by Vittorio Gregotti, Lodovico Meneghetti and Giotto Stoppino, 1954, and manufactured by SIM Novara.

10.   An 'Egg' armchair designed by Arne Jacobsen, 1957 and manufactured by Fritz Hansens, the steel form covered in foam, upholstered in synthetic fabric, on swivel aluminium base, manufacturer's label F.H. Made in Denmark by Fritz Hansens, Furniture Makers, Danish Control 0763.

6

7

8

9

10

With design making deeper and deeper inroads into industry during the twentieth century, it is only natural that a lot of thought should have gone into the 'high altar' of industrial life, the office desk. There has been endless variety in desk design during the post-war years, as seen in an exhibition at the Musée des Arts Décoratifs in 1984 entitled 'L'Empire du Bureau', the catalogue of which has become the bible of twentieth-century desk design. Each of the three desks seen here shows a different approach, with Mollino and his liking for revealed structure, the adaptability of the Olivetti desk and the typical French concern with elegance and luxury in Adnet's desk.

1. An oak and formica desk by Carlo Mollino, Torino, circa 1953, with splayed and buttressed legs below a formica top; 178cm. wide, 76cm. high.

2. A 'Serie Spazio' self-assembly L-shaped office desk by Olivetti, Ivrea, in metal and plastic, circa 1956; 180cm. wide, marked Olivetti DZGMT, Arredamenti, Metallici, 340133F.

3. A leather and red glass desk designed by Jacques Adnet for the office of the President of Sud Aviation, circa 1952, the leather by Hermès; 211.5cm. wide, 76cm. high, unsigned.

2

3

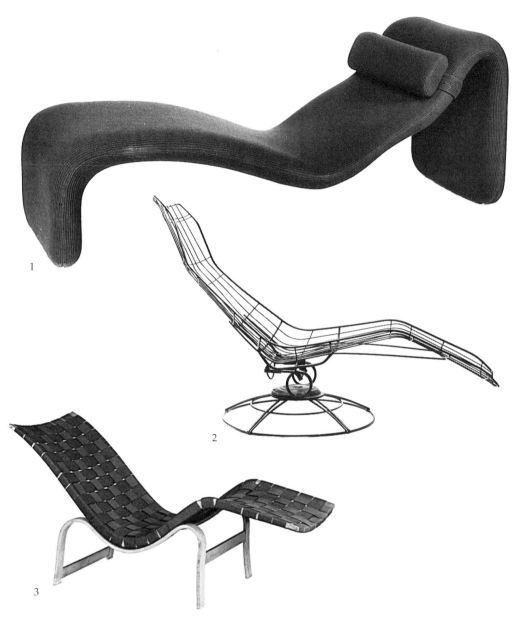

Comfort does not always seem to have been foremost in the minds of designers, and there is often a feeling that sheer ingenuity takes pride of place. The Hans Wegner cord, steel and metal armchair might be a sculptural triuniph, but requires youthful agility to get in and out of, and once in, can soon become uncomfortable. The Mies chair seems to defy all the laws of sitting, but is remarkably comfortable.

1. 'Djinn series', an upholstered chaise longue designed by Olivier Mourgue, the steel frame and trestle ends covered in urethane foam, and upholstered in nylon stretch jersey, circa 1965; 170 cm. long.

2. An American tubular steel reclining chair with sprung supports on domed, pivoting base; 190 cm. long.

3. A laminated birchwood chaise longue designed by Bruno Mathsson, the curving frame slung with interlaced webbing; 151 cm. long. Designer's printed label, stamped Made in Sweden.

4. 'Mies', a rubber, ponyskin and chromed steel chair and foot stool designed by Archizoom for Poltronova, circa 1969, natural rubber stretched over the frame, with ponyskin pillow; 130 cm. long; 73.5 cm. wide; 76 cm. high, unsigned.

5. A cord, stainless steel and painted metal armchair, designed by Hans L. Wegner, 1958, and manufactured by Doberck & Sons, Copenhagen; 115 cm. high.

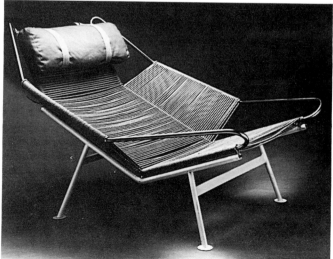

Fantasy has often been as important as practicality in post-war design, and trompe-l'oeil *or sheer disguise has produced some amusing but bizarre results. The Wurlitzer with its neon-lit plastic casing is a diversion in itself even without a record playing mechanism.*

1.   A geometric coffee table by O. Rosa for San Polo, circa 1955, the top inset with multicoloured textured ceramic tiles, on painted wooden legs; 98.5 cm. wide. Signed in the ceramic San Polo, Venezia, Italy, O. Rosa.

2.   A Bush Radio Ltd. table television, Type 22, with a nine inch screen enclosed in a brown bakelite casing constructed by British Moulded Plastics Ltd, circa 1949; 39 cm. high.

3.   'Egocentrismo', a printed wood, metal and wood circular table on tripod base by Piero Fornasetti, Milan, circa 1958; 75 cm. diam., 49.5 cm. high, applied maker's paper label.

4.   A multi-selector phonograph (juke-box) by Wurlitzer, 1940's. Model No. 1015. 149 cm. high, 81 cm. wide.

5.   A 'trompe l'oeil' commode by Piero Fornasetti, circa 1958, with wrap-around composition of a Palladian styled building on tapering metal feet; 100 cm wide, 85 cm. high, unsigned.

6.   A suite of leather and brass furniture retailed by Hermes, circa 1950; table – 80 cm. diam; chairs 82.5 cm. high.

1

2

3

4

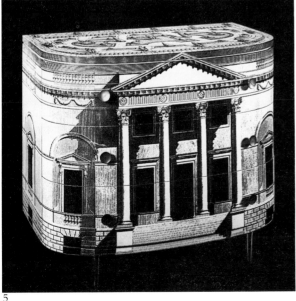

5

6

1

Both Italian and French ceramics of the 1950s were colourful and richly decorated with modernist imagery borrowed from the fine arts. Shapes become more and more sculptural, and many of the Italian potters worked on a very large scale. The pottery seen here is far from the more restrained art of the potter as practised in other European countries, and Britain particularly.

1.   'Visages Blanc', a large double-faced ceramic vase by Jean Lurçat; 39 cm. high, signed Jean Lurçat, numbered 8/25, inscribed Sant Vincens B.R.

2.   A stylized pottery 'Zodiac' jug and a crystalline glazed bowl by Guido Gambone; 44.5 cm. high and 27.7 cm. diam., painted monogram G and Vietri, Italy.
      A large earthenware 'cista' by Claudio Ferri, the hand-built base and cover forming a gourd with cylindrical neck and foot; 47 cm. high, painted C. Ferri, Firenze.

3.   A fine earthenware vase designed by Jean Lurçat, executed by Sant-Vincens, circa 1955; 38 cm. high, Painted Dessin J. Lurçat Sant-Vincens B/R 8/25.

2

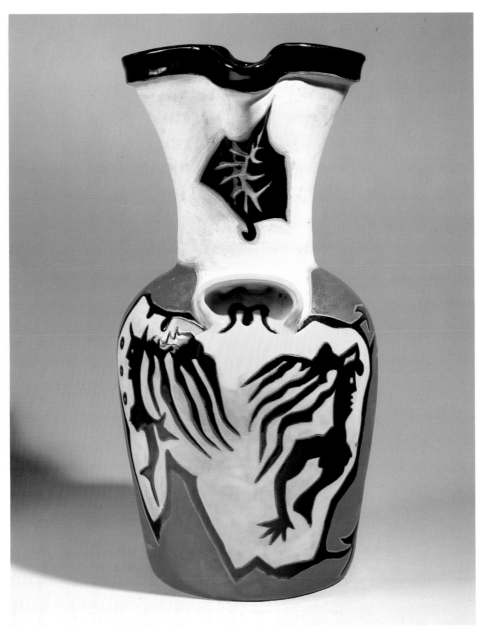

3

The variety of studio ceramics during the post-war years has been very great, with some potters using their surface for sheer decoration, others using clay to make sculpture, and at the same time there has been an important revival of the purer art of the potter deeply concerned with vessel forms and glazes, harking back to older traditions in order to create a new art form.

1. A Tapio Wirkkala speckled stoneware vase with incised geometric decoration; 15 cm. high. Incised artist's monogram TW circa 1955.

2. An Edition Picasso pottery wine jug incised and painted in blue and black with a knight and a caparisoned horse; 21 cm. high; impressed and painted Edition Picasso and Madoura marks, 264/300.

3. Two Guido Gambone pottery jugs, one with upright spout and arrow-tail handle, the other with narrow spout and bowed handle, both painted with polychrome abstract designs, circa 1955; 30 cm. and 25.5 cm. high. Painted marks, Gambone Italy on taller jug.

4. A Fausto Melotti pottery vase with high-fired drip glaze decoration, circa 1955; 46.5 cm. high, raised impressed mark on base, Melotti Milano Italy.

5. A double-mask ceramic vase attributed to Vibi, one side moulded with the double masks of comedy and tragedy; 27 cm. wide.

6.   A set of six Fornasetti 'Tema E Variazioni' black and white transfer-printed pottery plates; 26 cm. diam. Printed title and Fornasetti – Milano Made in Italy.

7.   A Marcello Fantoni tall, bottle-shaped stoneware vase, the matt black body decorated in sgraffito polychrome enamel colours; 58.5 cm. high, painted signature Fantoni 1959.

8.   'Adamo' and 'Eva', a set of twenty-four porcelain plates by Piero Fornasetti, circa 1960, each as twelve circular plates assembled to form a portrait; each plate 25.5 cm. diam., each painted Fornasetti – Milano, Made in Italy.

9.   Left: An earthenware abstract vase designed by Ivaldi for Ceramiche Italia, Albisola; 20.8 cm. high, printed mark.
   Centre: A black and white glazed bird form vase designed by Antonia Campé for Lavenia circa 1951; 36.1 cm. high.
   Right: 'Pinguino', a ceramic vase by Pucci Umbertide; 29.6 cm. high, inscribed 1262 Pucci – Umbertide. made in Italy.

10.   An Ariele ceramic abstract vase, the base dividing into three curving branches, circa 1955; 42 cm. high, painted signature Ariele, Torino Italy N138.

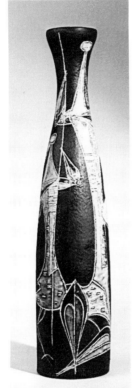

7

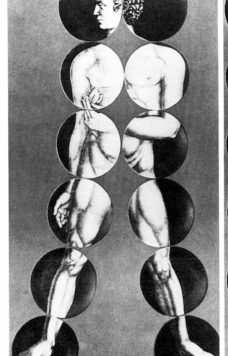

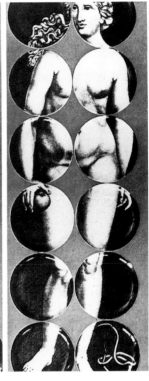

8

9

10

The world of serious studio pottery has been dominated by two potters of middle-European origin, both of whom lived and worked for most of their lives in England. Hans Coper and Lucie Rie worked separately and together, each of them with strong individual talents that combined harmoniously when they worked as a team.

1. A selection of Lucie Rie porcelain and stoneware bowls and bottles, 1970–80; bottle lower right 22 cm. high, all with LR monogram.

2. Four Hans Coper stoneware vases; 23, 19, 49.8, and 21 cm. high, all with impressed HC monogram.

1

Design innovation in the years after the Second World War has stemmed mainly from Italy and Scandinavia. During the 1950s Scandinavian glass, furniture and textiles impressed the design world with a clearness of purpose, emphasis on natural woods and honest craftsmanship. By contrast with the clean lines of Scandinavian glass at this period, Italian glass was more in tune with the asymmetry and glaring colour spectrum of modern art. During the '60s and '70s classics of modern design seem to have come mainly out of Italy.

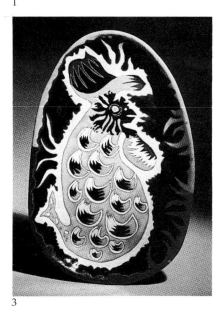

1.   An Iittala glass bowl designed by Tapio Wirkkala, the 'tree bark' decoration the result of having been made from a carved wooden mould, circa 1955; 24.5cm. diam., engraved Tapio Wirkkala 2450.

2.   A white metal necklace by Georg Jensen Silversmithy, probably designed by Henning Koppel, constructed of linked broad flattened ovals; impressed Georg Jensen 750 1190, 2.7 troy ozs.

3.   A pottery platter by Jean Lurçat, the asymmetric oval shape painted in brilliant colours with a cockerel; 53.5cm. long, painted signature Dessin J. Lurçat Sant Vincens DN 11/50.

4.   Two heavy clear glass Skrufs Thalatta vases designed by Bengt Edenfalk, with air-trapped decoration; left, 26.5cm high, engraved Unick Thalatta, Bengt Edenfalk Skrufs Sweden 525–63; right, 23.5cm. high, engraved Thalatta, Bengt Edenfalk, Skrufs Sweden 4/5/59.

5.   A rosewood and laminated birch low table by Tapio Wirkkala, a leaf form inlaid in the rectangular top, on tubular steel, chromium-plated legs; 40cm. high, top 124 × 62cm.

6.   'Amalussanta', a chromium-plated and painted metal floor lamp designed by Vittoro Gregotti for Bilumen, 49 multicoloured discs surrounding the neon strip light; 180–5cm. high.

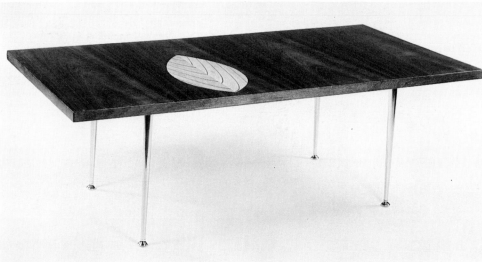

7. A Carlo Mollino bentwood and laminated 10-ply ash chair, manufactured by Appelli and Varesio, feet strengthened in two places by metal plaques, the spring seat clamped to the rear legs by two curved metal strips held with decorative brass bolts. Mollino (1905–73) was a pioneer of Italian design in the '50s, using organic sculptural forms.

8. A Daum twin-light lamp in clear and frosted glass with pâte de verre and brass mounts, 1950; 58 cm. high, engraved Daum France.

9. Three Finnish white metal vases and a white metal three-branch candelabra designed by Tapio Wirkkala; candelabra 24.2 cm. high, stamped TW monogram, Hämeenlinna town mark and date code for 1961; vases dated from left to right, 1961, 1957 and 1958.

6

7

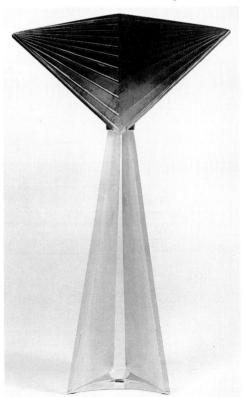

8

9

The International Studio Glass movement has spread across the world from America where it began in the late 1960s. The main reason it began was the invention of a small, easily transportable kiln which could be used by the artist at home, reducing the need for glass to be made within the industry. Glass also became a subject to be taught on university campuses, and many artists who previously might have sought to express themselves in another medium were attracted to it.

1. A selection of contemporary glass by Liz Lowe (two vases, left), Annette Meech (bowl), Catherine Hough (disc-shape), Tessa Clegg and Elizabeth Crowley (cylindrical vase), and two scent bottles by David Taylor, smaller bottle on right 14.4 cm. high; all 1985.

2. left to right: A Diana Hobson pâte de verre bowl form; 10.7 cm. high, signed, 1985.
A small Diana Hobson pâte de verre bowl form; 9 cm. high, signed, 1985.
A sculptural mould-blown glass vase by Tim Shaw, with diamond saw-cutting and sandblasted decoration; 46 cm. high, signed, 1985.
Pod 11, an Arlon Bayliss glass sculpture with spiralling metal foil inclusions; 51 cm. long, engraved Pod 11 9–84 Arlon Bayliss.

3. A cast-glass folded bowl by Tessa Clegg, the shaded blue glass with dark blue speckling; 29 cm. diam., engraved signature, dated 1985.

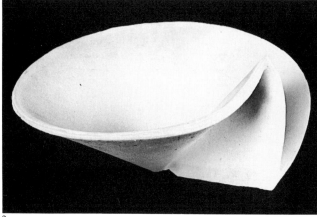

4. 'Lounge Lizard Lover', a clear glass carved and engraved bowl form by David Prytherch; 26.8 cm. long, inscribed and signed, dated 1985.

5. 'Split Triangle', a Colin Reid glass sculpture in two sections, kiln-formed glass cast in a mould, cut and polished, clear glass with orange and black transparent veiling; 90 cm. long, each section engraved Colin Reid 1985 R140 A & B.

6. Three ceramic and glass sculptures by Tatiana Best-Devereux, the ceramic conical forms enclosing cut and polished glass cones; 1985.

7. A glass bowl by Annette Meech, the rounded blown form scratched with an asymmetrical pattern; 25.1 cm. high, engraved Annette Meech 1345, The Glasshouse 1985.

8. A dish by Brian Blanthorn in fused glass, partly matt and partly irregularly striped in blue and dark blue; 33 cm. diam., engraved B.C. Blanthorn 29/9/85.

5

6

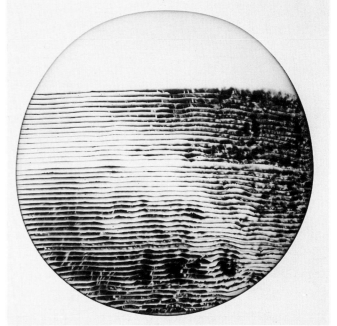

7

8

Price List

In some cases it has not been possible to give dates or prices for the objects illustrated. The prices shown below refer to the final bids at the time of sale, inclusive of any local taxes or premium. While every care has been taken in compiling this list, accuracy cannot be guaranteed.

The place of sale is indicated as follows:
- A: Christie's Amsterdam (prices in guilders)
- G: Christie's Geneva (Swiss francs)
- KS: London, King Street (pounds)
- M: Christie's Monaco (French francs)
- NY: Christie's New York (dollars)
- SK: London, Christie's South Kensington
- *: Dan Klein's private collection, sold at sotheby's on 29 November 1984

Prices from sales other than those in New York are also given in the dollar equivalent at the time of sale.

- B: bottom
- C: centre
- F: front
- L: left
- R: right
- T: top

Page	Place	Date	Price (local or sterling)	Price ($ US)
6	NY	4.12.81	13,157	25,000
7	KS	28.1.86	1,026	1,436
8	KS	17.4.84	432	604
8	NY	30.3.85	534	770
9	NY	–	–	–
9	NY	27.5.82	–	–
10	NY	3.4.82	17,111	30,800
10	NY	1.10.83	–	–
12	KS	30.4.85	2,916	3,499
13	NY	26.3.83	3,000	4,200
14	KS	30.4.85	–	–

ARTS AND CRAFTS AND LATE NINETEENTH-CENTURY MODERNISM

Page	Place	Date	Price (local or sterling)	Price ($ US)
15	KS	18.7.85	–	–
16	KS	28.1.86	324	421
17	KS	28.1.86	2,700	3,510
18	NY	14.6.85	–	–
19	NY	26.5.85	–	–
20	A	3.3.83	4,560	12,202
20	A	3.3.83	4,560	12,202
22 1	NY	14.12.84	–	–
23 3	NY	30.3.85	49,186	60,500
24 1	SK	25.5.84	1,300	1,800
24 2	KS	8.11.84	2,300	2,920
24 3FL	KS	18.7.85	280	392
3BL		18.7.85	216	302
3FC		18.7.85	594	831
3C		18.7.85	129	180
3FR		18.7.85	259	362
3BR		18.7.85	324	453
24 4L	KS	18.7.85	6,480	9,072
24 4C	KS	18.7.85	2,808	3,931
24 4R	KS	18.7.85	2,808	3,931
25 5	KS	18.7.85	280	392
25 6	KS	18.7.85	–	–
25 7	–	–	–	–
25 8	SK	7.6.85	2,000	2,520
25 9	KS	8.11.84	250	317
25 10	KS	18.7.85	2,700	3,780
26 1	–	–	–	–
26 2	KS	8.11.84	1,500	1,882
27 3C	KS	18.7.85	280	392
27 3L	KS	18.7.85	1,296	1,814
27 3R	KS	18.7.85	1,512	2,116
27 4	KS	18.7.85	1,728	2,419
28 1	KS	18.7.85	864	1,209
28 2	KS	18.7.85	550	770
28 3	SK	26.2.82	200	368
28 4L	KS	30.4.85	885	1,099
28 4CL	KS	30.4.85	864	1,073
28 4CR	KS	30.4.85	864	1,073
28 4R	KS	30.4.85	1,888	2,346
29 5	SK	28.10.83	260	389
29 6	KS	3.3.81	190	424

Page	Place	Date	Price (local or sterling)	Price ($ US)
29 7L	KS	30.4.85	3,456	4,294
29 7C	KS	30.4.85	1,944	2,415
29 7R	KS	30.4.85	810	1,008
29 8	KS	8.11.84	1,000	1,269
30 1	KS	16.3.82	–	–
31 2	KS	30.4.85	32,400	40,257
32 1	KS	30.4.85	594	738
32 2L	KS	8.11.84	220	263
32 2R	KS	8.11.84	420	503
32 3L	KS	8.11.84	129	154
32 3C	KS	8.11.84	237	384
32 3R	KS	8.11.84	172	206
32 4	KS	18.7.85	378	529
32 5L	KS	18.7.85	151	211
32 5C	KS	18.7.85	118	165
32 5R	KS	18.7.85	561	785
33 6	SK	30.4.82	–	–
33 7	NY	13.12.85	4,769	6,820
33 8	KS	30.4.85	380	472
33 9	KS	30.9.85	1,728	2,433
33 10	SK	30.4.82	–	–
34 1	A	3.3.83	36,480	97,446
34 2	NY	24.5.84	–	–
35 3	A	3.3.83	7,980	20,887
35 4	A	3.3.83	27,360	71,613
35 5	NY	17.12.83	27,500	38,500
36 1	KS	23.9.81	1,600	3,044
36 2	NY	16.12.83	5,445	7,700
36 3	NY	1.10.83	8,817	13,200
36 4	NY	24.5.84	–	–
37 5	A	3.3.83	1,596	4,177
37 6	NY	5.12.81	2,157	4,100
37 7	NY	1.10.83	–	–
37 5	NY	1.10.83	882	1,320
38 1	A	3.3.83	3,990	10,443
38 2	KS	8.11.84	4,000	5,078
38 3	KS	18.7.85	540	756
39 4	NY	15.2.84	2,287	3,300
40 1	–	–	–	–
40 2	KS	23.9.81	2,400	5,919
40 3	KS	23.9.81	8,000	13,064
41 4	KS	23.9.81	3,000	4,899
41 5	KS	22.11.82	5,400	8,819
41 6	–	–	–	–
41 7	–	–	–	–
41 8	A	3.3.83	1,368	3,580
42 1	A	15.5.85	–	–
43 2	KS	18.7.85	2,808	3,931
43 3	KS	23.9.81	18,000	32,686
44 1	A	3.3.83	969	2,536
44 2	A	3.3.83	513	1,342
44 3	KS	17.4.84	453	643
44 4	KS	17.4.84	350	497
44 5	–	–	–	–
44 6TL	NY	1.10.83	11,780	17,600

Page	Place	Date	Price (local or sterling)	Price ($ US)
44 6TL	NY	1.10.83	5,731	8,580
44 6BL	NY	1.10.83	–	–
44 6R	NY	1.10.83	11,756	17,600
45 7	KS	3.9.85	–	–
45 8	KS	17.4.84	–	–
45 9	G	10.5.82	–	–
45 10	NY	17.12.83	6,631	9,350
45 11	KS	18.7.85	216	302
46 1	NY	24.5.84	–	–
46 2	NY	16.12.83	23,338	33,000
47 3L	NY	14.6.85	9,442	12,100
47 3R	NY	14.6.85	8,583	11,000
48 2	NY	24.5.84	–	–
48 3	–	–	–	–
49 5	–	–	–	–
50	NY	14.12.84	–	–

ART NOUVEAU

Page	Place	Date	Price (local or sterling)	Price ($ US)
51	KS	18.4.86	1,026	1,539
53	KS	28.1.86	–	–
54 TC	NY	17.12.83	3,120	4,400
54 BC	NY	17.12.83	1,985	2,800
54 L	NY	17.12.83	3,120	4,400
54 R	NY	17.12.83	4,680	6,600
55	G	8.5.83	–	–
55	G	13.5.84	–	–
57	KS	18.4.86	1,728	2,592
58	–	–	–	–
59	KS	30.4.85	6,696	8,035
60 5	KS	17.4.84	1,300	1,846
61 6	NY	15.12.84	3,227	3,850
61 7	KS	30.4.85	1,404	1,744
61 8	KS	3.3.81	4,500	10,037
61 9	KS	17.4.84	1,500	2,130
61 10	NY	10.12.82	10,197	16,500
62 1	G	8.5.83	3,000	14,778
62 2	KS	8.11.84	5,250	6,664
63 3	KS	17.4.84	9,180	12,852
63 4	NY	5.12.81	9,180	17,442
64 1	KS	6.5.81	2,800	5,852
64 2	KS	30.9.85	1,500	2,100
64 3	KS	30.9.85	1,800	2,520
64 4	KS	30.9.85	800	1,120
64 5	KS	30.9.85	864	1,209
64 6	KS	30.9.85	1,300	1,824
65 7	NY	27.5.82	–	–
65 8	KS	29.6.83	2,000	3,055
65 9	G	11.11.84	1,089,000	435,600
65 10	KS	12.7.82	1,000	1,734
66 1	KS	8.11.84	7,000	8,834
66 2	G	10.5.82	–	–
67 3	NY	9.10.82	14,319	24,200
68 1	NY	11.12.82	217	8,256
68 2	NY	26.5.83	618	990
68 3	NY	17.12.83	–	–
68 4	NY	9.10.82	2,082	3,520
68 5	NY	17.12.83	3,276	4,620
69 6	NY	3.4.82	–	–
69 7	NY	26.5.83	618	990
69 8L	KS	12.7.82	170	294
69 8C	KS	12.7.82	180	312
69 8R	KS	12.7.82	250	433
69 9	SK	24.9.82	1,000	1,713
70 1	G	8.5.83	–	–
70 2	G	11.11.84	–	–
71 3	NY	6.12.80	106,837	250,000
71 4	G	10.5.82	44,000	101,516
71 5	G	10.5.82	57,200	129,125
72 1	KS	29.6.83	2,800	4,277
72 2	KS	29.6.83	380	580
72 3	NY	5.12.81	–	–
72 4	KS	15.12.81	420	800
73 5	KS	15.12.81	4,200	8,007
73 6	KS	16.12.84	170	203
73 7	KS	6.5.81	1,000	2,090
73 8	KS	11.1.85	–	–
74 1T	KS	18.7.85	480	672
74 1B	KS	18.7.85	650	910
74 2	KS	17.4.84	5,000	7,102
74 3	–	–	–	–
74 4	NY	24.5.84	–	–
75 5	NY	5&6.2.80	14,035	32,000
75 5	NY	5&6.2.80	11,617	26,000
76 1	NY	2.10.81	–	–
76 2	SK	27.1.84	300	380
76 3	NY	20.3.81	–	–
76 4	NY	9.10.82	–	–
76 5	NY	27.6.81	789	1,500
77 6	KS	18.7.85	432	604
77 7	NY	3.4.82	–	–
77 8	KS	12.7.82	850	1,474
77 9	NY	17.12.83	–	–
78 1	NY	4.10.80	–	–
78 2	KS	17.4.84	8,500	12,074
78 3	NY	5&6.2.80	–	–
78 4	NY	10.12.82	–	–
79 5L	NY	17.12.83	15,602	22,000
79 5BC	NY	17.12.83	9,154	13,000
79 5R	NY	17.12.83	9,289	13,200
79 5TC	NY	17.12.83	3,251	4,620
80 1	NY	31.3.84	1,510	1,870
80 2	KS	17.4.84	750	1,065
80 3	–	–	–	–
80 4	A	3.3.83	1,026	2,685
81 5	KS	30.4.85	864	1,073
81 6	M	8.12.85	–	–
81 7	M	8.12.85	–	–
81 8	M	8.12.85	–	–
82 1	G	10.5.82	–	
82 2	–	–		–
82 3L	G	28.11.82	2,500	4,083
82 3CL	G	28.11.82	2,200	3,595
82 3CR	G	28.11.82	3,500	5,716
82 3R	G	28.11.82	1,700	2,776
83 4	NY	31.3.84	839	1,210
83 5	SK	29.10.82	–	–
83 6B	G	10.5.82	1,650	11,583
83 6T	G	10.5.82	2,240	15,246
83 7	NY	4.10.80	916	2,200
84 1	NY	2.10.81	2,173	4,000
84 2	NY	10.12.82	1,024	1,650
84 3	KS	8.11.84	1,600	2,031
84 4	NY	2.10.81	434	800
84 5	KS	6.5.81	350	634
85 6	KS	17.4.84	380	540
85 7	KS	18.7.85	648	907
85 8	KS	8.11.84	800	1,015
85 9	KS	15.12.82	1,400	2,669
85 10	NY	4.10.80	1,458	3,500
85 11	A	3.3.83	3,420	8,951
86 1	KS	17.4.84	2,600	3,693
86 2	KS	17.4.84	12,000	17,046
87 1	KS	8.11.84	4,200	5,332
87 2L	KS	16.3.82	–	–
87 2CL	KS	16.3.82	–	–
87 2CL	KS	16.3.82	–	–
87 2CR	KS	16.3.82	–	–
87 2R	KS	16.3.82	–	–
88 1	NY	9.10.82	976	1,650
88 2	NY	15.6.85	1,731	2,090
88 3	KS	18.7.85	594	831
88 4	KS	18.7.85	–	–
88 5	KS	30.4.85	420	521
88 6C	KS	30.4.85	216	268
88 6LR	KS	30.4.85	129	160
89 7R	NY	24.5.84	–	–
89 7L	NY	24.5.84	382	528
89 7F	NY	24.5.84	111	154
89 8	–	–	–	–
89 9	KS	6.5.81	190	397
89 10	SK	28.10.83	350	523
89 11	–	–	–	–
89 12	NY	24.5.84	–	–
90 1	M	8.12.85	77,700	8,108
90 2	M	8.12.85	61,050	6,371
91 3	M	8.12.85	111,000	36,270
91 4	M	8.12.85	–	–
91 5	M	8.12.85	–	–
92 1	NY	10.12.82	–	–
92 2	NY	2.10.81	4,619	8,500
92 3	NY	1.10.83	–	–
92 4	–	–	–	–
93 5	NY	27.5.82	1,580	2,860
93 6	NY	5.12.81	3,157	6,000
93 7	NY	27.5.82	3,457	6,050
93 8	–	–	–	–
93 9	KS	17.4.84	650	923
94	NY	14.12.84	–	–

TRADITIONALISM

Page	Place	Date	Price (local or sterling)	Price ($ US)
95	KS	30.4.85	378	461
96 L	KS	18.7.85	194	271
96 C	KS	18.7.85	162	226
96 R	KS	18.7.85	216	302
97	KS	30.4.85	561	673
98	KS	18.4.86	–	–
99	KS	18.4.86	31,320	47,293
100 FCR	KS	30.9.85	–	–
100 C	KS	30.9.85	–	–
100 L	KS	30.9.85	–	–
100 FCL	KS	30.9.85	–	–
100 TL	KS	30.9.85	–	–
100 TR	KS	30.9.85	–	–
100 R	KS	30.9.85	–	–
101	KS	18.7.85	1,620	2,268
102	KS	28.1.86	16,200	23,166
103	KS	28.1.86	–	–
104 1	NY	4.12.81	–	–
104 2	NY	4.12.81	–	–
104 3	NY	24.5.84	1,115	1,540
104 4	NY	10.12.82	1,366	2,200
104 5	NY	14.6.85	2,396	3,080
104 6	NY	11.12.82	1,639	2,640
104 7	NY	10.12.82	375	605
105 8	NY	10.12.82	1,024	1,650
105 9	NY	10.12.82	819	1,320
105 10	NY	16.12.83	–	–
105 11	NY	16.12.83	–	–
105 12	–	–	–	–
105 13	NY	26.5.83	962	1,540
106 1	NY	14.6.85	189,062	242,000
106 2	NY	10.12.82	6,832	11,000
107 3L	NY	24.5.84	19,927	27,500
107 3R	Ny	24.5.84	17,536	24,200
107 4	NY	14.12.84	–	–
108 1	NY	4.12.81	–	–
108 2	NY	14.6.85	385	492
108 3	KS	8.11.84	220	279
108 4	NY	14.12.84	–	–
108 5L	NY	14.11.84	–	–

Page	Place	Date	Price (local or sterling)	Price ($ US)
108 5R	NY	14.11.84	–	–
109 6	NY	4.12.81	2,368	4,500
109 7	NY	10.12.82	2,322	3,740
109 8	NY	24.5.84	–	–
109 9	NY	10.12.82	129	209
110 1L	NY	14.6.85	1,374	1,760
110 1C	NY	14.6.85	2,568	3,300
110 1R	NY	14.6.85	1,369	1,760
110 2	NY	14.6.85	4,708	6,050
110 3	NY	16.12.83	7,390	10,450
111 4	NY	14.6.85	5,992	7,700
111 5	NY	24.5.84	–	–
111 6	NY	10.12.82	8,198	13,200
111 7	NY	14.6.85	1,424	1,830
112 1	NY	26.5.83	–	–
112 2	NY	5&6.2.80	–	–
112 3	NY	14.11.80	–	–
112 4	NY	14.6.85	–	–
112 5	NY	4.12.81	–	–
112 6	NY	5&6.2.80	2,222	5,200
112 7	NY	14.12.84	–	–
113 1	NY	24.5.84	14,347	19,800
113 2	NY	24.5.84	9,565	13,200
113 3L	NY	14.6.85	7,480	9,350
113 3R	NY	14.6.85	6,848	8,800
113 4	NY	16.12.83	565	8,800
113 4	NY	16.12.83	505	715
114 1L	G	12.5.85	2,860	11,119
114 1CL	G	12.5.85	2,640	10,488
114 1B	G	12.5.85	2,420	9,379
114 1F	G	12.5.85	–	–
114 2L	KS	23.9.81	800	1,453
114 2B	KS	23.9.81	2,600	4,721
114 2F	KS	23.9.81	1,200	2,179
114 2R	KS	23.9.81	1,350	2,451
115 3	G	12.5.85	–	–
115 4	G	12.5.85	16,500	63,954
115 5L	KS	23.9.80	800	1,922
115 5R	KS	23.9.80	900	2,162
115 5B	KS	23.9.80	850	2,042
115 5F	KS	23.9.80	1,100	2,642
116 1	SK	5.8.83	1,400	2,079
116 2	SK	27.4.84	650	911
116 3	KS	18.7.85	216	302
116 4	KS	30.4.85	6,264	7,783
117 5	A	3.3.83	627	1,641
117 6	NY	26.3.83	1,883	2,750
117 7L	NY	24.5.84	–	–
117 7C	NY	24.5.84	–	–
117 7R	NY	24.5.84	628	880
117 8L	G	12.5.85	–	–
117 8R	G	12.5.85	–	–
117 9	NY	15.12.84	–	–
118 1	KS	30.4.85	324	401
118 2	KS	30.4.85	540	707
118 3	KS	30.4.85	2,700	3,354
119 4	NY	31.3.84	2,440	3,520
119 5LR	KS	30.4.85	2,160	2,592
119 5BC	KS	30.4.85	1,080	1,296
119 5TC	KS	30.4.85	810	972
120 1	SK	30.9.83	550	823
120 2	KS	18.7.85	1,300	1,820
120 3	SK	17.12.82	1,298	2,090
120 4L	KS	18.7.85	194	271
120 4R	KS	18.7.85	237	331
120 5	SK	23.3.84	650	934
120 6	–	27.1.84	–	–
121 7	KS	30.9.85	–	–
121 8L	KS	12.7.82	432	749
121 8R	KS	12.7.82	–	–
121 9	KS	16.3.82	150	271
121 10	SK	27.4.84	1,700	2,382
121 11	KS	12.7.82	2,592	4,497
122 1	SK	24.9.82	980	1,679
122 2	KS	30.9.85	8,500	11,972
123 3	KS	18.7.85	2,376	3,326
123 4L	KS	18.7.85	410	574
123 4CL	KS	18.7.85	216	302
123 4BC	KS	18.7.85	453	634
123 4FC	KS	18.7.85	864	1,209
123 4CR	KS	18.7.85	90	126
123 4R	KS	18.7.85	270	378
124 1	KS	30.9.85	594	712
124 2	SK	29.10.82	–	–
124 3	KS	30.9.85	216	259
124 4	NY	26.3.83	614	990
124 5	KS	18.7.85	150	210
125 6	A	3.3.83	1,710	9,936
125 7	G	11.11.84	–	–
125 8	KS	30.4.85	864	1,073
125 9L	KS	30.4.85	151	187
125 9C	KS	30.4.85	345	1,463
125 9R	KS	30.4.85	432	537
125 10	G	28.11.82	2,800	16,339
126 1	KS	18.7.85	20,520	28,728
126 2	NY	15.6.85	25,360	35,200
127 3	NY	30.3.85	9,918	12,100
128 1	NY	24.5.84	677	935
128 2	KS	18.7.85	750	1,050
128 3	KS	30.4.85	–	–
128 4	NY	9.10.82	–	–
128 5	A	3.3.83	513	2,981
128 6	G	28.11.82	8,500	13,881
129 7	NY	9.10.82	683	1,100
129 8	KS	29.6.83	7,000	10,692
129 9	KS	17.4.84	4,000	5,682
129 10	KS	22.11.82	1,700	2,776
129 11C	NY	5&6.2.80	87	200
129 11O	NY	5&6.2.80	–	–
130	NY	15.6.85	–	–

ART DECO

Page	Place	Date	Price (local or sterling)	Price ($ US)
131	KS	17.4.84	1,188	1,663
133	KS	18.4.86	–	–
134	–	–	–	–
136 1	KS	17.4.84	1,300	1,846
136 2	KS	12.7.82	300	562
136 3	–	–	–	–
136 4	KS	16.12.80	1,700	3,986
136 5L	KS	17.4.84	700	994
136 5C	KS	17.4.84	400	568
136 5R	KS	17.4.84	1,400	1,988
137 6	–	–	–	–
137 7	SK	25.6.82	–	–
137 8	NY	26.5.83	9,108	14,300
137 9	–	–	–	–
137 10	KS	17.4.84	1,900	2,698
137 11	–	–	–	–
138 1	NY	15.12.84	25,817	30,800
138 2TR	NY	5&6.2.80	416	950
138 2TC	NY	5&6.2.80	1,140	2,600
138 2TL	NY	5&6.2.80	526	1,200
138 2BR	NY	5&6.2.80	964	2,200
138 2BC	NY	5&6.2.80	–	–
138 2BL	NY	5&6.2.80	833	1,900
139 3	G	13.5.84	13,200	52,747
139 4FL	NY	24.5.84	637	880
139 4FR	NY	24.5.84	3,985	5,500
139 4FCR	NY	24.5.84	4,144	5,720
139 4BL	NY	24.5.84	2,231	3,080
139 4C	NY	24.5.84	1,036	1,430
139 4LCF	NY	24.5.84	1,594	2,200
139 4BCR	NY	24.5.84	5,579	7,700
139 4BR	NY	24.5.84	2,391	3,300
139 4BLC	NY	24.5.84	3,188	4,400
140 1	NY	27.5.82	438	605
140 2	–	–	–	–
140 3	NY	3.4.82	3,728	6,600
140 4	NY	26.3.83	753	1,100
140 5	NY	26.3.83	4,046	7,000
141 6	KS	17.4.84	1,100	1,562
141 7	G	8.5.83	6,500	3,065
141 8	KS	17.4.84	1,350	190
141 9	–	–	–	–
141 10	–	–	–	–
142 1	NY	15.6.85	5,154	6,600
143 2L	KS	23.9.81	3,200	5,811
143 2R	KS	23.9.81	2,800	5,084
143 3	–	–	–	–
143 4	KS	29.6.83	3,500	5,346
144 1	NY	5.12.81	–	–
144 2	–	–	–	–
144 3	NY	26.3.83	–	–
144 4	NY	26.5.83	6,531	10,450
144 5	A	3.3.83	228	1,324
144 6L	A	3.3.83	228	1,324
144 6BC	A	3.3.83	342	1,987
144 6R	A	3.3.83	342	1,987
144 6FC	A	3.3.83	171	993
145 7	SK	25.2.83	650	993
145 8	NY	10.12.82	580	935
145 9	KS	12.7.82	1,188	2,060
145 10	SK	27.7.84	720	944
145 11	SK	24.2.84	850	1,250
145 12	–	–	–	–
146 1	KS	30.4.85	5,184	6,441
146 2	KS	29.6.83	1,728	2,639
147 3	NY	30.3.85	–	–
148 1	KS	17.4.84	1,800	2,556
148 2	–	–	–	–
148 3	NY	26.5.83	2,913	4,620
148 4	NY	15.12.84	18,487	22,000
149 5	NY	31.3.84	–	–
149 6	KS	16.3.82	1,500	2,710
149 7	NY	4.10.80	20,833	50,000
149 8	NY	27.5.82	2,444	4,400
150 1	NY	15.12.84	–	–
150 2	NY	17.12.83	13,943	19,800
151 3	NY	27.5.82	11,611	20,900
151 4	NY	15.12.84	23,109	27,500
152 1	NY	31.3.84	5,347	7,700
152 2	KS	16.3.82	–	–
152 3	KS	17.3.84	16,000	11,034
152 4	NY	9.10.82	5,857	9,900
152 5	NY	9.10.82	13,017	22,000
153 6	KS	29.6.83	1,300	1,985
153 7L	KS	23.9.81	800	1,452
153 7R	KS	23.9.81	850	1,543
153 8	KS	17.4.84	2,800	3,977
153 9	NY	3.4.82	9,943	17,600
153 10	KS	15.12.81	3,500	6,672
154 1	NY	3.4.82	–	–
154 2	KS	17.4.84	6,000	8,523
155 3	NY	9.10.82	18,224	30,800
156 1	NY	24.5.84	–	–
156 2	KS	29.6.83	5,000	7,749
156 3	–	–	–	–
156 4	–	–	–	–
156 5	KS	22.11.82	1,700	2,776
156 6	–	–	–	–

Page	Place	Date	Price (local or sterling)	Price ($ US)
157 7	NY	1.10.83	–	–
157 8	–	–	–	–
157 9	NY	3.4.82	–	–
157 10	KS	12.7.82	850	1,474
157 11	NY	3.4.82		2,800
157 12	–	–	–	–
158 1	NY	31.3.84	45,674	66,000
159 2	NY	27.5.82		
159 3	NY	17.12.83	15,492	22,000
160 2	NY	1.10.83	55,110	82,500
160 3	NY	17.12.83	1,971	2,800
160 4	NY	26.5.83	–	
160 5	NY	1.10.83	808	1,210
161 1	NY	10–11.12.84	284	1,980
161 2	NY	9.10.82	5,532	9.350
161 3	KS	16.3.82	950	1,716
161 4	NY	4.10.80	7,916	19,000
161 5	NY	10.12.82	1,692	2,860
162 1	–	–	–	–
163 2	NY	26.5.83	–	–
164 1	NY	17.12.83	21,690	30,800
164 2	KS	15.12.81	400	762
164 3	NY	17.12.83	–	–
164 4	NY	26.3.83	4,897	7,150
164 5	NY	26.3.83	1,164	1,700
165 6	NY	26.3.83	3,767	5,500
165 7	NY	9.10.82	1,952	3,300
165 8	NY	1.10.83	–	–
165 9	NY	1.10.83	3,674	5,500
165 10	KS	29.6.83	1,900	2,902
166 1	KS	17.4.84	3,200	2,252
166 2	NY	10.12.82	9,112	15,400
167 3	KS	17.4.84	8,500	5,983
168 1	–	–	–	–
168 2	G	13.5.84	–	–
168 3	KS	16.3.82	2,500	1,383
168 4	KS	30.4.85	3,672	2,949
169 5	KS	22.11.82	1,080	661
169 6	KS	15.7.80	1,700	713
169 7	KS	22.11.82	130	79
169 8	NY	26.5.83	346	550
169 9	NY	26.3.83	1,896	2,750
169 10	NY	24.5.84	20,724	28,600
170 1	NY	9.10.82	–	–
171 2	KS	23.9.81	3,800	2,092
172 1	NY	27.5.82	911	1,650
172 2	KS	23.9.81	30,000	16,519
172 3	NY	27.5.82	668	1,210
172 4	NY	1.10.83	1,910	2,860
172 5	NY	3.4.82	–	–
172 6	KS	16.12.80	1,300	3,048
172 7	NY	17.12.83	1,282	1,770
173 8L	NY	17.12.83	1,992	2,750
173 8R	NY	17.12.83	1,594	2,200
173 9	NY	17.12.83	637	880
173 10	KS	22.11.82	700	1,143
173 11	NY	14.12.84	–	–
173 12	KS	17.4.84	300	426
174	–	–	–	–

BAUHAUS AND ITS INFLUENCE

Page	Place	Date	Price (local or sterling)	Price ($ US)
175	–	–	–	–
176 L	NY	26.3.83	1,130	1,650
176 R	NY	3.4.82	–	–
177	KS	18.12.85	453	643
178	G	11.11.84	–	–
179	KS	18.12.85	3,672	5,140
186	KS	18.4.86	1,188	1,782
181	KS	18.4.86	810	1,215

Page	Place	Date	Price (local or sterling)	Price ($ US)
182 1	KS	30.4.85	2,160	3,020
182 2	NY	26.5.83	–	–
183 3	NY	1.10.83	13,961	20,900
184 1	NY	15.12.84	6,424	7,700
184 2	KS	17.4.84	500	710
184 3	NY	24.5.84		
184 4	KS	22.11.82	1,200	1,959
184 5	KS	17.4.84	1,900	2,699
185 1	KS	30.4.85	1,296	1,594
185	KS	–	–	–
185 3	KS	8.11.84	1,000	1,198
185 4	KS	18.7.85	5,940	8,316
185 5	A	3.3.83	–	–
186 1	NY	24.5.84	–	–
187 2	KS	30.4.85	8,100	10,064
187 3	NY	15.12.84	9,220	11,000
188 1	KS	22.11.82	250	442
188 2	NY	31.3.84	3,437	4,950
188 3	KS	17.4.84	300	426
188 4	KS	29.6.83	1,500	2,295
189 5	NY	9.10.82	488	825
189 6	NY	1.10.83	8,783	13,000
189 7	KS	30.4.85	810	1,006
189 8	A	3.3.83	1,710	9,936
190 1	KS	29.6.83	1,700	2,596
190 2	NY	3.4.82	9,943	17,600
191 3	NY	1.10.83	30,861	46,200
192 1	NY	27.5.82	1,093	1,870
192 2	NY	27.5.82	388	660
192 3	NY	24.5.84	329	455
192 4	NY	24.5.84	1,115	1,540
192 5	NY	24.5.84	–	–
192 6	NY	31.3.84	763	1,100
193 7	NY	31.3.84	–	–
193 8	KS	17.4.84	650	923
193 9	NY	1.10.83	1,910	2,860
193 10	NY	9.10.82	2,473	4,180
193 11	NY	17.12.83	–	–
193 12L	G	13.5.84	–	–
193 12R	G	13.5.84	–	–
194 1	NY	31.3.84	18,333	26,400
195 2	NY	17.12.83	13,169	18,700
196 1	NY	5.12.81	1,473	2,800
196 2	KS	16.3.82	5,000	9,034
196 3	KS	17.4.84	1,500	2,130
196 4	KS	17.4.84	650	976
196 5	NY	26.5.83	2,200	3,520
197 6	NY	26.5.83	–	–
197 7	NY	5.12.81	4,210	8,000
197 8	KS	30.4.85	1,404	1,963
197 9	KS	17.4.84	2,800	3,977
197 10	KS	29.6.83	650	992
198 1	KS	22.11.82	4,800	7,838
199 2	NY	4.10.80	5,416	13,000
200 1	NY	3.4.82	2,983	5,280
200 2	NY	17.12.83	2,323	3,300
200 3	NY	10.12.82	552	890
200 4	NY	17.12.83	46,478	66,000
201 5	KS	17.4.84	700	994
201 6	KS	30.4.85	864	1,073
201 7	KS	22.11.82	2,000	3,266
202 1	NY	14.6.85	10,476	13,200
203 2L	NY	15.6.85	4,252	5,060
203 2R	NY	15.6.85	4,252	5,060
203 2C	NY	15.6.85	1,571	1,870
203 3	NY	15.12.84	69,327	82,500
204 1	NY	26.5.83	893	1,430
204 2	NY	–	–	–
204 3	A	3.3.83	2,508	6,564
204 4	NY	3.4.82	4,971	8,800

Page	Place	Date	Price (local or sterling)	Price ($ US)
205 5	NY	9.10.82	2,863	4,840
205 6	NY	2.10.81	1,086	2,000
205 7	NY	27.5.82	–	–
205 8	A	3.3.83	1,824	4,774
205 9	A	3.3.83	2,964	7,758
206 1	NY	31.3.84	–	–
206 2	NY	4.10.80	–	–
207 3	NY	15.12.84	12,016	14,300
207 4	NY	4.10.80	–	–
208 1	KS	17.4.84	2,000	2,841
208 2	KS	16.3.82	–	–
208 3	NY	27.5.82	3,950	7,150
208 4	NY	3.4.82	–	–
209 5	A	3.3.83	912	2,387
209 6	KS	8.11.84	2,800	3,554
209 7	KS	15.7.80	1,000	2,372
209 8	NY	9.10.82	16,272	27,500
209 9	KS	30.4.85	540	670
210 1	KS	8.11.84	4,800	6,093
211 2TC	KS	29.6.83	7,000	10,692
211 2BC	KS	29.6.83	3,000	4,582
211 2TL	KS	29.6.83	2,600	3,971
211 2BR	KS	29.6.83	3,200	4,888
211 2TR	KS	29.6.83	3,000	4,582
211 2BL	KS	29.6.83	2,400	3,666
212 1	KS	8.11.84	500	634
212 2	KS	8.11.84	850	1,079
212 3	KS	30.4.85	162	200
212 4	KS	18.7.85	1,188	1,663
212 5	–	–	–	–
213 6	KS	18.7.85	216	302
213 7	KS	18.7.85	2,700	3,780
213 8	SK	27.4.84	350	509
213 9	SK	30.10.81	60	110
214	*	28.11.84	–	–
215 –	–	–	–	

POST–WAR DESIGN

Page	Place	Date	Price (local or sterling)	Price ($ US)
216	KS	18.7.85	2,808	3,931
217 L	NY	31.3.84	–	–
217 R	KS	30.4.85	3,672	4,590
218	KS	16.4.84	6,500	9,233
219	NY	24.5.84	9,565	13,200
220	NY	5.12.81	578	1,100
222 1	*	29.11.84	700	840
222 2L	G	8.5.83	6,200	3,020
222 2C	G	8.5.83	6,500	3,167
222 2R	G	8.5.83	7,800	3,799
223 3	*	29.11.84	3,800	4,560
223 4L	*	29.11.84	300	360
4C	*	29.11.84	240	288
4R	*	29.11.84	280	336
224 1	*	29.11.84	650	780
224 2L	*	29.11.84	320	384
2C	*	29.11.84	400	480
2R	*	29.11.84	420	504
224 3CL	KS	18.7.85	280	392
224 3L	KS	18.7.85	280	392
224 3CR	KS	18.7.85	190	266
224 3R	KS	18.7.85	130	182
224 4L	KS	18.7.85	150	210
224 4R	KS	18.7.85	194	271
224 5L	KS	30.4.85	756	939
224 5K	KS	30.4.85	420	521
225 6L	*	29.11.84	180	216
6R	*	29.11.84	100	120
225 7	NY	26.3.83	–	–
225 8	*	29.11.84	360	432
225 9L	*	29.11.84	180	216

Page	Place	Date	Price (local or sterling)	Price ($ US)
225 **9R**	*	29.11.84	80	96
225 **10L**	*	29.11.84	220	264
225 **10Cl**	*	29.11.84	280	336
225 **10CR**	*	29.11.84	100	120
225 **10R**	*	29.11.84	80	96
226 **1**	KS	16.4.84	850	1,207
226 **2L**	NY	17.12.83	528	750
226 **2C**	NY	17.12.83	669	950
226 **2R**	NY	17.12.83	338	480
227 **3**	KS	16.4.84	2,600	3,693
227 **4CR**	NY	10.12.82	687	1,100
227 **4CL**	NY	10.12.82	–	–
227 **4C**	NY	10.12.82	–	–
227 **4L**	NY	10.12.82	962	1,540
227 **4R**	NY	10.12.82	687	1,100
228 **1R**	KS	18.7.85	550	770
1L	KS	18.7.85	480	672
228 **2**	*	29.11.84	1,000	1,200
228 **3**	*	29.11.84	2,000	2,400
228 **4L**	NY	1.10.83	257	385
228 **4R**	NY	1.10.83	955	1,430
228 **5**	NY	1.10.83	–	–
229 **6L**	NY	26.3.83	452	660
229 **6C**	NY	26.3.83	452	660
229 **6R**	NY	26.3.83	376	550
229 **7**	KS	18.7.85	918	1,285
229 **8L**	NY	31.3.84	–	–
229 **8C**	NY	31.3.84	–	–
229 **8R**	NY	31.3.84	572	825
230 **1L**	*	29.11.84	1,900	2,280
230 **1R**	*	29.11.84	1,700	2,040
230 **2**	*	29.11.84	1,500	1,800
231 **3**	*	29.11.84	25,000	30,000
231 **4L**	*	29.11.84	500	600
231 **4R**	*	29.11.84	1,300	1,560
232 **1**	KS	16.4.84	150	213
232 **2**	NY	30.3.85	901	1,100
232 **3**	KS	18.7.85	324	453
232 **4**	KS	18.7.85	345	483
232 **5L**	KS	16.4.84	400	568
232 **5R**	KS	16.4.84	320	454
233 **6**	KS	16.4.84	240	341
233 **7**	KS	16.4.84	300	426
233 **8**	NY	15.6.85	2,568	3,300
233 **9**	NY	15.12.84	–	–
233 **10**	KS	30.4.85	270	324
234 **1B**	NY	17.12.83	7,746	11,000
234 **1F**	NY	17.12.83	2,478	3,520
235 **2**	KS	8.11.84	6,500	8,251
235 **3**	–	–	–	–
236 **1**	NY	17.12.83	1,056	1,500
236 **2**	KS	30.4.85	–	–
236 **3**	KS	16.4.84	750	1,065
236 **4**	KS	30.4.85	280	3,479
236 **5**	NY	26.3.83	–	–
237 **6L**	KS	16.4.84	50	71
237 **6R**	KS	16.4.84	50	71
237 **7**	NY	9.10.82	1,031	1,650
237 **8L**	KS	16.4.84	300	426
237 **8R**	KS	16.4.84	110	156
237 **9**	KS	16.4.84	850	1,207
237 **10**	KS	16.4.84	260	369
236 **1**	NY	17.12.83	9,154	13,000
239 **2**	KS	16.4.84	800	1,136
239 **3**	NY	30.3.85	5,477	6,600
240 **1**	KS	18.7.85	756	1,058
240 **2**	KS	16.4.84	700	994
240 **3**	KS	18.7.85	486	680
240 **4**	NY	15.12.84	1,844	2,200
240 **5**	KS	16.4.84	900	1,278
241 **1**	KS	16.4.84	550	781
241 **2**	SK	25.3.83	130	189
241 **3**	NY	17.12.83	1,471	2,090
241 **4**	NY	2.10.81	1,521	2,800
241 **5**	NY	15.6.85	2,996	3,850
241 **6**	NY	31.3.84	1,172	1,430
242 **1**	KS	16.4.84	2,400	3,410
242 **2L**	KS	16.4.84	800	1,136
242 **2C**	KS	16.4.84	320	454
242 **2R**	KS	16.4.84	1,500	2,131
243 **3**	NY	24.5.84	3,028	4,180
244 **1**	KS	18.7.85	216	302
244 **2**	SK	4.8.81	180	327
244 **3L**	KS	30.4.85	280	347
244 **3R**	KS	30.4.85	280	347
244 **4**	KS	30.4.85	600	855
244 **5**	KS	16.4.84	220	312
244 **6**	KS	30.4.85	648	894
245 **7**	KS	30.4.85	450	559
245 **8**	NY	17.12.83	1,063	1,500
245 **9L**	KS	16.4.84	140	198
245 **9C**	KS	16.4.84	–	–
245 **9R**	KS	16.4.84	–	–
245 **10**	KS	30.4.85	65	80
246 **1CL**	KS	16.3.82	300	450
246 **1CR**	KS	16.3.82	1,300	1,950
246 **1T**	KS	16.3.82	1,700	2,550
246 **1BCL**	KS	16.3.82	1,800	2,700
246 **1BR**	KS	16.3.82	850	1,275
246 **1BCR**	KS	16.3.82	220	330
246 **1C**	KS	16.3.82	1,600	2,400
246 **1BL**	KS	16.3.82	1,300	1,950
247 **2L**	KS	23.9.81	2,500	4,525
247 **2CF**	KS	23.9.81	2,000	3,620
247 **2CT**	KS	23.9.81	7,000	12,670
247 **2R**	KS	23.9.81	2,000	3,620
248 **1**	KS	18.4.86	324	489
248 **2**	NY	22.3.86	110	133
248 **3**	KS	18.4.86	750	1,125
248 **4L**	KS	18.4.86	432	648
248 **4R**	KS	18.4.86	864	1,296
248 **5**	KS	18.4.86	–	–
249 **6**	KS	18.4.86	1,836	2,754
249 **7**	KS	18.4.86	–	–
249 **8**	KS	18.4.86	1,836	2,754
249 **9L**	KS	18.4.86	324	486
249 **9CL**	KS	18.4.86	864	1,296
249 **9CR**	KS	18.4.86	486	729
249 **9R**	KS	18.4.86	432	648
250 **1L**	KS	18.1.86	194	271
250 **1LC**	KS	18.1.86	172	240
250 **1LB**	KS	18.1.86	–	–
250 **1RB**	KS	18.1.86	25,702	35,982
250 **1C**	KS	18.1.86	–	–
250 **1R**	KS	18.1.86	–	–
250 **2L**	KS	18.1.86	810	1,134
250 **2CF**	KS	18.1.86	810	1,134
250 **2CF**	KS	18.1.86	432	604
250 **2CB**	KS	18.1.86	518	725
250 **2R**	KS	18.1.86	378	529
250 **3**	KS	18.1.86	410	574
250 **4**	KS	18.1.86	1,404	1,965
251 **5**	KS	18.1.86	3,780	3,292
251 **6L**	KS	18.1.86	918	1,285
251 **6C**	KS	18.1.86	432	604
251 **6R**	KS	18.1.86	150	210
251 **7**	KS	18.1.86	237	331
251 **8**	KS	18.1.86	–	–

Index